"We had so much fun working with Cindy and creating products together that warmed our customers' hearts...ours too! Her pillows were a WP trademark! I'm so happy to have Cindy's beautiful book to refer to often!"

~ Mickey Kelly Murray
WHISPERING PINES,
THINGS FOR THE CABIN...
OWNER/MERCHANDISE DIRECTOR

"Cindy was a joy to work with. She was extremely creative with a great sense of fashion. In addition, she was committed to learning the business management end of things. She attended business workshops and used everything she learned in her business. She sought financial advice from the bankers and accountants. All of her hard work on the business end led to her being even more successful with her most creative coats. Cindy was one of my most interesting and favorite customers during the years we worked together."

~ Gary Sisson
FIRST SECURITY BANK OF BOZEMAN

"When I was at university, all I wanted was a Cindy Owings' coat. I was inspired by the quirky brand, the vibrant wool colors of her outerwear, Cindy's bohemian work studio on the north side of Bozeman, and her expansive creativity in it.
   Generously, she let this impressionable and inexperienced college student photograph her winter collection on trade; and that morphed into a live stage installation fabricated entirely from cardboard, flashlights, and fishbowls for a uniquely choreographed fashion show which was my final architectural thesis.
   Many of the photos are in this book, and my coat still hangs in the closet today, decades later."

~ Audrey Hall
PHOTOGRAPHER

"Designers create for the woman who considers herself unique and enjoys art to wear. Cindy Owings Designs went a step further and invited the buyers to participate by selecting their own color combinations on her outerwear. Stores enjoyed knowing they were offering one-of-a-kind pieces to their customers. These are my sentiments and why I was proud to offer COD."

~ Deborah Cook
MIDWEST REGION SALES REPRESENTATIVE

Background: Unprocessed wool fleece shorn from a Navajo Churro sheep named Con Leche.

The Purple Blanket

Whimsical coat tales from a tiny Montana business that achieved national acclaim

Cindy Owings

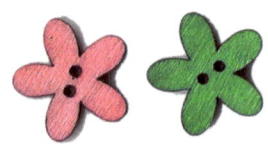

This book is dedicated to
Maya, my daughter and Graham, my husband
Barb Jones, Jones & Company, LTD
Peach Gilbert, Mabels
Deborah Cook (& the late Leah Cook), Minneapolis Gift Mart
Mickey Murray, Whispering Pines Catalog

You all believed in me when I wondered!

A special note of thanks to my graphic designer, Erica Evans Mita of Sparkle Bomb Studio, for the thoughtful organization of the visual side of my story.

*When my customers come to me, they want to know
they have crossed the threshold of some magic place.*
~ Coco Chanel

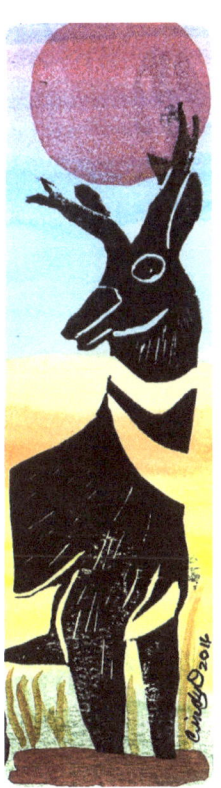

*Vain trifles as they seem, clothes have, they say,
more important offices than to merely keep us warm.
They change our view of the world
and the world's view of us.*
~ Virginia Woolf

The Purple Blanket:
Whimsical coat tales from a tiny Montana business that achieved national acclaim

Copyright © 2021 by Cindy Owings

Published by

Bitterroot Mountain Publishing House LLC
P.O. Box 3508, Hayden, ID 83835

Visit our website at www.BMPHmedia.com

All rights reserved. No part of this book may be reproduced, stored in a retrieval system, or transmitted in any form or by any means—electronic, mechanical, digital, photocopy, recording, or any other—except for brief quotations in printed reviews, without prior written permission of the publisher.

For questions or information regarding permission for excerpts please contact Bitterroot Mountain Publishing House at Editor@BMPHmedia.com.

This is a work of non-fiction. Although the author and publisher have made every effort to ensure the accuracy and completeness of information contained in this book, we assume no responsibility for errors, inaccuracies, omissions, or any inconsistency herein. Any slights of people, places, organizations are unintentional.

All photos are courtesy of Cindy Owings Design (COD), except those listed in the acknowledgments section. A list of photo credits and permissions appear on page 131. The publisher accepts no responsibility in the selection and display of the photographs in this book.

ISBN: 978-1-940025-55-1 (Print)
ISBN: 978-1-940025-56-8 (eBook)

Library of Congress Control Number: 2021921220

1. Creative Fashions - Coats   2. Unique Designer Coats - Biography   3. Artistic Designer Clothes   4. Women's Fashion - Inspirational Entrepreneurs   I. Title

Printed in the United States of America

10 9 8 7 6 5 4 3 2 1

CONTENTS

Preface		8
1	Beginnings	12
2	A Washing Machine and a Pot of Purple Dye	16
3	Coat Business Fledges	22
4	And, Flies	28
5	Anatomy of a Coat	34
6	COD Coats Travel to the Big Apple	38
7	Take Me Seriously Already	46
8	A Blanket Becomes a Coat	54
9	Heady Times	60
10	COD's Underbelly	66
11	Coats and the People Who Made Them	72
12	Gifts of Discovery	82
13	Reaching Out to Share and Receive	88
14	Oh, Precious Scrap	102
15	Petunias Grow Forever, Almost	112
16	Endings Circle Around to Beginnings	118
Afterword & Acknowledgments		128

Preface

The rivers, yes, the rivers of the west course through my life. Rounded stones and downed tree branches mark river edges. Pools of backwater swirl at unexpected corners. Fresh is the smell of clear water as it plunges out of the mountains. All the rivers I know flow north, except the Snake.

My family lived on the banks of the Snake River in southeastern Idaho. It flows south and west to become part of the Columbia. One summer evening, my brother and I were dressed in our pajamas. I was reading a bedtime story. We were playing pretend camping in a tent we had made out of a card table and some old blankets. Late into the night, we were startled awake, confused. The house bucked and rolled. It was an earthquake. This earthquake portended an even greater upheaval. On August 17, 1959, the whole of southeastern Idaho swayed from its grounding. This would be the massive quake that created Quake Lake out of Hebgen Lake in Montana just north of our home. The quake, known as the "Yellowstone Quake," was momentous. Entire sliding mountains buried campers and Highway 287 was rearranged.

I grew up a "Dam Kid." My family lived in remote mountainous places, next to rivers, and dams. My father worked as a civil engineer for the Bureau of Reclamation. My mother was a housewife who read every book in the public library and lived for political discussions. During my youth, we lived on the Gunnison, Big Thompson, and North Fork of the Gunnison River in Colorado. For five years, we lived on the banks of the Snake. As a high school senior, my friends and I leapt from sandstone cliffs into the Colorado River near Page, Arizona, where we lived. For three years, we lived in pear country along the Rogue River in Medford, Oregon, the first city in my life. Here we had our first telephone and television, and as a townie, I walked to school on a sidewalk. Wild Horse, Nevada, was the wildest place we lived.

In my hallway hangs a black-and-white photo of my first-grade class. I spent this first year in a one-room schoolhouse in Irwin, Idaho. I am sitting toward the rear at my desk, my head leaning on my steepled hands. I am

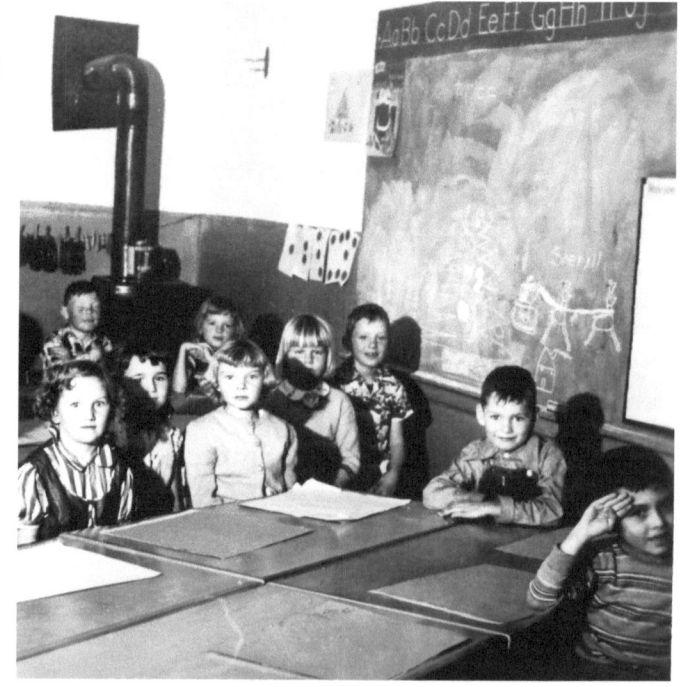

This is Cindy's first grade class in an one-room schoolhouse.

wearing a pinafore dress and my normally straight hair was curled. Damp mittens hung on a line above the wood stove. One kid in a striped shirt was saluting the camera; another had a big, silly smile. The rest of us were dead serious, much the way we spent each school day, in earnest concentration. For better or for worse, this manner of intense sincere focus followed me through my teen years and on into adulthood, manifesting in a quiet determination and sense of how I would walk in the world. I needed to learn to laugh a bit, however.

We moved so many times that I invented a way to safeguard my treasures. I collected and labeled shoeboxes and filled them with projects. Painting supplies filled a few. Parts of mini-theatre stage sets filled even more boxes. My postcard collection filled two shoeboxes. For hours, I would sit with my Aunt Margaret while she taught me how to hand-sew clothes for clothespin and Ginny dolls, little 5-inch-tall girly girls with curled hair and sweet faces. Tiny skirts, jackets, hats, and bags filled multiple shoeboxes. It was from making this doll clothing with my aunt that I grew to love sewing. I also learned to sew from my mother and high school home economics classes.

I was born in 1946. The 1950s, following World War II, were years of calm and hope. Women wore housedresses. Men wore fedoras. Kids signed up to learn tap and square dancing. In summer, we raced outdoors to build forts and rafts, and played kick-the-can into darkness. We were wild creatures setting off to explore even wilder country, with no fear, with only pure excitement for discovery of the unknown. I learned geography in fifth grade by collecting postmarked stamps from pen pals across the world. Each postmark was placed on a huge map of the world. We listened to radio dramas and then made up our own plays.

Our national tranquility was shattered with the shooting of President Kennedy in 1963. The Beatles appeared on *The Ed Sullivan Show* in 1964, the year I graduated from high school. I was voted the "Book Queen of the Year." I designed and sewed a fancy dress for the dance. As a girl, I was expected to become a teacher, nurse, or better yet, a housewife. My parents had raised two kids who were encouraged to think independently. When I did follow my own ideas of how my life would go, it made my parents have second thoughts, I'm sure.

I attended Colorado State University, where I studied political science. The mid-1960s was a time of unrest on college campuses. Women were beginning to speak out. Inspired by the Women's Movement, I followed the artwork of Judy Chicago and read everything I could by Gloria Steinem and Betty Friedan.

In my freshman year, my advisor told me I wasn't cut out for college. He said, "You should quit and go to beauty school."

I had never been treated with overt discrimination before. The beauty school suggestion rankled me no end. The encounter was one of the few times in my life when I knew I had to fight for my own right to be who I wanted to be. I changed majors (and advisor) and forged ahead to graduate in 1968 with a Bachelor of Science Degree in Speech Pathology. I had chosen this major because I had volunteered to work in a preschool for deaf children on campus. The experience helped me envision a certain fulfillment through working with children with speech and language problems.

In my second year of college, I was selected to be a participant in People to People: International Travel Programs for Students, and I lived with families in Denmark, Norway, and Sweden. It was at the "homestays" that I got my first exposure to socialism. Also, the bright, colorfully patterned Scandinavian textiles I saw along the way inspired me. And the tablecloths, bedding, and fabrics covered in simple flower patterns and geometric designs were unforgettable.

I lived with a fishing family on a tiny island off the coast of Kristiansand, in Norway. When I arrived by bus in the city, the Evensens picked me up, and we rowed in a tiny boat to their home across the sound. I woke up the next morning to a breakfast of yogurt and strawberries. I had never eaten yogurt before. Mrs. Evensen had made the yogurt by letting raw milk ferment under the kitchen sink.

Following my time in Scandinavia, I met my friend, Jan, in Belgium, and then we completed our European trip by hitchhiking through Germany, Austria, Luxemburg, and France. The trip, with all its eye-opening moments, political awakenings, and exposure to sights I only dreamed of seeing, gave me pause. How would I integrate my newly acquired appreciation for the arts and, for that matter, my dyed pink hair, into my life back home?

Straight out of college, I married and landed a speech clinician job, and then moved with my husband to Madison, Wisconsin, for my husband's graduate study. On trips to Northern New Mexico to visit my husband's family, I got my first exposure to the work of Navajo weavers. I wanted to learn to weave, so I started weaving with Annaliese Steppet, a well-known Austrian fiber artist living in Madison. I then purchased a large floor loom that followed me to Missouri, back to Wisconsin, and finally to Montana.

Madison, along with Berkeley, California, was a hotbed of protests against the war. I took part in the anti-war marches with my husband, college students, friends, and coworkers at school. I will never forget the awful sting of mace in my eyes. Within two years, my husband was drafted out of graduate school into the Vietnam War. Following basic training, we moved to Fort Leonard Wood in southern Missouri, the Ozarks, where I worked as a speech pathologist in the public schools. I recall that women weren't allowed to wear pants and that the teachers' dress code applied only to women.

In Lebanon, Missouri, there were two distinct sides of town: one for white people, and one for black people. My naïve eyes were opened wide for the first time to the accepted culture of the South. With a friend, I started an after-school arts-and-crafts program. The class was my first opportunity to honor my beliefs and share my creativity. Kids would come tumbling in to put their hands in wet clay, dip paper in wheat paste, and make graffiti wall art with huge paintbrushes. We invited kids of all races, backgrounds, and experience to share in the common language of creating with your hands.

Following the Vietnam War, we returned to Wisconsin. I worked in a Title I program in the public schools with kids who had difficulty learning and those who had speech problems. To guide children to the realization that they could pronounce intelligible *s-s-s* or *er-er-er* sounds was an absolute delight for me, especially when those little round faces lit up at the success they achieved. And did I ever laugh and explore with deaf children as they discovered the softness of a goat tongue slurping against their cheeks. Seemingly small accomplishments, but every day my work with struggling children with disabilities fulfilled my own dream of helping others.

Meanwhile, I continued to hone my skills in the fiber arts realm. The University of Wisconsin offered a rich and varied program in the study of textile arts. Renie Breskin Adams, a nationally known fiber artist, inspired a whimsical approach to crocheted fiber art. I took her classes, and she guided me in combining woven elements with embroidered and crocheted techniques in pieces that illustrated my dream of returning to the Rocky Mountains, for example. Renie pushed her students to question the boundaries of textile as art through the exploration of materials and techniques. The fiber arts department housed one of the most extensive collections of international textiles in the world, the Helen Louise Allen Textile Collection. Viewed from the outside, my fiber studies may have been considered a "hobby," but to me, my thread studies were steps on the way to another career.

My daughter, Maya, was born in 1976, the same year we moved to Bozeman, Montana. I stopped working in speech pathology at that time. As a young mother, I carried my baby girl on my back, hiking the mountain trails around Bozeman. I learned to hand-spin raw wool with Margaret Emerson, the intrepid leader of my hiking group. I experimented with woven tapestry techniques and hand-dyed ikat weaving in the Japanese tradition.

Three years later, I got divorced, and suddenly was on my own. This life change was so painful that I actually fell out of bed one night writhing on the floor with a powerful ache in my heart. I thought I was near death, but I transformed the sorrow of loss into a determination to continue my exploration of the textile arts. I rented studio space in downtown Bozeman above what used to be Phillips Book Store. It was here that I began to explore hand-painted silk techniques and dyeing of wool, silk, and cotton yarn.

Eventually, my daughter and I moved into a tiny shotgun-style house on Lindley Place. In these houses, each room is lined up behind the front room, hence the name "shotgun." The living room became my studio. Neighbor kids ran to and fro. I grew vegetables in the backyard, and life was filled with potlucks and financial struggles. It was a time in Bozeman when artists lived Bohemian lifestyles and creativity reigned in all aspects of life. With friends, we created excuses to throw parties that turned into large extravagant performance events to raise money for certain charities and causes. At these happenings, we wore wild clothing, painted costumes, and choreographed dances. Being part of the Montana arts community sustained and influenced my work and life.

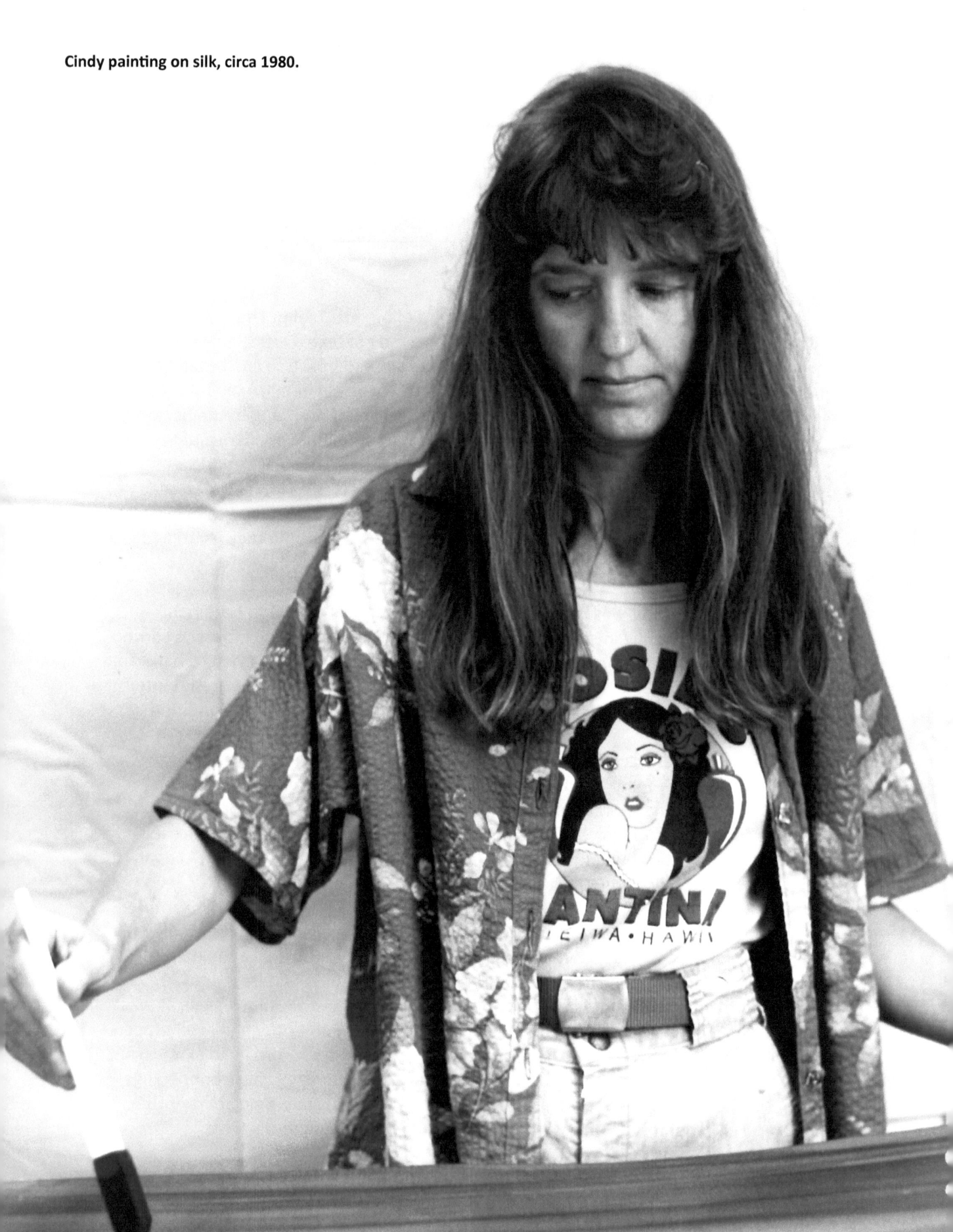
Cindy painting on silk, circa 1980.

CHAPTER 1

Beginnings

In 1883, Bozeman, Montana, became an official town named for John Bozeman, a Southern gold miner who saw profits in guiding other miners over the cut-off trail from Wyoming Territories through the mountains. He established a town in the Valley of the Flowers (Gallatin Valley) so-named by the Bannock Indians as a way station for Gold Rush travelers on their way to Virginia City. Bozeman, the man, was later shot by a friend on the Yellowstone River because he had taken up with the friend's wife. The town of Bozeman, with its colorful early history, eventually became known for its pea harvest and canning operations. On Lindley Place, a short south-side street along Bozeman Creek, rows of cannery worker houses in the shotgun style sprouted up. In 1980, almost a hundred years later, I owned and lived in one of these shotgun houses, and the first room off the street became my textile design studio.

Early in my fiber arts career, I taught myself to paint with dye on silk fabric. Fabric artists who made clothing, scarves, bags, and wall pieces from lively colored, resist-dyed silks had reinvented this ancient art form. Silk painting was brought to the United States from India, Bali, and Burma. Wonderful effects could be achieved as dye was brushed onto smooth silk satin. Touch a sloppy brush in dye and then to silk and white turns into a luscious color. Liquid color marries, melts, and thaws into silk fibers. It isn't enough to say the process is magic. It is more like alchemy on the run. I painted in earnest. From my own hand-painted fabrics, I made jackets, blouses, and dresses. Regional galleries sold my work and customers came directly to my studio. Determined to build a self-sustaining art business that could provide a living for my daughter and me, I worked a part-time job at The Textile Merchant, a Scandinavian contemporary decorative fabric store, while maintaining a determined dedication to studio work.

In the early 1980s, Bozeman, Montana, was a one-horse town, with a lot of cowboys with 10-gallon hats who actually came with cows. I spoke a different language than most of those with whom I brushed shoulders in this small western town. I yearned to have my textile work seen in the context of the greater fiber arts world. Wider recognition could mean I wasn't so dependent on local support. Far afield, I applied for and was selected to attend the American Crafts Council wholesale show in Dallas, Texas. My chance to wear city clothing, my suitcase was packed to the gills with long flowing skirts and light tops, my hair burgundy, fresh from my hairdresser friend, Cinder's imagination.

The show was filled with imaginative textiles, pottery, blown glass, and wood furniture. All mediums were represented. As I visited with other vendors, I was surprised to discover that many did not necessarily make each of their pieces themselves. They hired people to help. What a concept, I thought. The results of this show provided substantial sales for me. And the eye-opening experience nudged me to continue my dyeing exploration in a different direction. I began to think of my work in multiples of one design, and I was prodded to rethink my work processes.

Soon the focus of my design work shifted away from dyeing silk fabric to dyeing handspun wool and silk yarn. My yarns ended up in cloth woven on a large 10-harness Maccober Loom in my Lindley Place living room. With handspun, hand-dyed yarns, I crocheted and knit bulky sweaters reminiscent of South American jacket-type sweaters. I spent hours experimenting with mixing dyes to create unique colors. My washing machine provided a ready pot for dying lots of fiber. The dye soaked into the fiber as the clamor of the dye processes permeated our home. My entire house became a dye studio without conscious intention. It seemed to just happen.

Yarn was pre-rinsed in the bathtub. The dyes were mixed with a glass mortar and pestle in the kitchen sink. Finished colored yarns were hung to dry on every available towel holder and rack in the house. Water boiled on the kitchen stove, as mountain-gathered plant material became dye colors. The house was filled with the wonderful, in my opinion, fragrance of pine tree lichen, golden tansy, and sumac berries, as the wild flora boiled down into natural dyestuffs. As she ate her lunch, Maya would smile and roll her big black eyes at my simmering pots, wondering if her sandwich was made with dyed bread. Suffice it to say, my daughter lived and breathed my dedication to the fiber arts.

A year later, on my walk to work at The Textile Merchant, the springtime air was filled with the sweet fragrance of willows, lilacs, and budding flowers. I loved this time of year for the transformation in Bozeman from winter to the warmth of almost summer. If I listened closely, I could hear the sound of the creek making its way north to flow under Main Street two blocks away. Shaded by Lindley Place's old cottonwoods and ash trees, I had decided to walk a longer route in order to pass by the Bozeman Army Navy Store on the south side of Main Street. I was a regular visitor, only interested in gauging the infrequent inventory of wool English hospital blankets.

The store door was propped open, so I strolled inside. All Army Navy stores smell the same, a sort of waxed canvas aroma, that permeated the piles of olive green pants, jackets, and sweaters, locking metal boxes, and heavy-soled boots of many shapes and sizes. My eyes scanned the displays. There, piled high before me, was a 5-foot-tall stack of folded off-white wool blankets. Shivers ran down my spine. I could feel my hair frizz. It was as if a bolt of lightning had shot through my body, leaving me as limp as a wet rag. For no reason at all, I knew without a doubt that these blankets represented my own future Gold Rush in the Valley of the Flowers.

I finally admitted to myself that the creation and sale of lightweight silk clothing in a cold Rocky Mountain state like Montana was crazy. Why didn't I make wild and wonderful wool coats instead? I asked myself. After all, people who lived in this state spent most of their time outside in outerwear that was either of the outdoor sports style or drab overcoat gray, navy, or sometimes red varieties. It was not a huge leap for me to dream up the idea to translate my dye skills into coloring white wool blankets. The storeowner gave me a deal on the purchase because I bought the entire stack of blankets. I raced back to get my car so I could bring my new friends home. It didn't matter that I was late to work. It didn't matter that there was no space in our tiny home for 20 blood-stained English hospital blankets. It only mattered that these hard-to-find, limited-supply blankets now belonged to me.

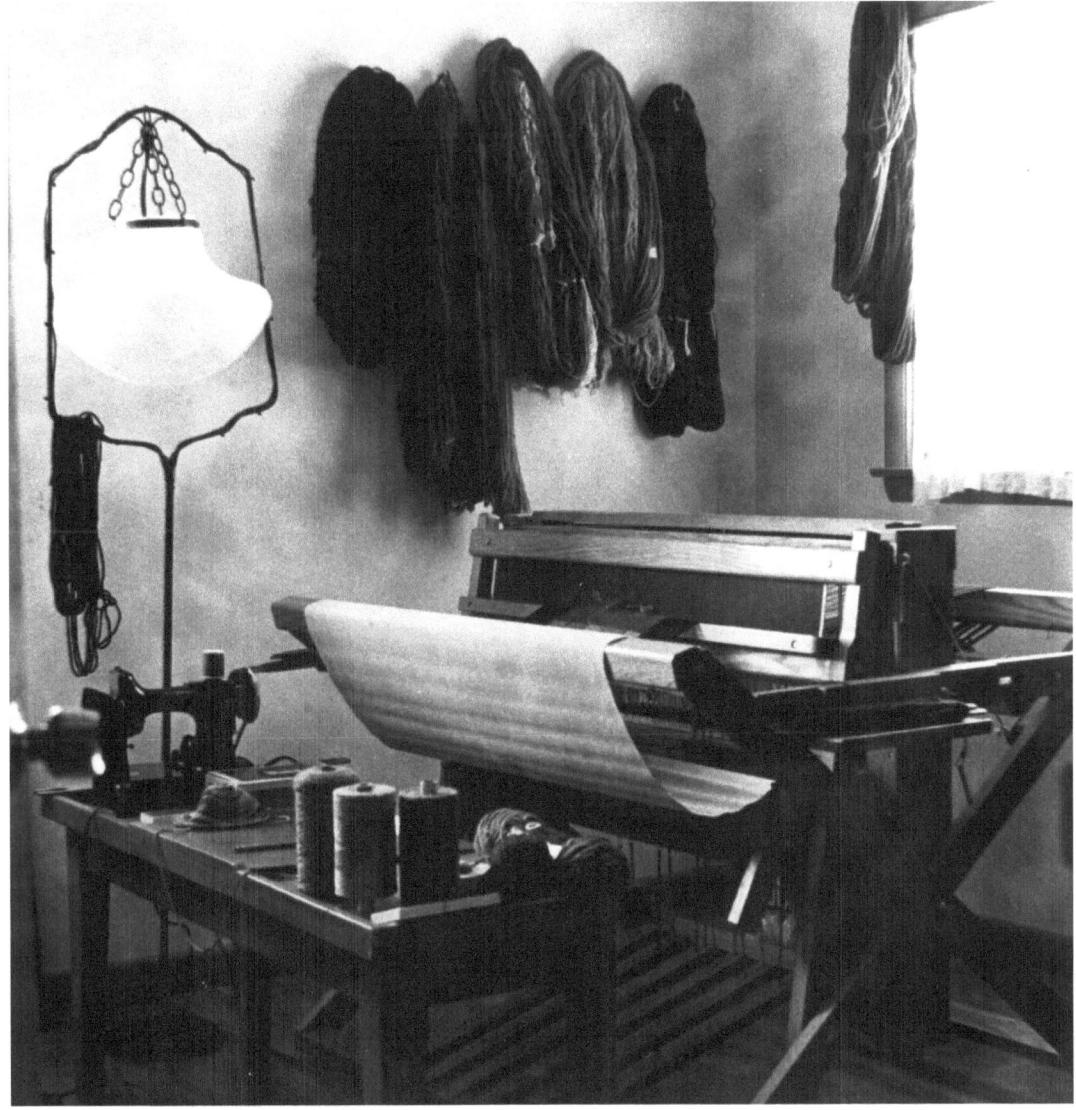

A 10-harness Maccober loom setup in Cindy's living room.

CHAPTER 2

A Washing Machine and a Pot of Purple Dye

Big things were percolating inside our house. A long rickety table took up the entire living room and served as the heart of my design studio. Sketchbooks and canning jars filled with colored pencils shared the space with dyed wool fabric swatches, threads, and ribbons. Large floor-to-ceiling wooden shelves covered the back wall. These were filled with yarns and raw wool used for spinning. A couple of shelves were stacked with my extensive library of design books on dyeing, weaving, spinning, and fabric printing. These books were my open door to the world of contemporary fiber arts. My isolation from what was happening in textiles at a national level was profound. Only through reading books and magazines that covered textile art exhibitions and happening was I able to stay current.

    I may have lacked a connection to the greater arts world, but on the flip side, Lindley Place, a picturesque, quiet, one-block-long street, provided the perfect place to raise a kid, to connect with a community. Many of the oldest homes in Bozeman line this street, and many of these homeowners felt a strong attachment to this neighborhood. In the early 1980s when my daughter was five years old, the street teamed with children her age. I walked out one summer morning to find her and a neighbor sitting on branches high up in our apple tree. Both tomboys, the two young girls spent hours together, in their ubiquitous bicycle beanies, overalls, and scruffy sneakers, building, climbing, digging, and riding their bikes. They were the Tom Sawyers of the street, where many neighbors were woodworkers, potters, painters, and librarians. Several people worked from their homes, so our family fit right in with our steaming dye pots and strung-up weaving looms.

    Purple is made of red and blue, the warmest and coolest colors on the spectrum. It is said that those seeking spiritual fulfillment and peace of mind surround themselves with purple. The first white wool blanket to go into the boiling hot water I poured into the washing machine was dyed a deep dark purple. Pots of dye are magic and mystery because the outcome can never be predicted with any amount of exactness. The not knowing is what attracted me to dyeing. I anxiously lifted the blanket into the dark water. The dye seeped into the folds, puddling here and there. I turned the washer on to gently move the blanket in the dye. Then I mixed the chemicals for setting the dye and poured them into the sloshing dye bath.

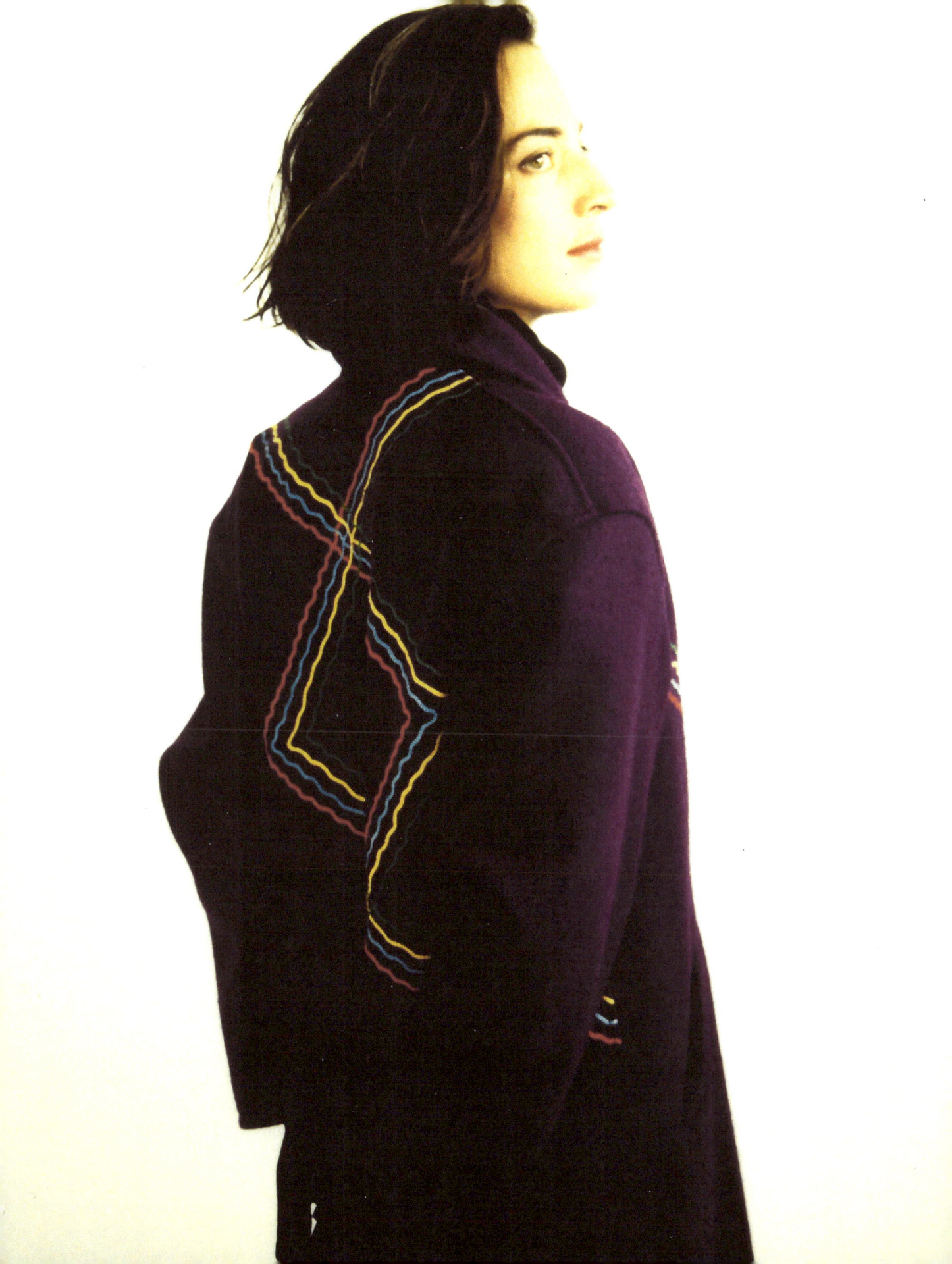

I paced one end of the house to the other. Waiting for my first dyed blanket to come out of the washing machine was like waiting for the birth of a baby. I had no idea whether this crazy scheme could work. In my own knowledge of the fiber arts world, or elsewhere, for that matter, no one was dyeing large amounts of wool fabric in a washing machine. Maybe it was a first. What if it worked? What if the blanket did turn out to be dyed a color of enough intensity, then what? I reminded myself that there was not enough blanket fabric in one blanket to make an entire coat. Cutting around blood spots and worn areas had definite limitations. Good grief, what was I thinking? Excited as I was, I worried that my idea might succeed, or it might fail. It was the not-knowing come to visit.

When I pulled the purple blanket out of the washing machine, it had felted in the hot water and agitation. It looked something like a stiff elk or bison hide with irregular edges and humps in the middle. And, of course, it had shrunk, and so had my confidence in this whole project. As I hung it on the clothesline to dry, I tried to convince myself that dyeing and felting these blankets was a good idea. I tried a second blanket in the washer dye bath. This time, the color was a rich dark green. Once again, of course, the blanket felted. Well, that's easy I told myself. Find beauty in the shrinkage and felting qualities of the process. Change your paradigm. I ended up dyeing all of the blankets each a different color.

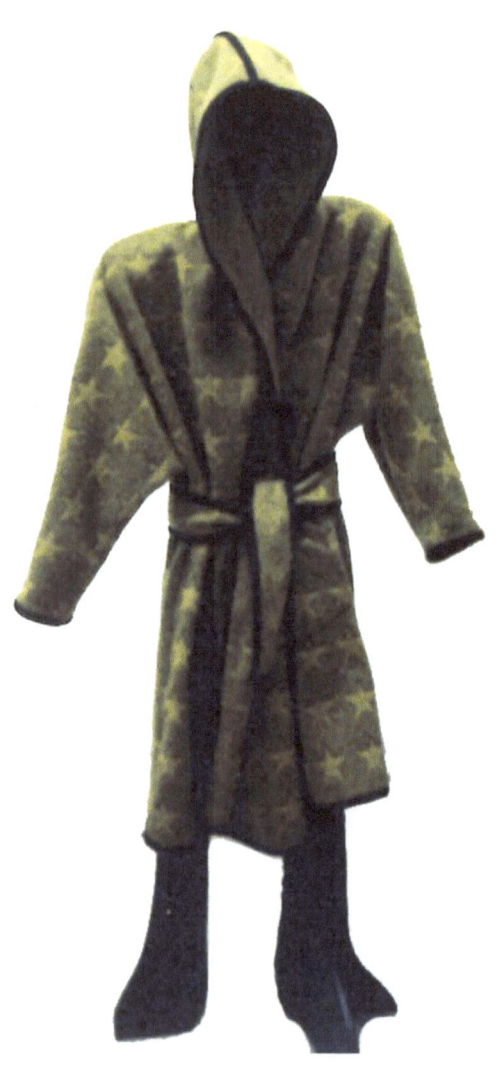

The star fabric was designed by COD and woven at Baron Woolen Mills, a legendary mill established in Bringham City, Utah, in 1871.

Eventually, when all the blankets were dry and steamed to flatness, I racked my brain for ideas on how to use them as coats. Individually, they were too small to make an entire coat. Sometimes ideas flow like water. Sometimes ideas just sprout up from nowhere. I took a long walk outside to clear my thoughts. Playing with ideas as I walked, it came to me that a bit of research might help. Sometimes ideas must have a definite source. I dove into my library of design books to find inspiration. I looked at paintings by Mondrian, Georgia O'Keefe, the African-American quilters of Gee's Bend, Alabama, and quilts by Amish women in Nebraska. As I studied the images of these artists, it dawned on me that blocks of colors were the basic building blocks of the work, and for me, the magic of these designs. Solid planes of color inspired me to see the beauty of each colored blanket for what it could become. A coat did not have to be one color—it could be many colors.

As the magpies swooped and screamed around their young outside my studio in the tall trees, I was thinking, could I make a coat of many colors, and if so, how? This was when the fun began. I quickly started sketching coat design ideas where each coat combined four to five colors. From a roll of newsprint, I started playing with pattern pieces until I came up with a simple short-jacket design. The body was purple, the sleeves were dark green, and the collar/facing was burgundy. I hired a friend to sew the sample together, because she worked at a local backpack manufacturing business and owned an industrial straight-stitch machine that could handle layers of thick felted wool. My Great Aunt Sally's 90-year-old portable Singer sewing machine would be grossly inadequate.

When my friend brought the sewn-together jacket back to me, it looked like a bunch of colored rags hanging together in a clumped mess. Holding it up, she declared, "You have to be kidding?"

Somewhat sheepishly, but with confidence, I replied, "No, this will work, Diane. Wait and see. I will have more for you soon."

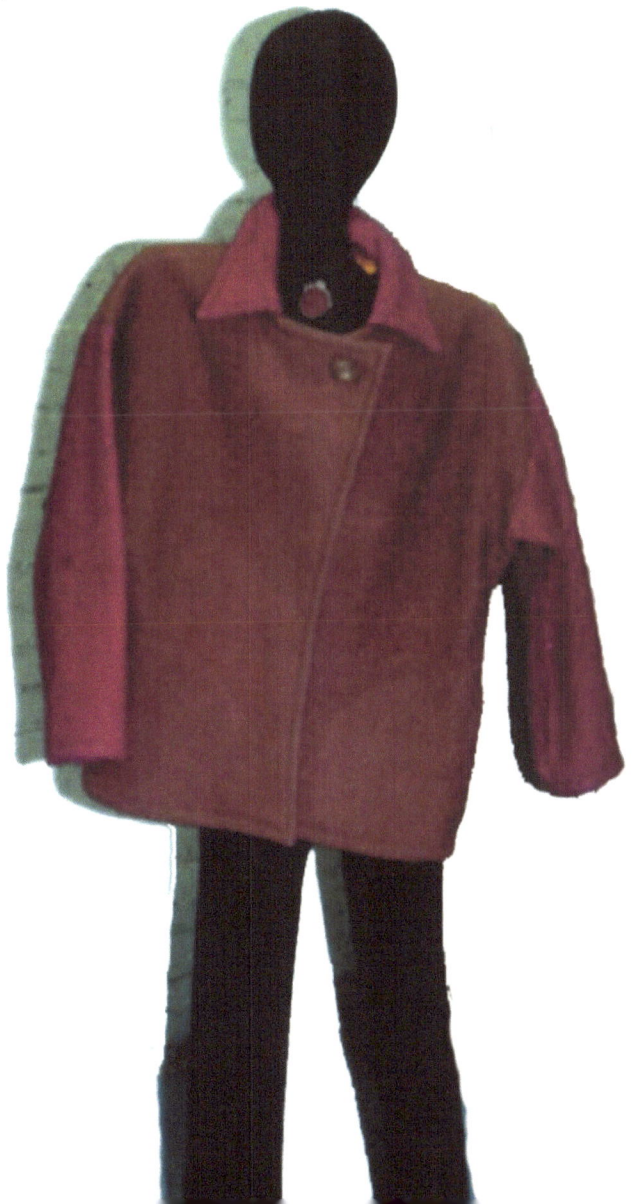

This coat is one of COD's first, made from hand-dyed English hospital blankets.

Again, I called on patience and courage. I dug deep to find my pool of inner knowing. There were no fashion mentors in my life at this point. Nor was the fashion world bursting with color. London fashion designers were the only creators of edgy experimental styles with color and patterns. In the United States, black was the new black, still. Steam irons can do amazing work on fabric. By the time I had steamed and formed the thick seams, flattening the edges, I held the jacket up, tears coming to my eyes. The transformation was magical. This first coat was a true piece of beauty, in my eyes. I raced to the backyard under my beloved apple tree. I held the coat to my chest like the newborn it was. I danced and skipped. I knew this coat was the first sister of many to follow.

Using sections from all 20 dyed blankets, I cut color combinations of sleeves, collars, pockets, and bodies. Next, I created a map of how the new coat parts would be joined. I hired my friend, Diane, to sew five short jackets. She was doubtful, but she still sewed them together in two weeks. When

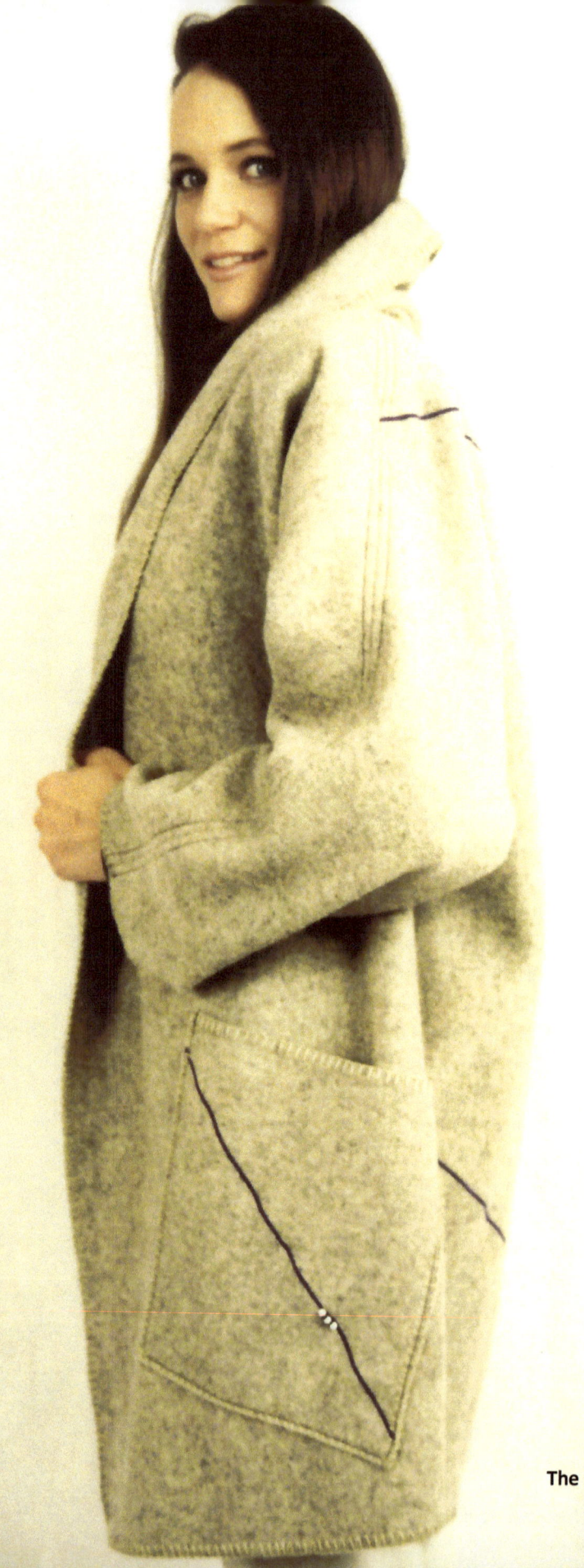

The model is showing one of COD's first three-quarter length blanket coats.

the new coats were completed with wooden button closures, steamed to perfection, and looking presentable, I called Barb Jones at Jones & Company, Ltd., an upscale women's clothing store in downtown Bozeman.

Barb sounded skeptical, but said, "Sure, I'll take a look at one of your coats. Drop by tomorrow while I'm in the store."

Throwing the coat over her snazzy garb, Barb stood in front of the store's full-length mirror, turning to and fro, pulling at the hem and pockets. She raised the collar as if to shut out a cold Montana wind. Then she turned to me, smiled big, and ordered six coats, in different color combinations. I delivered the first half dozen, and the new collection sold within a week. Barb then ordered a dozen coats, and that quickly turned into two dozen.

Barb Jones had been familiar with my hand-painted silk clothing. And I had shopped in her store. When she bought my first coats, however, she definitely went out on a limb. Her confidence in my work was an unexpected gift. There were no indicators in the fashion world that "color blocking" in clothing was an accepted trend. I personally had no idea that color blocking was even a fashion concept. The idea was fresh, new, and exciting, but untried. However, Barb had a trained eye and she knew what her customers liked.

The beautiful purple blanket became my talisman. As an artist, an idea that turns into a passion can be a curse of sorts. There is a certain internal conversation with one's self around creation. Yet I have to admit had my dyed blankets not turned into a marketable item I wouldn't have cared. My road, yes, was the one less traveled, but it was still my road. The wool blankets and the dyeing process were what most interested me.

The story turned a hairpin corner right here because I decided to transform my passion into a business in order to make a living. My experience with selling handmade clothing in Montana was limited. Was I shooting in the dark to think I could market hand-dyed, felted, multicolored coats locally and even beyond? My passion had morphed into a grand vision. I knew my dyed wool blankets held promise, but would clothing retailers agree? I had no business experience, but I could conjure ideas. I had some idea of how to design and sew. Even at that, my skills were self-taught and limited. Regardless, coats of many colors would become my life-blood for the next 23 years. Sewn into the folds of that first coat were all my doubts, my struggles, and my hard work. That was the magic of the purple blanket. The purple blanket was also the mystery. How would I pull off building a coat business from nothing?

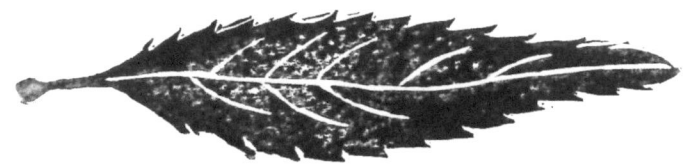

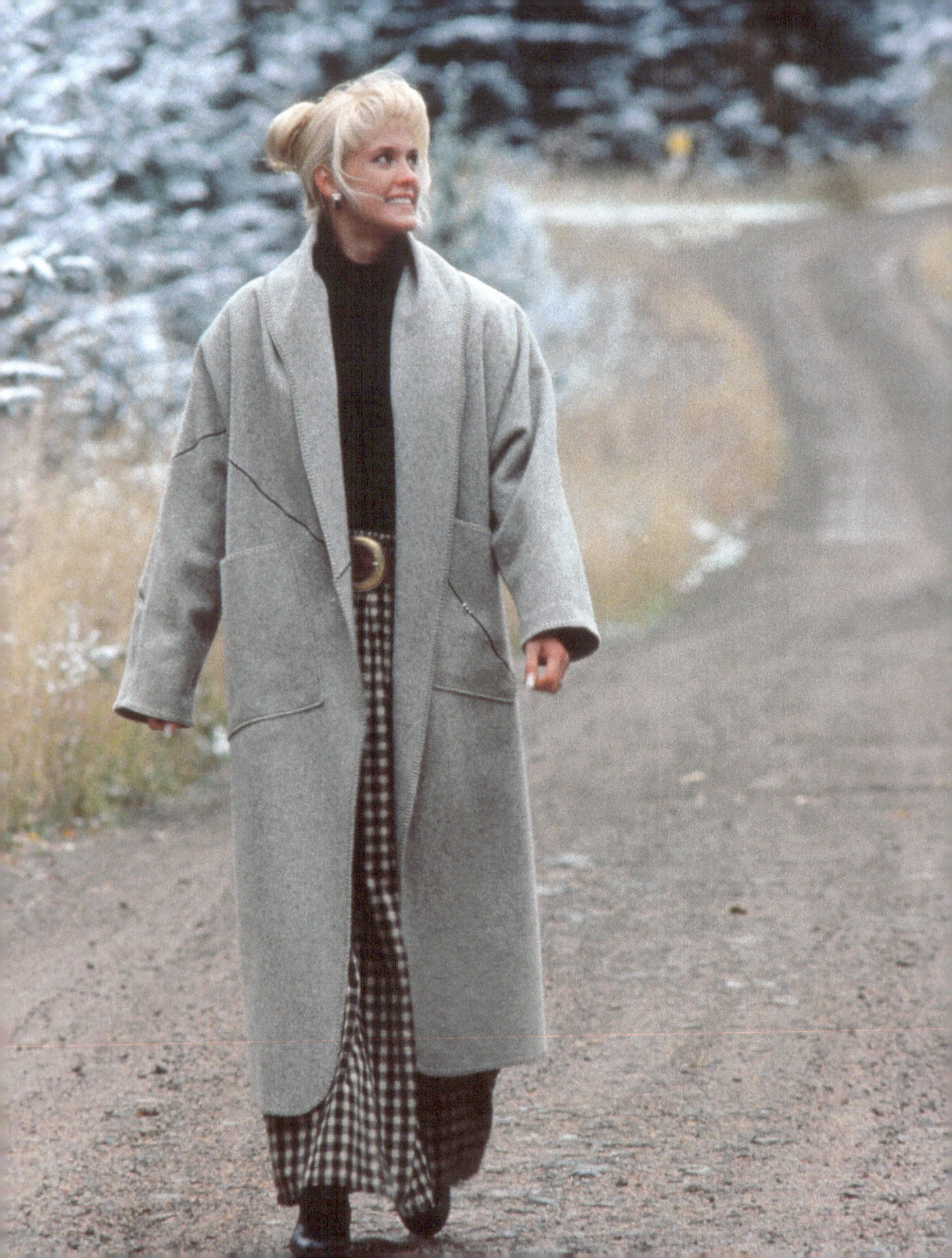

CHAPTER 3

Coat Business Fledges

All good things come to an end, or evolve. My washing machine started to clunk and grind. Most likely it was overtaxed as one heavy blanket after another was dyed in scalding water. Washing white underwear was now out of the question. The Army Navy Store went out of business, so my source of white wool blankets disappeared. Our Lindley Place house was no longer big enough to accommodate fabric layout, hanging cardboard patterns, dyeing, and sewing coats. Maya remembers how she took it for granted that our house would be filled with hanging wet blankets, sewing machines, and stacks of fabric. Recalling her childhood, she says, "Even though my home was pretty different from the homes of my friends, I really only worried about my mom and me never having money like my friends."

My job at The Textile Merchant became impossible to continue because my coat business had become a 12-hour-a-day job. Money was going out in all directions. And income from the coat business came in at a trickle. Still, I refused to work a "real job." I trusted the future of my coat business to provide the lifestyle I wanted.

Neighborhood trees turned yellow and burnt-orange as I sat on my couch in the early 1980s to contemplate my situation. Momentous decisions had to be made. First, how could I locate wool coat fabric to replicate thick wool blankets? The Internet did not exist at this time, so research required lots of library time. I spent hours at both the MSU (Montana State University) and Bozeman libraries and soon became all too familiar with commercial industry listings of tomes 4 to 5 inches thick. The volumes were filled with topics covering wrenches to caskets to rose suppliers. Fabric source listings were often outdated. The search became frustrating and discouraging. I left the library each visit with a file folder full of contacts, phone numbers, and addresses. Upon following up with phone calls, I found many wool fabric companies had gone out of business. My mind spun in so many circles around sourcing, I lost track of time. I had no place to turn for answers. The fabric search took more than six months. During this time, with frayed nerves, I paced our house front to back. And I made no coats.

Following World War II, ranchers in the United States had stopped raising sheep because there was little call for wool. Growers turned to corn and grains. America focused on manufacturing steel for cars and rubber for tires. America's wool industry was scarfed up by the wool industries in New Zealand and Australia. The Southern Hemisphere's large-tract

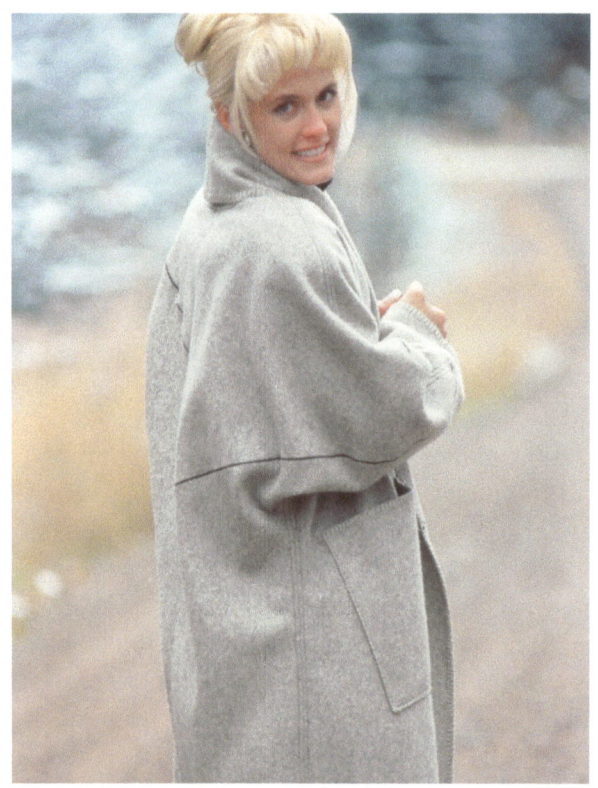
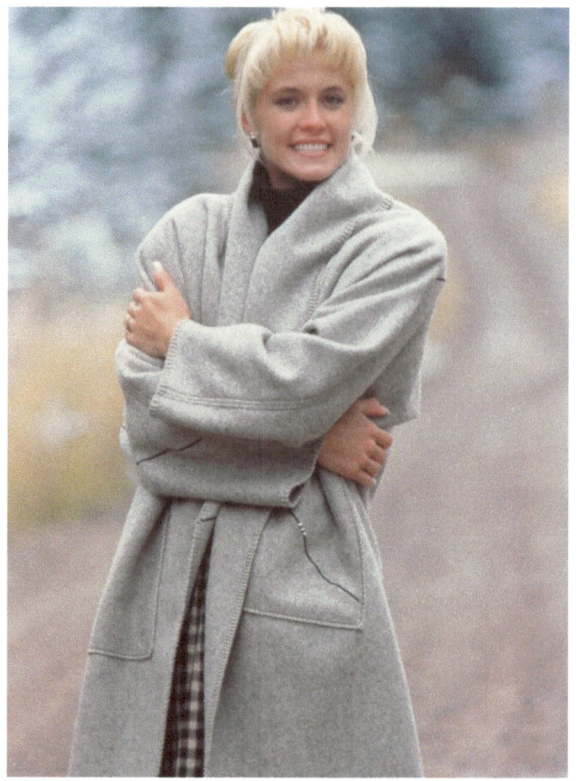

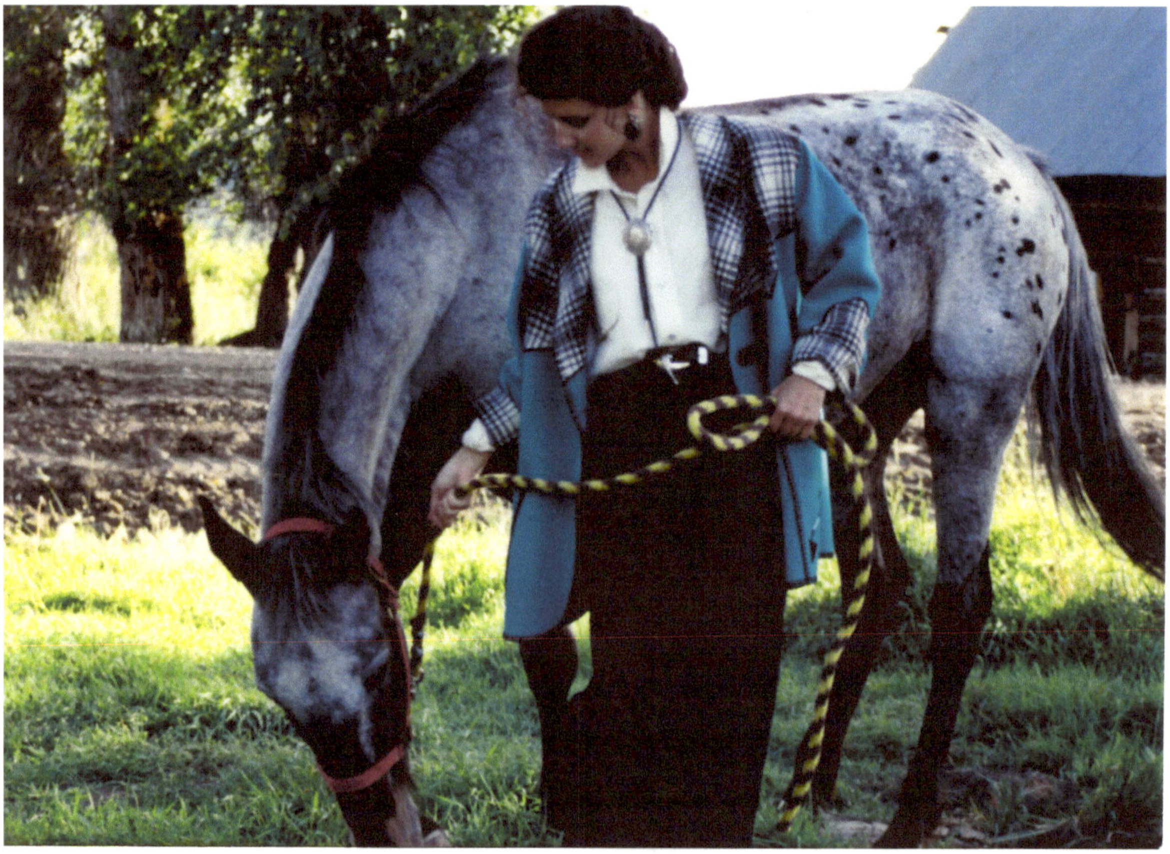

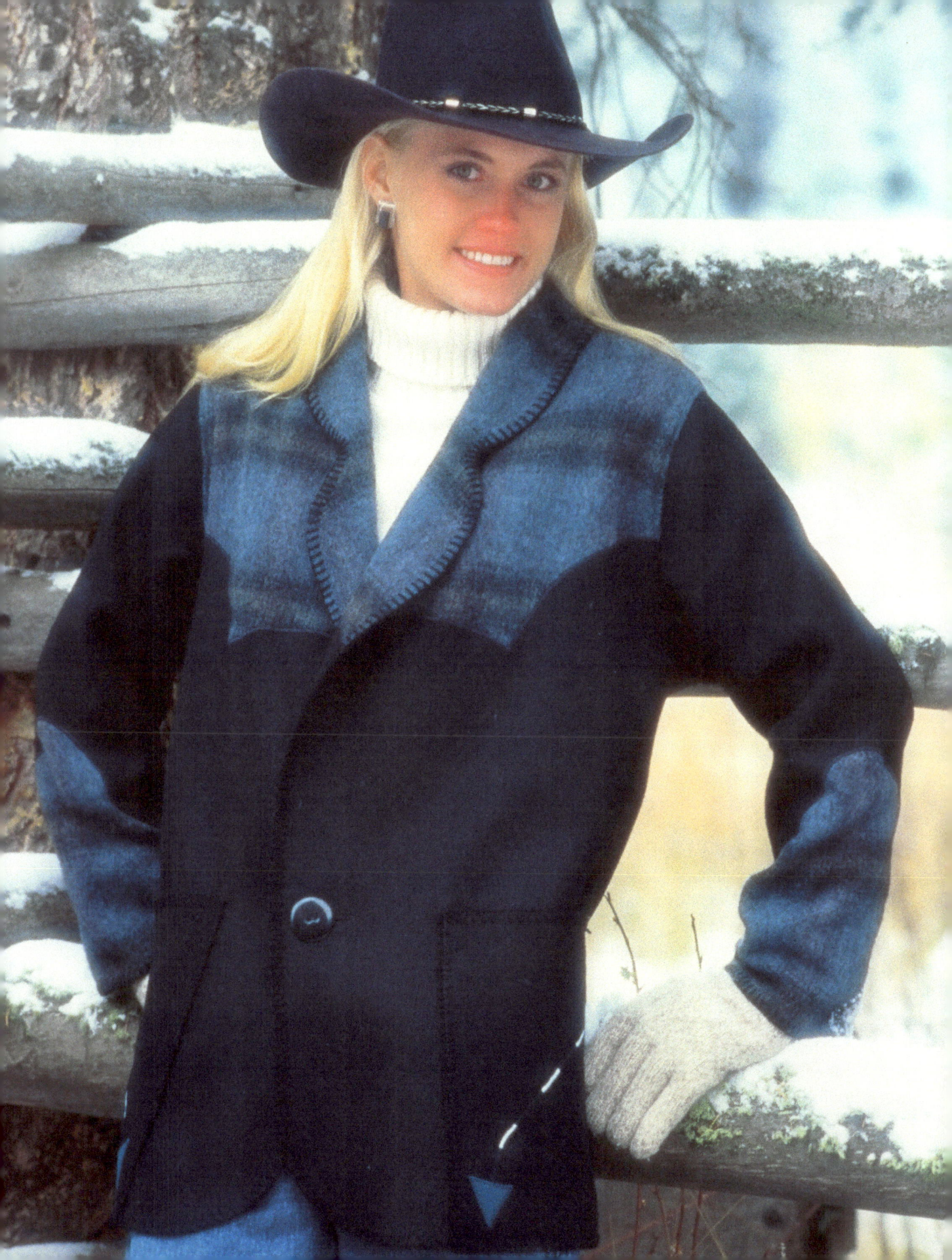

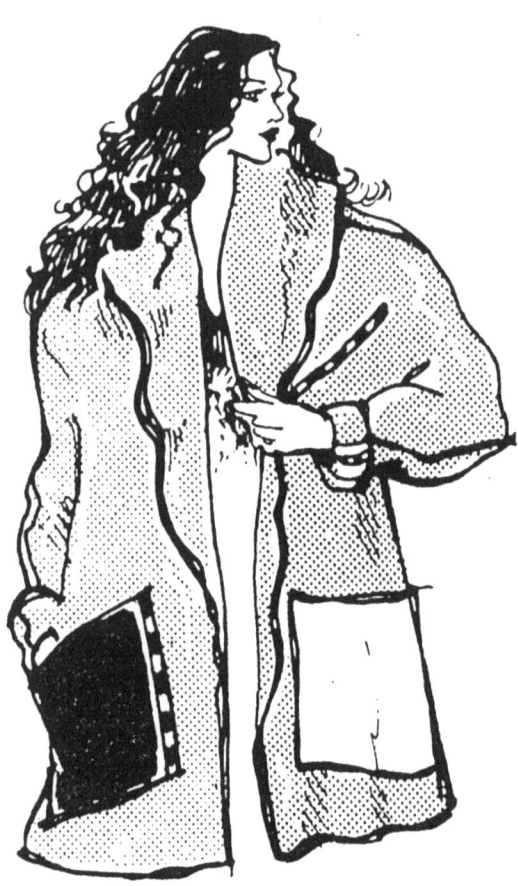

sheep raisers sold highly sought after merino wool to China. At this time, Americans were enamored with polyester and nylon, not natural fibers. The U.S. fabric industry was defined by clothing manufacturing focused on T-shirts, activewear, uniforms, jeans, and nylon outerwear. Wool? Who in the United States wove large amounts of wool outerwear fabric anymore? It turned out nobody did. I was even more bereft at losing my source for wonderful English wool blankets. The wool situation gave me pause to question continuing, but it did not deter me, as I had fallen deeply in love with wool.

My telephone bill skyrocketed as I called one fabric distributor after another from one end of the country to the other. An unexpected hurdle emerged. What were the magic words that could convince fabric suppliers to take me seriously as an outerwear manufacturer? After all, the "rag trade" was located in either Los Angeles or New York City, not a remote state like Montana. Now, where is Montana? "Isn't it part of Canada?" asked one fabric merchant after another. Montana, the place I loved so dearly as home, turned out to be a liability when I attempted to connect to the larger world of serious fashion suppliers.

Finally, a Canadian friend directed me to Victor Woolen Mills in Quebec, Canada. I looked up information on the mill and found they wove a wide range of colors in two different weights of wool melton fabric. I was familiar with felted wool fabric, or melton, because it was used in the manufacturing of pea coats, short double-breasted jackets worn by U.S. Navy sailors. An iconic black-and-white photo of my parents holding me as a baby shows my dad wearing a dark-navy pea coat. It was 1946 and he had just been released from the Navy. In fact, I secretly modeled my own wool coat designs after my dad's pea coat, as I was so filled with nostalgia.

When I called Victor Woolen Mills, the receptionist answered the phone in French. Upon hearing my English-only voice, she searched for a person who spoke enough English to answer my questions. My palms were sweaty and shaking as I held the phone. My heart raced. It bothered me that I had failed French in college. My own French communication skills were very limited. Through English peppered with some French, I was able to order 5 yards each of five colors of 24-oz. brushed wool fabric and 5 yards each of five colors of 12-oz. felted wool melton. The brushed wool was the same as a fuzzy blanket with a two-sided nap. The melton was tightly woven, felted, and heavily brushed, making it soft to the touch.

Finally, I breathed a sigh of relief having found a colorful wool fabric sold by the yard. I said, "Yes, yes, yes," loud and strong. I could move on from blankets. No more dyeing in the washing machine. No more living with wet blankets hanging around our house. No more frozen condensation on our windows. My daughter and I lived and breathed my blanket dyeing process for three long years. Maya jumped with joy when she found out our house could be a home again. While I knew I had to go in the direction of using commercially dyed wool fabric, this departure still made me sad. Nevertheless, I put my deep passion for the process of dyeing wool blankets on a shelf and moved on.

It turned out that COD (Cindy Owings Designs) was Victor's first U.S. customer. Our association lasted for about 10 years. On one occasion, I visited the mill. Quebec City's cobbled streets lined with old-world houses and shops reminded me of places I had seen in France. Nearby, in the tiny village of Saint-Victor, Victor Woolen Mills was the center of the area's economy. I was welcomed with enthusiasm by mill staff. The sound of the clattering looms in the cavernous weaving room was music to my ears. The aroma of raw wool washed over me as the yarn was woven into the fabrics my seamstresses would sew. I felt I had come home in some sense. The mill was the birthplace of COD's new coats, after all.

The second momentous decision had to do with the need for a workspace. It was clear that the coat business had taken over our home. The manufacturing had to move, but where? In the past, I had rented studio space for hand-painting silk at two different places on Bozeman's Main Street, but the locations were now restaurants and lawyer offices. While riding my bike around the Northeast neighborhood, I spotted a for-rent sign on a brick building on Peach Street. The building turned out to be the cold storage facility that had once supplied the growing town with fresh produce.

The huge rolls of wool fabric shipping from Victor Woolen Mills could now be delivered to a place outside our home. I hired a friend to build a sturdy wood and Masonite cutting table. It fit onto giant saw horses. I will never forget seeing all the new rolls of fabric piled high on the table. The distinctive smell of wool mixed with the smell of the history of this building. I loved the idea of working in a place that had been so vitally connected to Bozeman. The scene was one of those moments when it became crystal clear I had made the right decision.

The new space represented a huge step forward as well as a huge stretch to pay the rent. The move was a big risk. The big table piled with rolls of fabric gave me butterflies. All sorts of questions flew into my head. New fabric required new coat designs. New coat designs required an expanded marketing approach. New coat designs required industrial sewing machines and operators who knew how to sew. One new coat design is not just that. New designs carry with them a rainbow of considerations.

CHAPTER 4

And, Flies

Moving shop from our Lindley Place home, I heard the magpies screech around the tops of the trees. Fledging baby birds is serious business. The energy needed to raise a brood is all consuming for the parents. It takes a lot of energy to start a life. Now with a source for my coat fabric and a new workspace, I felt like a young bird, myself, having acquired the feathers necessary to take off, and fly.

Among the rainbow of considerations I now entertained was the creation of a name for my new venture. I asked a graphic artist friend to help me. After we batted around a lot of name possibilities, my friend finally said, "Why don't you just call it Cindy Owings Designs?"

How obvious, I thought. Brilliant! The name was simple and could be an umbrella for any artistic endeavor. The name stuck and went on to be the name of my coat business and all of its iterations for 23 years. With a new name came a new business location, new fabric, and new problems to be solved.

Eventually, each coat we made had a black-and-white line that coursed around the surface or edged blocks of color. The line was a design element that held meaning for me. The checkerboard "snake," as we called it, paid homage to the indomitable spirit of magpies, with their black-and-white pattern, that have graced my entire life in the West.

As for the process of fledge to flight at COD, the birth of the first coats made with commercially woven and dyed wool fabric took place at the Peach Street studio in the cold storage facility. Excited to be using new fabrics, I dove into making new patterns out of butcher paper that was cut and sewn from the Victor fabrics. The cutting table was cleared of all but paper for making patterns. The cold storage room ceiling fluttered with hanging drafts of patterns. Using pattern pieces from Vogue home sewing patterns, I cobbled together beginning designs.

At this time, I knew nothing about the art and science of making clothing patterns. My first attempts at fitting together sleeves to bodies produced a garment that conceptually was a coat. However, fit-wise, the pattern had a long way to go before becoming recognizable as a coat. I knew I was in over my head. I had to find someone who could help me with the technical end of garment sizing and pattern drafting.

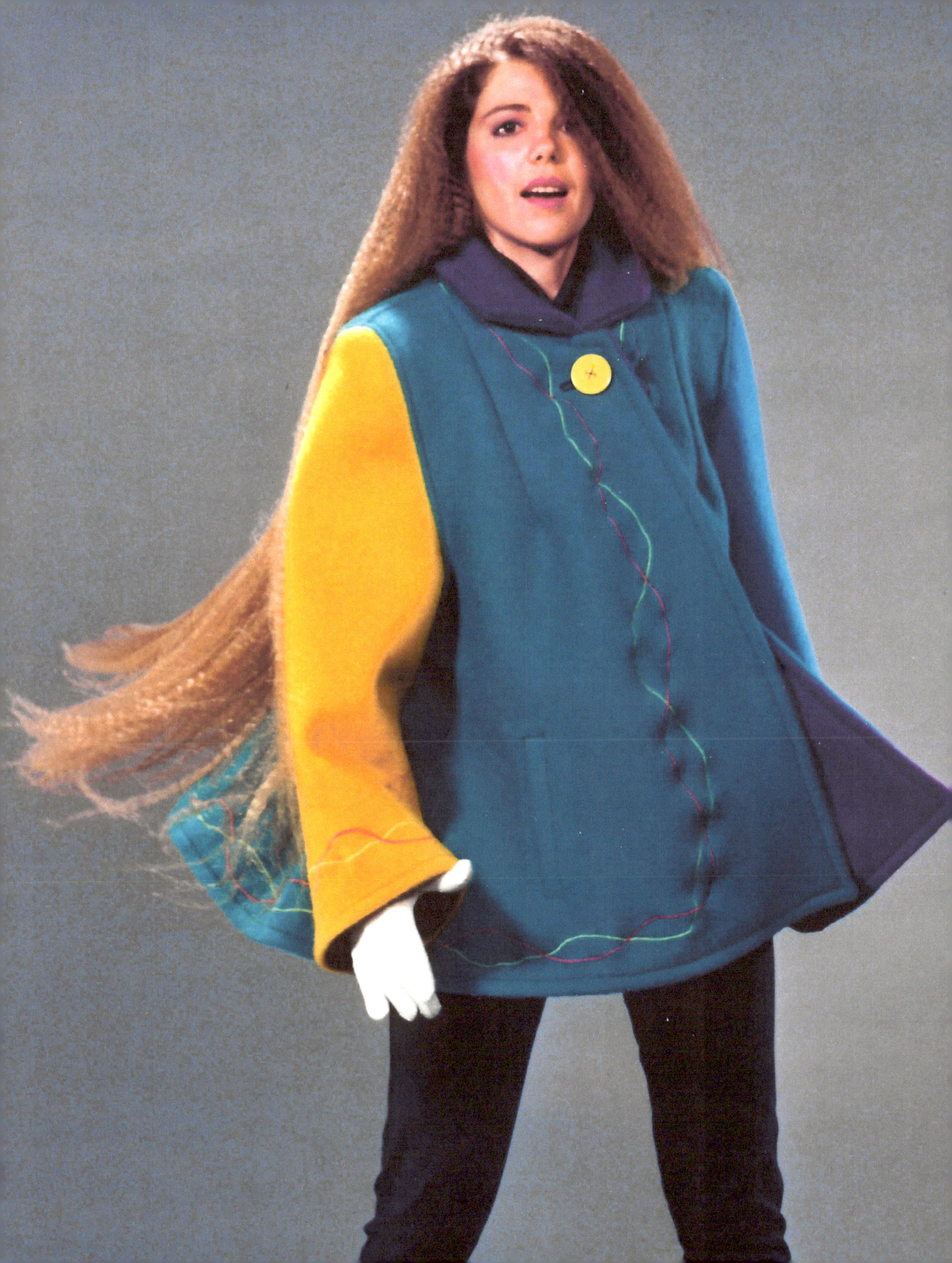

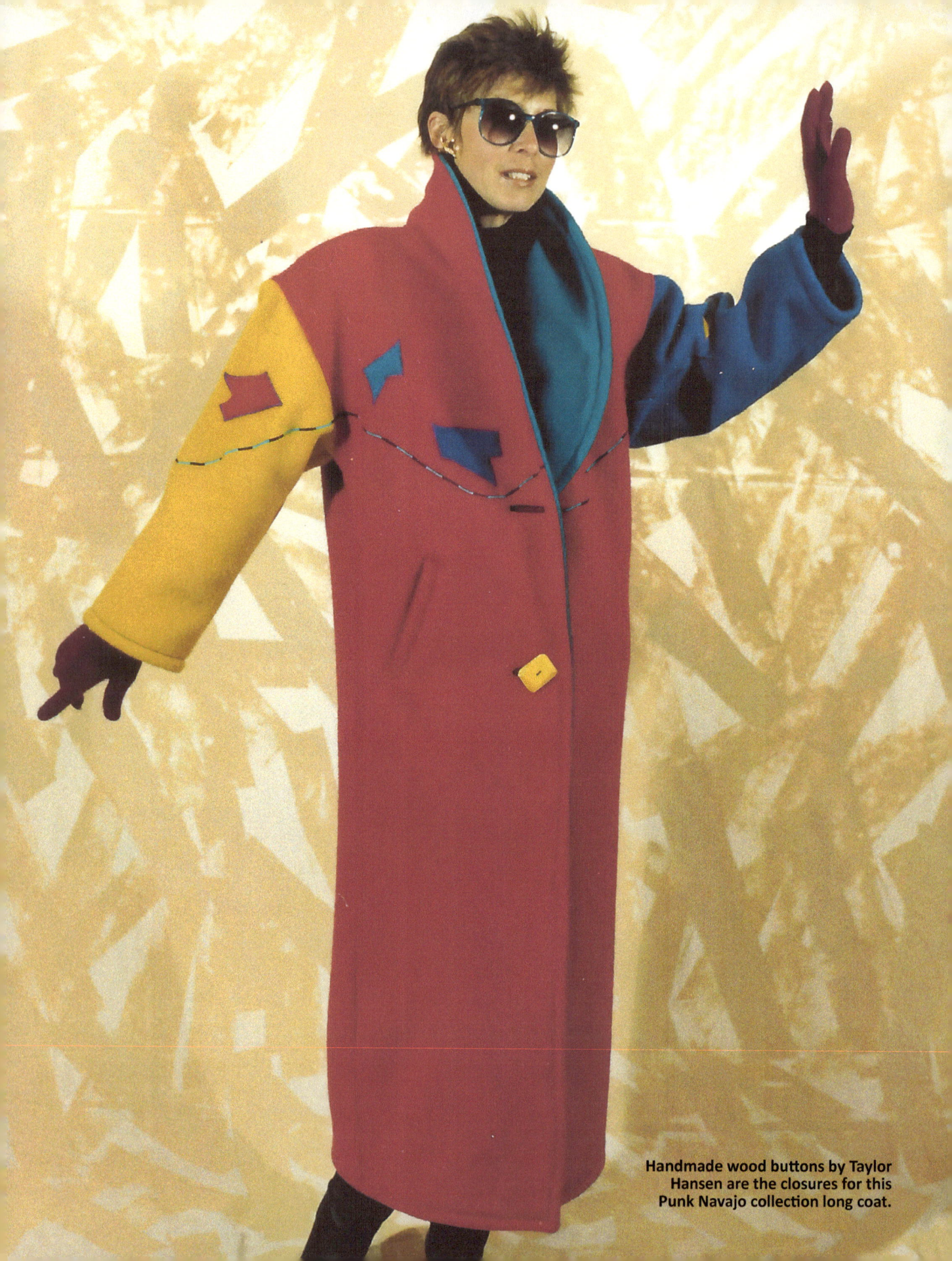

Handmade wood buttons by Taylor Hansen are the closures for this Punk Navajo collection long coat.

So I advertised for help and ended up hiring an experienced "sewist" (sewer and artist) who had a more precise and technical understanding of clothing construction than I did. She was an engineer with extensive knowledge of sewing processes and the creation of workable systems. She turned out to be a perfect addition to my business. She was adept at capturing my ideas for garments. She could turn these often crazy ideas into reality. I came to trust my first employee's skills and judgment implicitly. Eventually, she handled the entire production end of COD. From my ideas, she created patterns, sewed, and quality-checked our entire production of coats. In addition, she trained and supervised all new sewing room employees, becoming one of COD's most valued employees and assets.

The first five coats were made with the brushed fabric that resembled the nap of blankets. I designed three styles: a short jacket, a three-quarter coat, and a long overcoat. Each coat was made with three colors of fabric. The body was one color, the sleeves a different color, and the collar/facing a third color. All of the coats were lined with black satin. The surfaces of the coats were not decorated. The coats were quite plain, actually, except they were colorful.

At about this time, the name, Cindy Owings Designs, was shortened to COD. I made this change because I created each label for each coat by hand-painting the name on silk, and the full name was way too long to draw on a 2-inch x 3-inch label. Visually, COD was easier to read and was more playful. The letters also carried more than one meaning. Cash on Delivery (COD) guarantees customer payment. The letters are universally recognized. I painted large sheets of labels that were cut apart and sewn into the interior of each coat. Now coats can be identified by their year of origin through how the interior label was made. Early coats had hand-painted silk labels. Later coats had labels printed by Hands On Printing, in Four Corners, Montana, 10 miles outside of Bozeman. Finally, the coats all had commercially woven black-and-white labels, once again a subliminal homage to magpies.

The renaming of Cindy Owings Designs made me feel ownership in some strange way. The magpies were now adults. They could make choices about their territories, how they are nourished, and how fast to fly. I felt confident that my coats would fly. And, fly they would. Sometimes they flew too high and fast for even me, a doting parent, to comprehend. With all my might, I hung on, as my coat designs reached new heights.

At this point, COD coats were being sold in a few towns in Montana, including Billings, Bozeman, and Missoula. We hadn't made enough coats out of the new wool fabric to claim five coats could be a "collection," but still I called as many stores as I knew about in the state to gauge interest in our new coats. A few stores said they would give the coats a try. They ordered two or three. I wasn't discouraged, but knew we had to sell more than this. Jones & Company in Bozeman remained a steadfast supporter, selling as many as we could make.

Throughout my years of toying with the artistic creation of clothing, I also experimented with the marketing of my products. I was not afraid to send up trial balloons

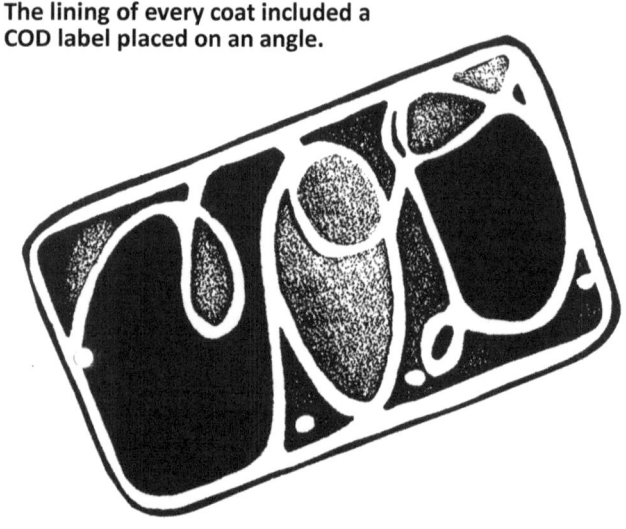

The lining of every coat included a COD label placed on an angle.

in the form of contacting retailers and sales reps in the rag trade to get feedback. One such request went out to an acquaintance in Denver, Colorado, who owned a wholesale showroom in the Merchandise Mart. She had sold tie-dyed cotton socks a friend and I had made some years back. Tie-dyed socks were a long way from wool coats, but oh well, nothing tried, nothing gained. I called the Denver sales rep to ask her whether she had any ideas about marketing my wool coats. And it turned out she did.

It's trite to say, it's not so much what you know, but who you know. Serendipity, who you know, who they know, with a bit of "nice" sprinkled on top, is what moves the world. Remember, these were the years before social networking on the Internet. Living in Montana during the launch of my rag trade outreach and my marketing efforts was a liability. What designer in her right mind would choose to live in the wilds of Montana and attempt to run a fashion business from such a remote location? But staying in Montana was very important to my artistic development. My sense of place in the mountains was the heart of my creativity. The warmth of wool buffered the cold snowy winters I loved. Crisp Rocky Mountain air buoyed my dreams. And close proximity to seven Native tribes inspired my choices of color in textiles.

The sales rep had a friend in New York City who sold Kenya bags. He had mentioned to her he was looking to share his booth at the upcoming New York Boutique Show. She suggested to me, "Give Frank a call. He just may like having you share his booth, and he needs the money."

"Wow, thank you," I said excitedly. "What a great lead and opportunity. I really appreciate your support." I hung up. I was shaking all over.

I quickly phoned the Kenya bag seller. He was hesitant, saying, "Well uh" and "Oh coats, hmm, for real?" I suspected the usual question, "You're...from...where?" However, I talked my way into the left side of Frank Hammelbacher's 10-foot-square booth at the New York show. I had no real idea what I had just agreed to. Kenya bags and COD wool coats go together like cats and dogs. No matter. Soon enough COD would be on the map, and that happened in the most extraordinary of ways. The show turned out to be one of the best decisions of my business life.

Opposite, Top Left: These Arrow Jackets, featuring COD's signature black and white snake design, were a best-selling item.

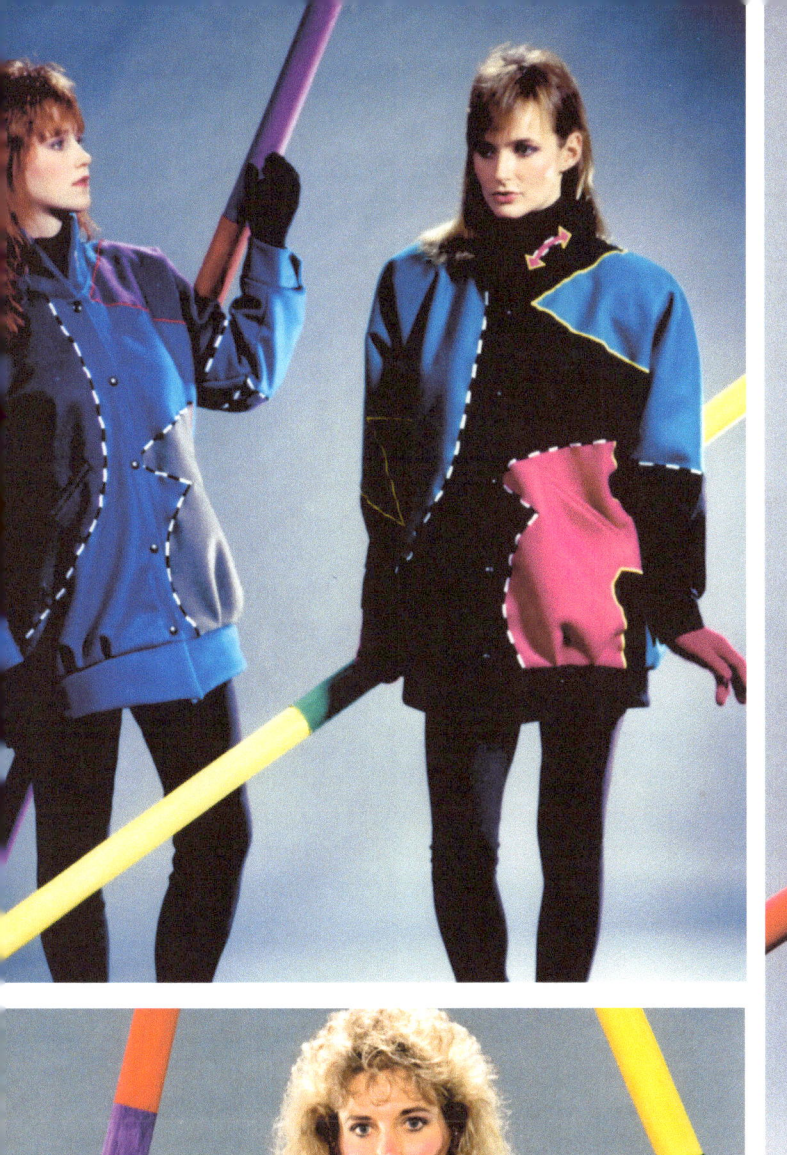
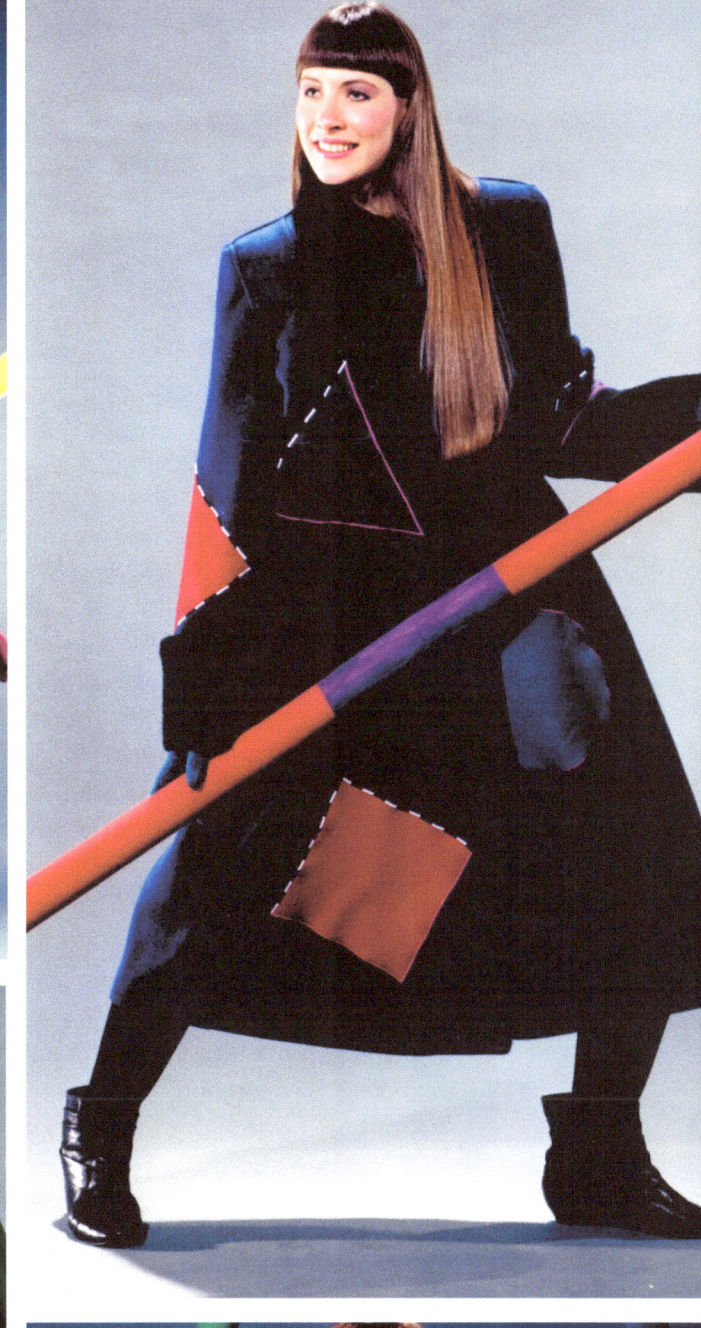
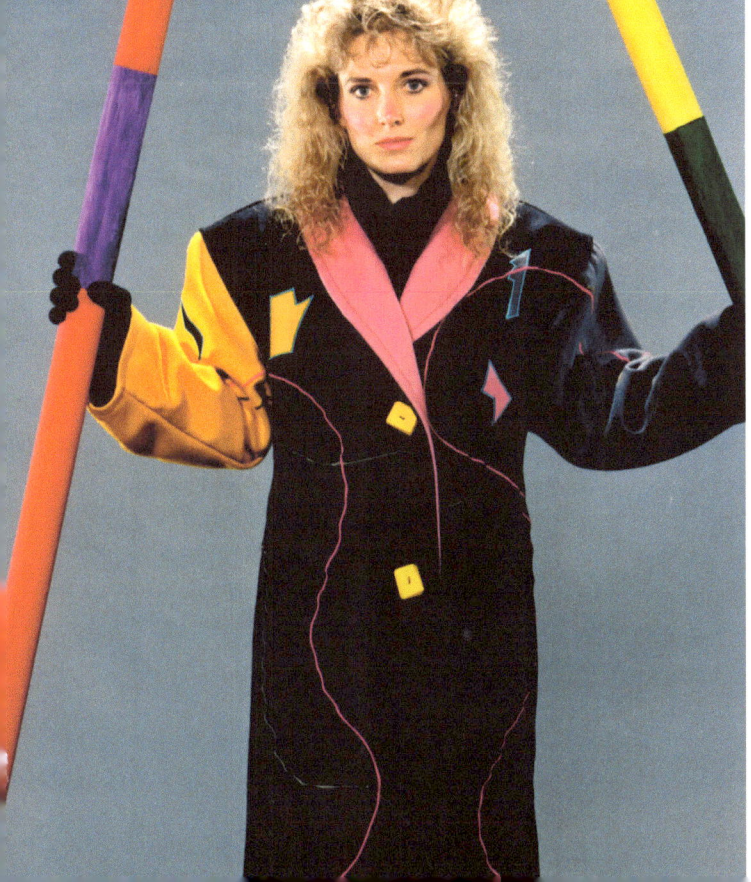
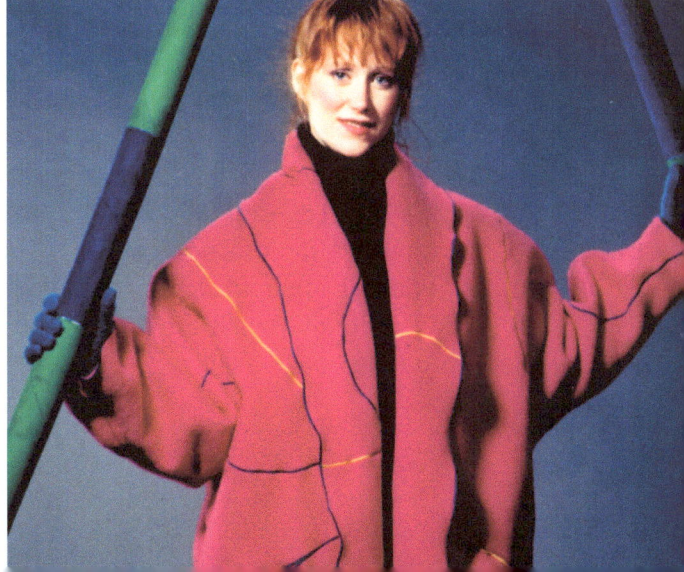

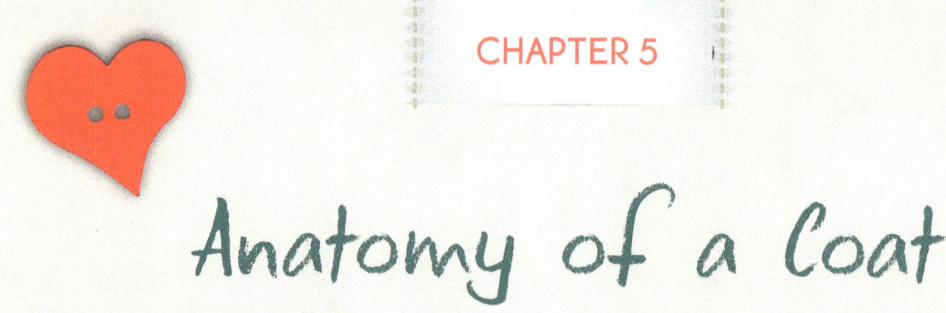

CHAPTER 5

Anatomy of a Coat

What's in a coat? The steps to reach a complete finished coat begin and end in an idea not at once known or fleshed out. Conceptually, for any cloth to become a garment, flat fabric must become three-dimensional. The manner in which the transformation occurs depends on adherence to general clothing construction steps and standards. Coat construction, however, presents a myriad of considerations of a different type specific to how wool fabric acts and performs when manipulated. A piece of 10-oz. wool melton becomes almost like cookie dough when sewn. The fabric, in other words, is malleable. Essential to forming around the human body, wool fabric can be pushed and pulled to shape shoulder seams, pocket openings, and curved back seams, for instance. Therein lays melton's beauty. Wool is "forgiving" when cut and sewn. The opposite is also true when sewing layers of melton wool. Wool loves to stick to itself. It stays in place in layers convenient in sewing seams.

Once the general idea of what a particular coat would look like was settled upon, the patterns could be sketched, in the flat. The basic anatomy of a coat includes the collar, sleeves, buttonholes, darts, pockets, neck facings, lining, and hemline. Along with the patterns, a discussion about the surface designs would ensue. Most COD coats involved elaborate "piecing" (in sewing parlance). For instance, in the case of the "Kissing Animal Series," the animal heads (four altogether per coat, front and back) made up the tops of the coat front and back patterns. The heads were not laid on top of a coat body, but pieced together in place by decorative satin-stitch outlines. It would be like working on a jigsaw puzzle fitting each piece in place to define the whole.

The quality of a COD coat not only depended on the sewers, but on the cutters, as well. The cutting required extreme attention to detail. In order for the piecing of colored wool fabric that COD would become known for to work, each cut piece required exact precision edges. Edges of fabric had to marry each other in an exact butted assembly. If a cutter sneezed, for instance, causing scissors to nick an edge, the entire piece must be re-cut. Wool melton holds an edge without stretching or puckering. Wool fabric could be layered to cut multiple pattern pieces using a vertical electric cutter. The quality of each cut piece depended on the skill of the cutting tool operator.

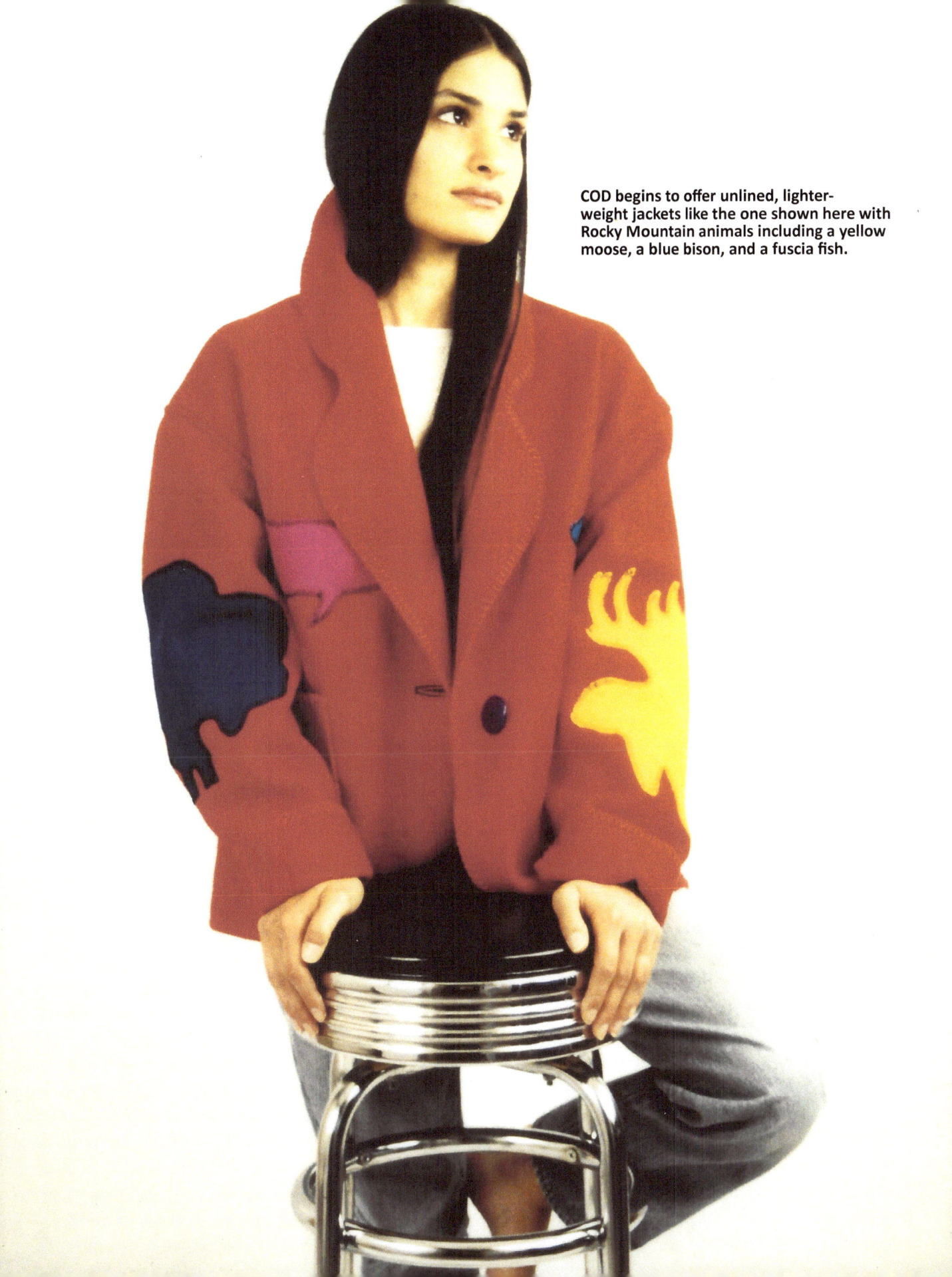

COD begins to offer unlined, lighter-weight jackets like the one shown here with Rocky Mountain animals including a yellow moose, a blue bison, and a fuscia fish.

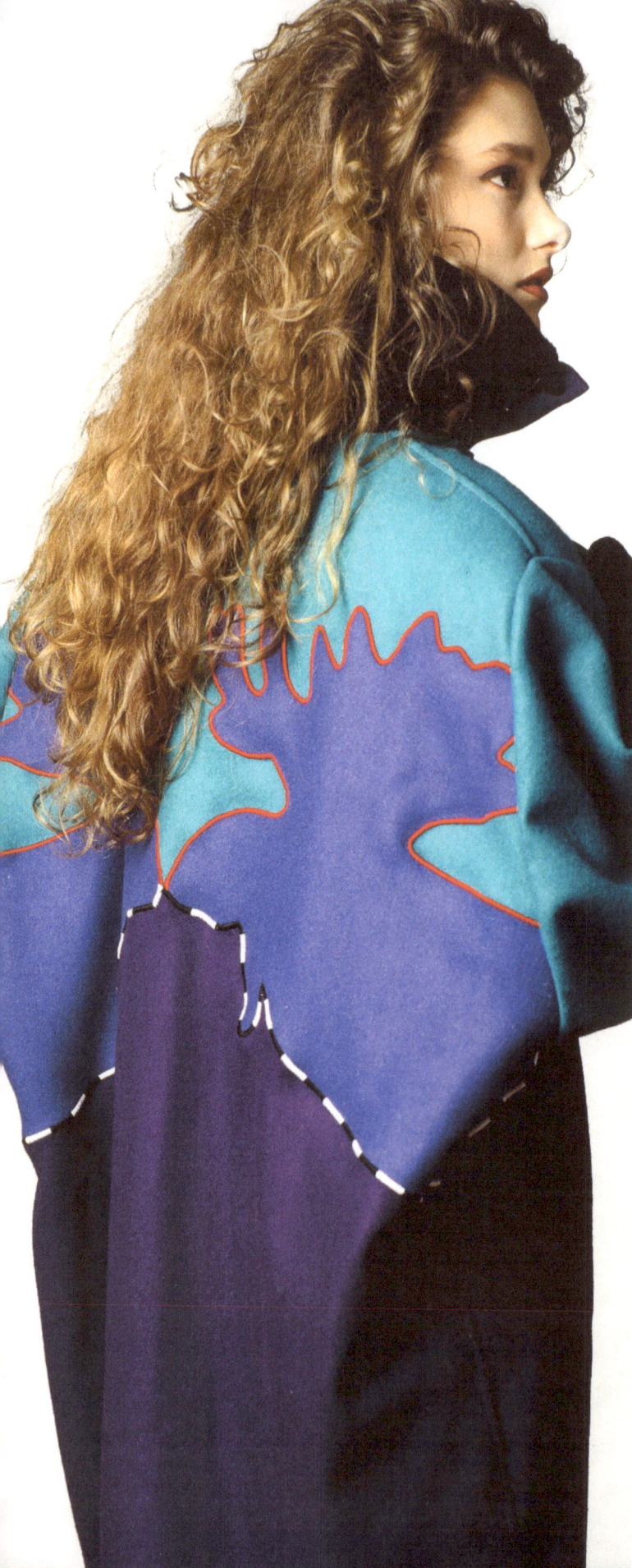

The flowing beauty and simplicity of a COD coat belied the mechanics of actually making the coat. Not only was the general concept of a coat discussed by the production staff, but the method of putting it together was addressed in minute detail as well. Our fleet of sewing machinery limited or defined our coat designs. COD's most valuable machines were our Bernina 217s. Swiss-made, these machines were considered to be the Cadillac of commercial embroidery/straight-stitch machines. All of our designs depended on operator skill. These machines could make a ¼-inch-wide satin stitch used in piecing and design definition. When a Bernina broke down, the one experienced sewing machine mechanic who repaired these machines fortunately lived north of Salt Lake City, Utah, not that far away. So we removed the sewing head from the motorized sewing table and piled more than one in my Toyota station wagon to be driven south for repair.

We used Brother and Juki straight-stitch industrial machines for wool fabric construction. Polyester satin linings were sewn together using a 5 Thread Serger. The Merrow machine, used for our blanket stitch, was also a valuable machine for edging, especially in pillow making, and the Omnistitch machine was used for free-form surface designs.

Left: Two moose are kissing on the back of this full-length coat from the Kissing Animal Series.

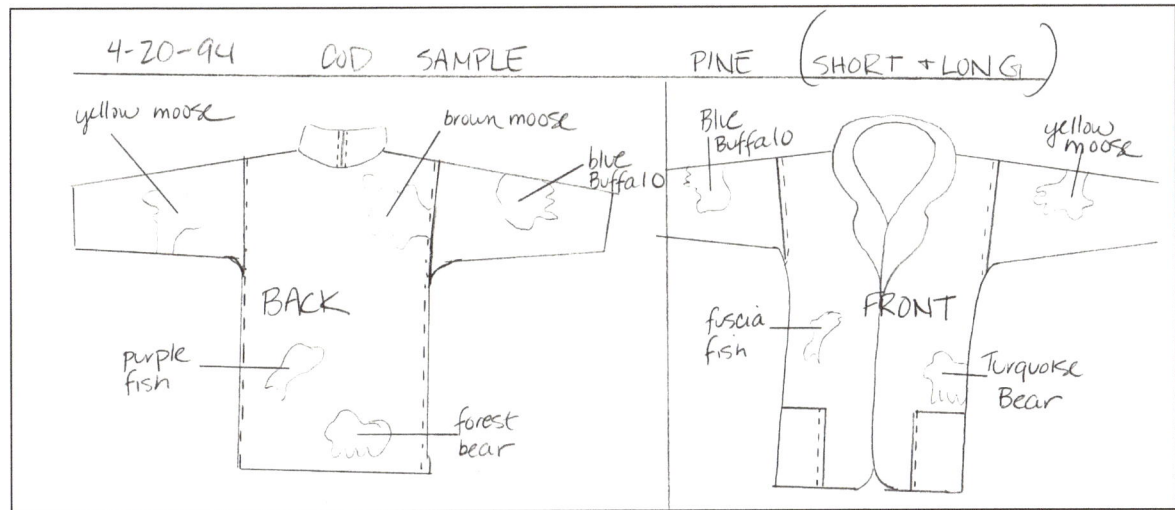

Above is a Rocky Mountain series sample drawing illustrating the placement of surface designs. A finished hooded jacket with color blocked animal backgrounds and mountains on the sleeves is to the right.

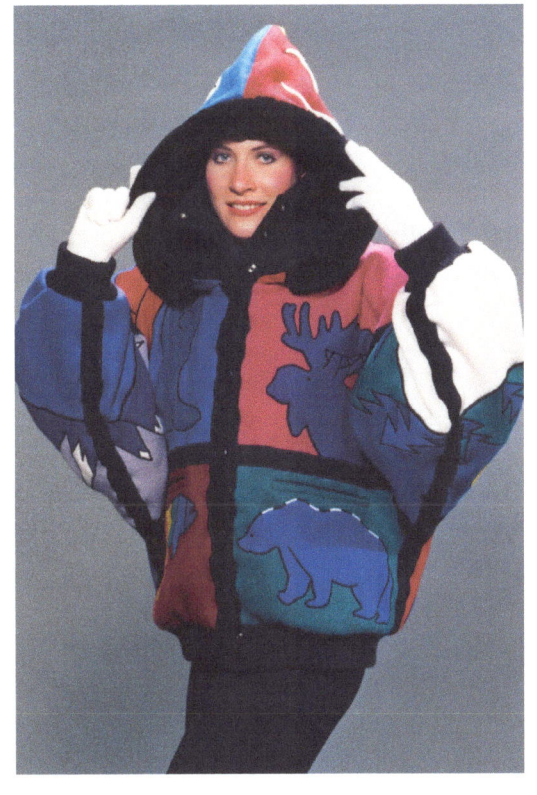

While COD became known for its wool coats, the changing seasons required the addition of lighter fabrics and new designs. Every six months, our design team created seasonal garments out of fleece, hand-printed cottons, satin, and canvas. It became a design conundrum to transfer the essence of a winter-heavy COD wool coat to a lighter fabrication. Sometimes we would be successful, other times not. Segueing from coats to a home line translated more easily than did spring clothing.

    If given the choice of sewing on luxurious Victor woolens and sitting down to an industrial sewing machine, as opposed to a quaint home sewing machine, I posit both are the *crème de la crème*. My love for both of these elements of COD coat-making filled my cup to running over. Sitting in front of an industrial sewing machine reminded me of opening a heavy steel door to an unknown world. The va-room-room powerful, throaty sound upon depressing the pedal is like it must feel for an engineer to drive a train. The harnessed power within an industrial sewing machine requires a strong response from the operator. On the other hand, sewing several layers of thick wool was as smooth and easy as sewing through a cube of butter. Always the smell of sheep lanolin drifted up from the dense wool, ever a comfortable reminder of its origin. Sewing coats was for me a sensual delight filled with the carnal enjoyment of colors and textures, ever playful with whimsy and surprise. Such are the bare bones of sewing a COD wool coat.

CHAPTER 6

COD Coats Travel to the Big Apple

One day not too long after moving the coat business out of our home, seven-year-old Maya gave me a gift. Scattered about our living room were all of the bags, suitcases, and boxes going to the trade show. I was busy preparing to leave for New York City to show my new coat designs at the New York Boutique Show. Her dark-brown eyes peeked out from under her ubiquitous bicycle beanie. Her pigtails stuck straight out from her head. Clasped in her little hand was an origami crane she had made at school. She said, "Mama, this is for you. It brings good luck." Not only did I need what the crane symbolized, but it also meant the world to me that my daughter understood on a deep level the journey we shared.

As the plane landed in Newark, New Jersey, in that fall of 1984, I was flooded with worry. How could I haul coats, suitcases, and mannequins from the airport to New York? I hadn't traveled to the East since before my daughter was born. Navigation of the city was intimidating, especially lugging the contents of my booth display. I was scared I might leave a bag behind. How in the world I could carry everything through the crowds of impatient commuters?

Upon landing, I decided to take a bus into New York. I hired a porter to carry my bags from baggage claim on a big rolling cart to the line of waiting people at the bus. We stowed everything in the bottom of the bus. I was grateful for the porter. I sat in a window seat. Traffic in the middle of the day was intense with honking and abrupt starting and stopping. The sounds of the city only increased my anxiety.

The bus began its climb onto the expressway roundabout. I happened to glance out the window just as we passed trashy wetlands below the bridge. There standing in the reeds and murky water was a beautiful white crane. I wrapped my hand around Maya's origami crane in my jacket pocket. All the worried anticipation I felt melted away. A sense of well-being washed over me with a feeling of acceptance, as I thought, what will be, will be.

At Penn Station, I was able to haul my luggage to the sidewalk outside to hail a taxi. Getting a cab was no small feat. Taxi drivers avoid people with mounds of luggage. Back home when I landed this opportunity to participate in a national show, I went about creating

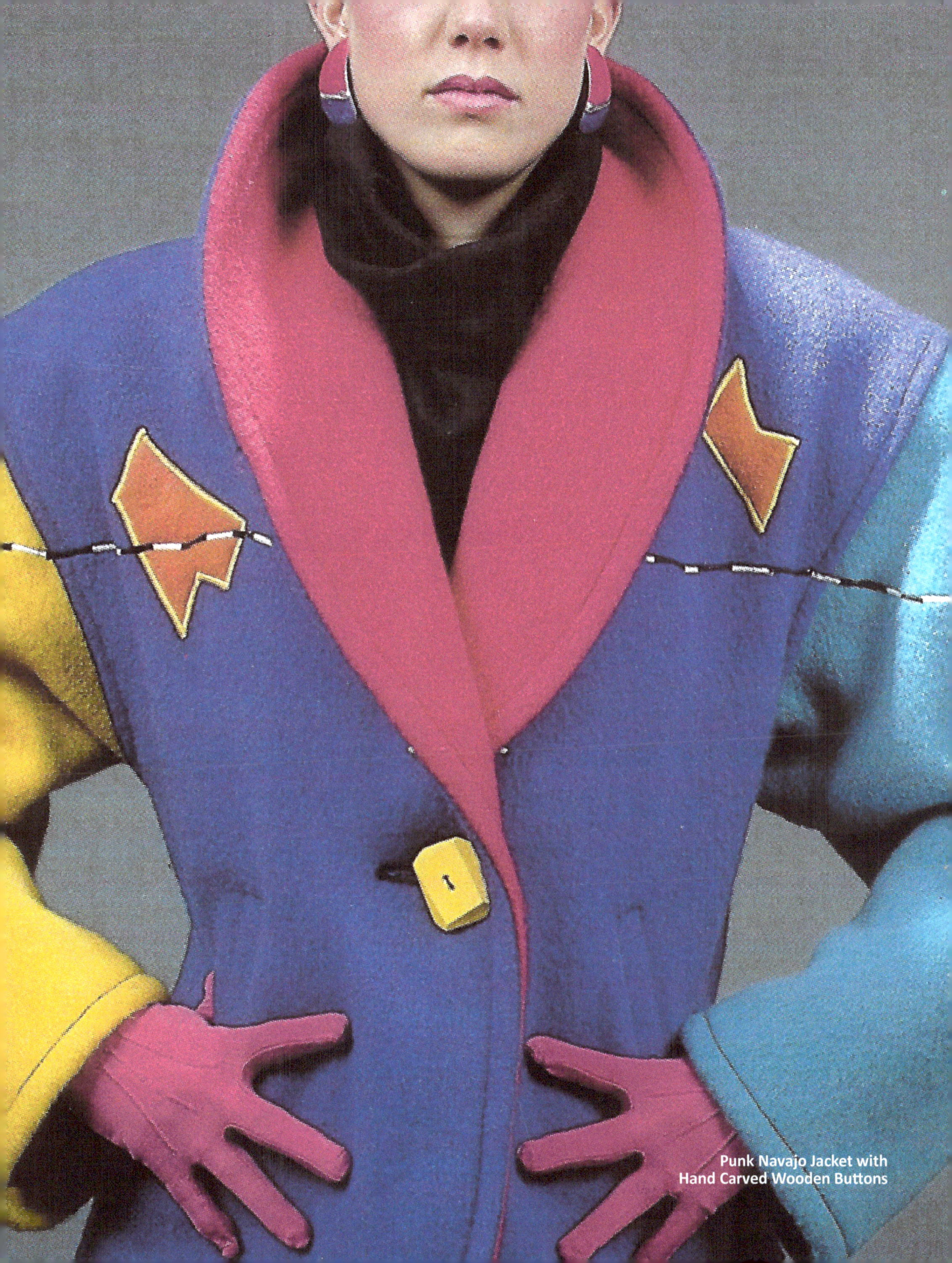

Punk Navajo Jacket with Hand Carved Wooden Buttons

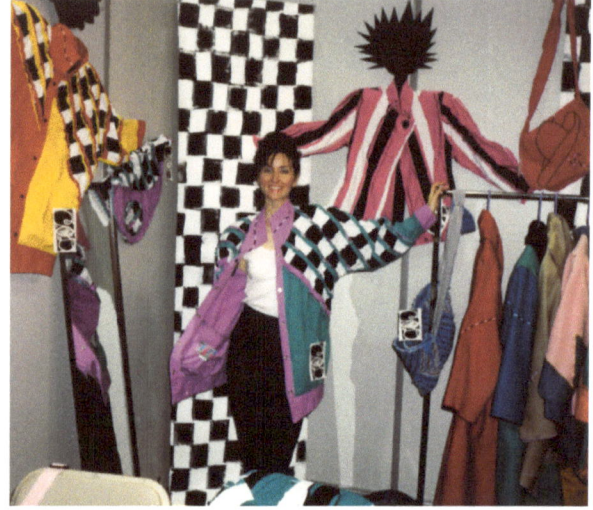

Model friend, Patricia, in NYC Spring Cotton Collection at show booth

the contents of my first exhibition booth. I hired a friend to build two mannequins out of ¼-inch plywood. They stood like paper dolls with a foot piece holding the body form erect. I painted them black, and I made large bags in which to transport them.

The sidewalk was burning hot. The smell of roasting hotdogs from a street vendor reminded me how hungry I was. Cars raced by, honking and screeching their brakes. A crush of people took up the sidewalk. Fast-walking city dwellers had to step around me and my mound of luggage. I was amazed and thankful when a Yellow Cab finally stopped. We crammed everything into the taxi. Off we raced to the Jacob Javits Center, a huge glass convention venue along the Hudson River. I looked around as buildings flew by. My heart pounded and I felt jittery and couldn't sit still during the cab ride. I could taste the energy of New York street life all around me. I had finally landed in the Big Apple as a new coat designer!

It took some doing, but I registered and found the Kenya bag seller's booth. Setting up at a five-day-long wholesale show was arduous. The Boutique Show (now defunct) often had hundreds of vendors. The aisles were filled with vendors' displays and empty boxes with packing materials strewn about. High-end vendors hired display services to set up their booths, so motorized carts raced around, pulling trailers filled with flowers, tables, chairs, and other display items. Music and announcements blared. The scene was one of total frenzy.

Frank, the Kenya bag seller, welcomed me into our booth. After a brief chat, I went about hanging my coats on the left curtained wall and setting up the black mannequins, which I then dressed in coats. It turned out that the colorful COD coats looked right at home with the patterned woven bags from Africa. Before I left home, I had prepared my packet of order forms, line sheets (drawings of styles with sizes and prices), and other sales materials, so that was all ready. Once everything was set up, I left the show to collapse on the couch at a friend's apartment.

New York City energized me. I loved the vitality of a large city and its contrast to my Rocky Mountains home. While I lived and worked in isolation (where my creativity was nurtured), city fashion inspired me. I visited department stores in my spare time to see what was happening in the world of *haute couture*. I touched designer clothing at Bergdorf Goodman, Saks Fifth Avenue, Henri Bendel, and Barney of New York. It was important for me to see exquisite sewing detail, fit, and drape of outerwear and dress fabrics. I spent so much time examining clothing at Bendel's that the salespeople looked askance at me.

I found clothing by English designers, Mary Quant and Zandra Rhodes, and American designer, Betsey Johnson. Eventually, my ritual when I visited New York became going from La Guardia Airport straight to the Betsey Johnson store in Soho. Her imaginative clothing, free spirit, and crazy can-can skirts swept me away. I often brought home what I called a fashionista coat to hang as a model in my studio. One day on a TV set, Betsey Johnson shook my hand as we were introduced, nearly bowling me over.

When the Boutique Show started the next day, the aisles teamed with determined, aggressive buyers dressed to the nines in sophisticated garb but wearing running shoes. Lots of black city clothing swished by. I wondered, myself, in my black pants and too-serious plaid blazer, if my outfit was right. Our booth display with the coats and Kenya bags was very simple, with no frills. It was nerve-racking to stand and wait for buyers to show interest. I paced back and forth to try to dissipate my anxiety. My hands were wet with nervous perspiration.

As a vendor, it was always a fine line between being too friendly or not. A friendly smile can be ignored. Buyers can be jaded and quick to decide on products of interest. Frank received a fair amount of attention and wrote many orders. I stood by and listened. It was a great learning experience for me as a novice vendor. A few buyers asked about my coats. They showed some interest, but walked on to see the next booth displays. It was difficult for me to keep my spirits up as one buyer after another walked on by.

The second day of the show, however, an attractive, self-assured blonde woman dressed in jeans and a T-shirt walked in to see the coats. "May I try them on?" she asked.

"But they're hanging on the wall," I protested.

"Well, take them down," she demanded.

Reluctantly, I dismantled my display. She proceeded to try on each coat. She pranced up and down the aisle, searching for a mirror (the one item I neglected to bring). As she waltzed around, people stopped to watch. She didn't say a word. I could hardly believe how lovely she looked in my coats. My heart raced. I asked myself, what is happening? Does she really like my coats? I had no way of knowing at the time that this blonde bombshell's presence and attention could put COD on the fashion map.

When all the coats I had brought to New York lay in a heap, the woman introduced herself. She said she was Peach Gilbert and owned a small shop on Madison Avenue called Mabel's. I had never heard of her shop, but it turned out that Mabel's, named after Peach's black-and-white cat, was famous in New York City. Although the shop was tiny, its black-and-white awning made it stand out. Mabel's was nestled next door to Yves St. Laurent. Her shop carried the *crème de la crème* of handcrafted clothing, accessories, and home items collected from artisans around the United States.

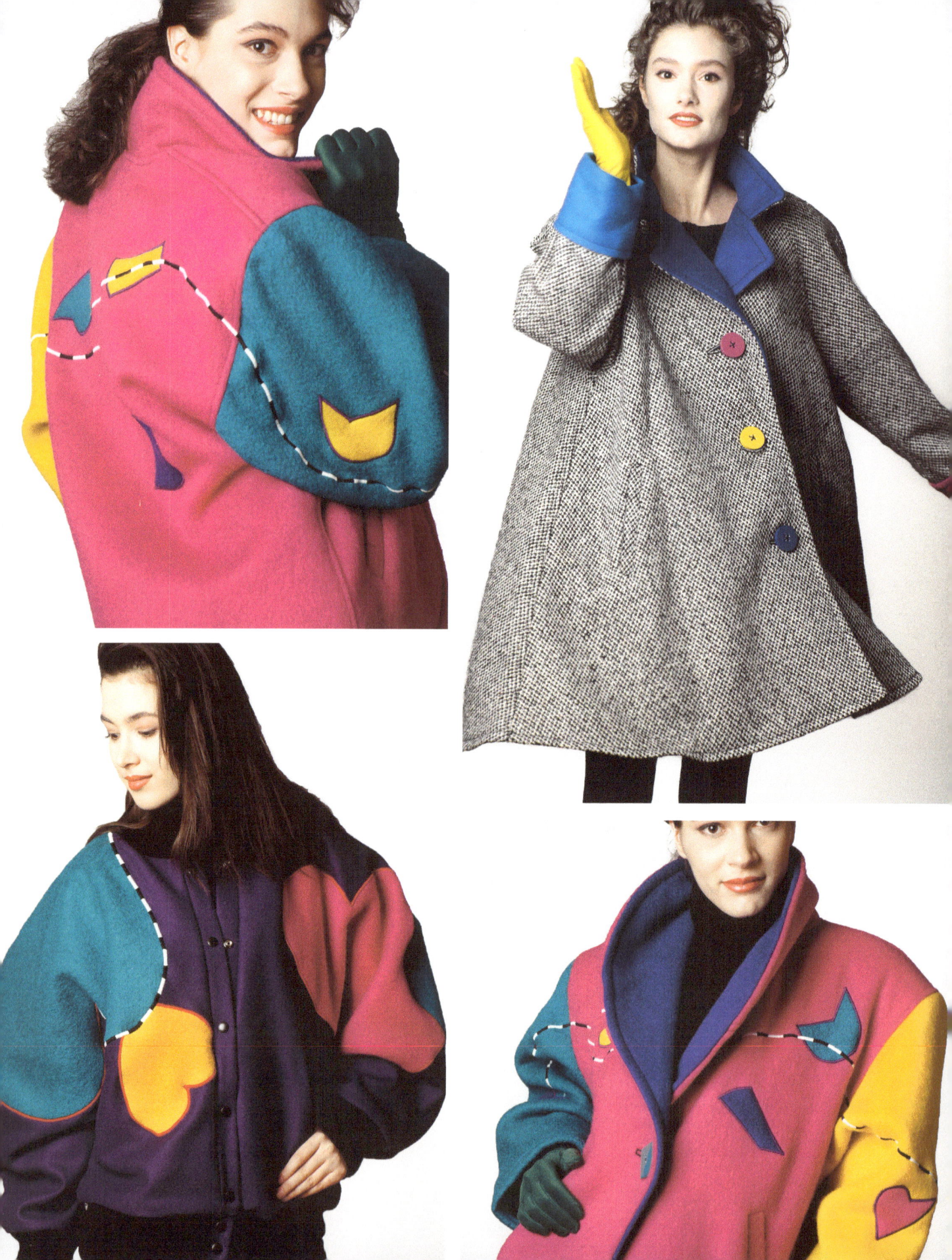

I walked into Mabel's five months later. Her store, to me, was more of a folk-art museum than a store, as it was filled with imaginative handmade clothing hung on racks, with kitty-themed ceramics perched on carefully painted shelves. Large whitewashed cabinets held whimsical, beaded, colorful leather items and unique hand-knit sweaters. Walls painted in *Trompe l'oeil* style welcomed customers into Venetian plazas and grassy knolls dotted with posies. Peach's taste was impeccable. She required a high standard of craftsmanship. Her selection of artisans' work was admired far and wide by customers and artisans alike. The black-and-white kitty store was mentioned in guidebooks as a must-see shop to visit in New York City.

That day at the convention center, Peach stood in front of the pile of coats. She said in a voice of authority and knowing, "If you do what I suggest, not only will you and I have a long association, but I will also make your coat designs better."

Hmm, I thought as I pushed the hackles on my back down. I could have turned around and walked away from this woman and her arrogance. Reasons to stay, reasons to leave, clicked through my brain. Suddenly, all of my being screamed out that I had nothing to lose. I felt my stomach do a flip. I was about to get sick. My vision started to blur. I straightened up to face whatever destiny was before me. I seized the moment, looked Peach in the eye, and asked, "Where do we begin?" Meanwhile, the buyers watching the drama unfold stood close to listen. A silence fell over the scene. I waited as jitters consumed me.

All of my New York sample coats were one or two colors. I had chosen to play it safe. Peach picked up a short coat and put it on. I got out my notebook to take notes. She pulled and tucked until the body was shaped and more fitted. She suggested different sleeve styles. Eventually, after we had examined each coat design, Peach placed an order for three short coats. She wanted coats in four bright colors per coat for her store. She also requested some kind of surface design on the outside. This was the first time I had thought about letting my imagination run wild on the outside of a coat. What a concept!

At home, I played with surface design by cutting scraps of wool to sew on the outside of coat pieces. When coat parts were sewn together and lying flat, I satin-stitched a black-and-white-checkerboard line that connected all the appliquéd pieces of cloth. Eventually, each coat we made had a black-and-white line that coursed around the surface or edged blocks of color.

The line was a design element that held meaning for me. The checkerboard "snake" paid homage to the indomitable spirit of the magpie, which has graced my entire life in the West. This checkerboard "snake" became COD's trademark design element. The Lindley Place magpie spirits flew around each coat we sewed. The surface decoration, in combination with the four-color-blocked coat body, characterized all my future coat designs. It was at this point that my coat designs entered a new stage, each coat becoming an artistic expression that combined elements of the West, including its flowing rivers, wild critters, and expansive space.

I suspected that all the buyers who remained to observe knew of Mabel's and its flamboyant opinionated owner. I realized that, while New York is a large city, in the world of quality handcrafted clothing, artisans and shop owners alike still knew of each other. From the point of dismantling my booth display for Peach, the potential customer, to the end of the show, I wrote a total of $3,000 in coat orders. In the larger scheme of COD's future business, this amount represented a small amount of orders. However, at the time, the amount was huge. Included in this stack of orders were shops in Connecticut, New Mexico, Washington, D.C., and Massachusetts. Buyers showed enough confidence in my designs to place small orders to be able to try COD coats to determine if the color-blocked unique outerwear could sell in their home environs.

Word travels fast. It was my guess that many orders I received were written because of Peach Gilbert's show of confidence in my work. If Peach hadn't been there that day, COD might not have had the success it did. The fashion industry can be fickle, uncaring, and quick to reject new designers. Many retailers refuse to spend the time it takes to understand and appreciate a new look.

My professional association with Peach lasted for about a decade. In that time, she and I collaborated on a new coat design each year. I proposed long trapeze coats with black-and-white cats frolicking around the hem. One year, we designed a three-quarter-length swing coat with hearts skipping along the ever-present black-and-white line circling the coat's body. One of Mabel's customers appeared in this coat on the TV show, 48 Hours, as she handed out sandwiches to homeless people on the streets of New York City. Our biggest seller was a cream-colored, ankle-length, fleece bathrobe, with Mabel's kitty faces circling the hem, with black blanket-stitched edging.

My connection with Peach became one of my most treasured professional and personal relationships. Not only did she open my eyes to high fashion, but she also invited me into her home for many wonderful meals with her and her husband, Eddie. It was because of Peach's keen eye for whimsy, style, and design that COD flourished the way it did in the beginning. I will forever be grateful to Peach for her patience and generosity of spirit. She was tough and bighearted at the same time. Mabel's was open until the late 1990s, when she closed the shop because her rent had reached the astronomical price of $24,000 a month. She cared for me as a designer and a friend. She saw something in my work that I couldn't see myself.

Being as remote from the fashion industry as I had been, I knew that having a mentor was essential to my success. I was exhilarated by the thought that others believed in my dream to make coats of many colors. If someone is going to buy it, I knew they really had to believe in it. I had been discovered. Maya's origami crane must have been perched on my shoulder when Peach Gilbert walked into our booth that day.

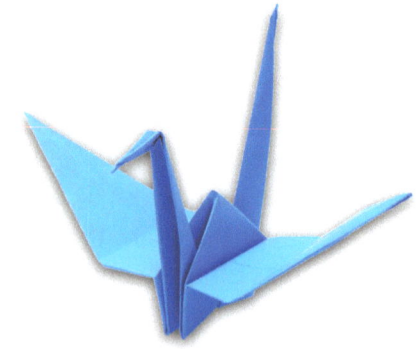

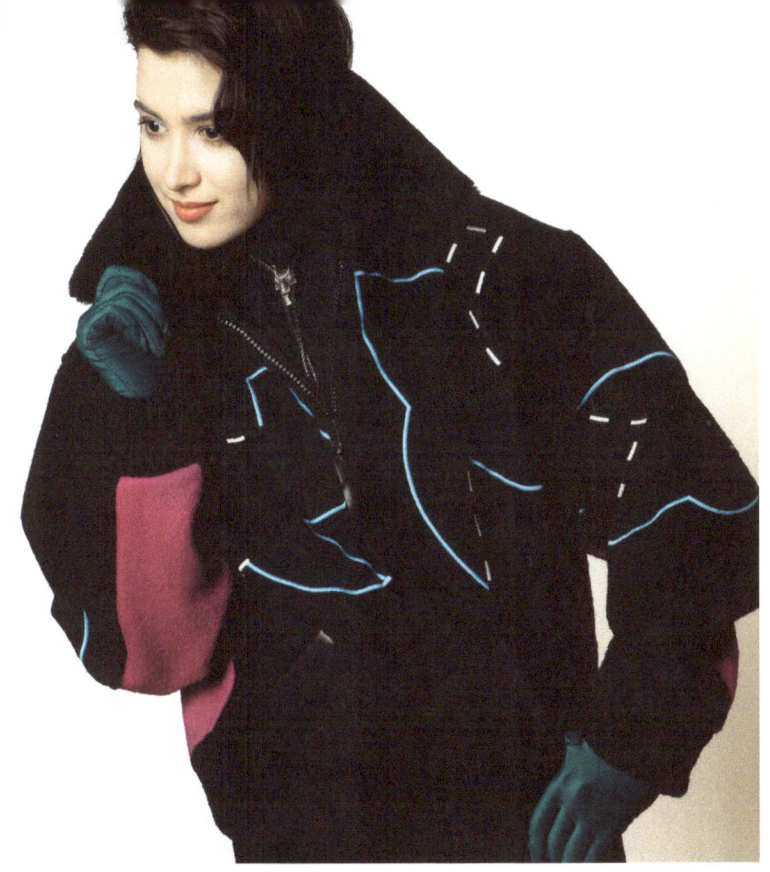
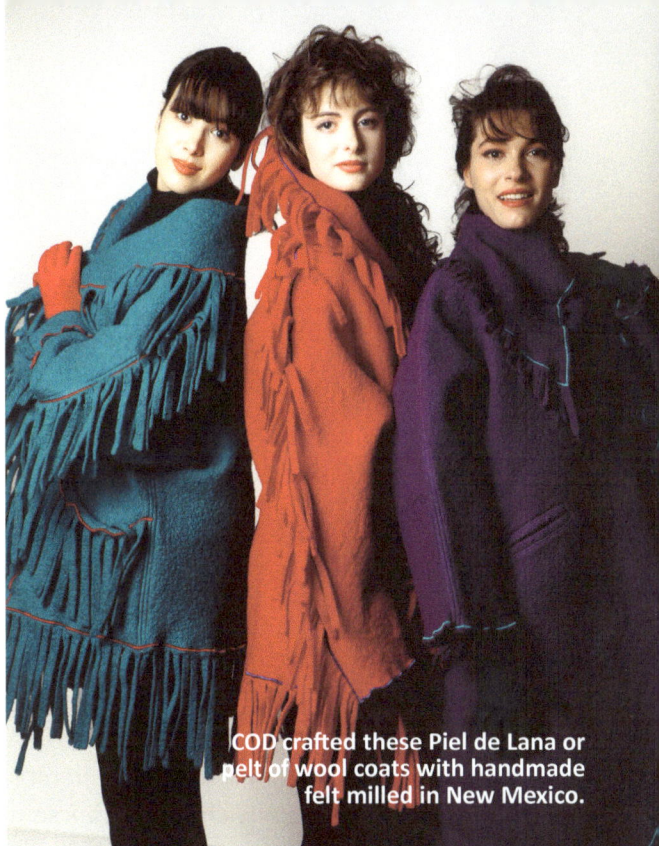

COD crafted these Piel de Lana or pelt of wool coats with handmade felt milled in New Mexico.

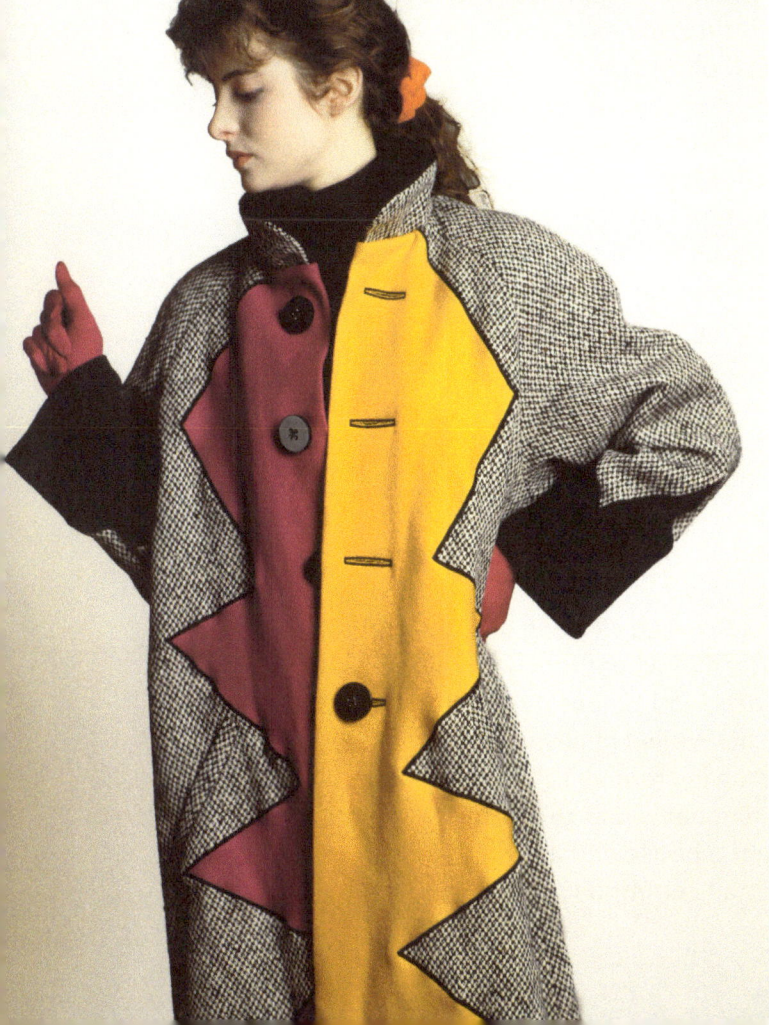
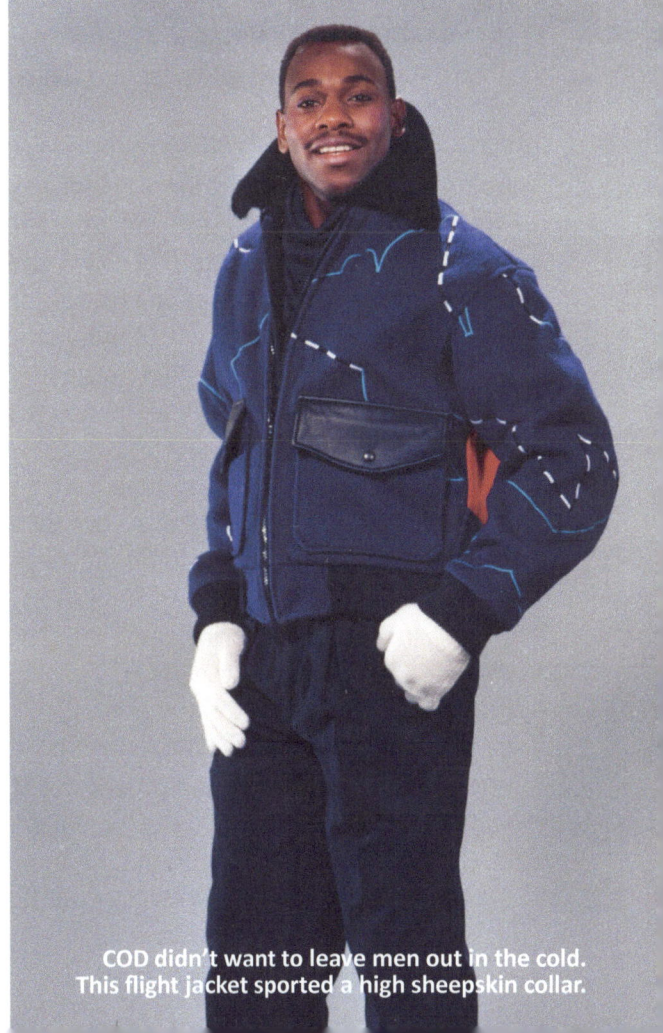

COD didn't want to leave men out in the cold. This flight jacket sported a high sheepskin collar.

CHAPTER 7

Take Me Seriously, Already

As I looked down on Manhattan from my airplane window, I felt like a different person in my bones. I watched the Hudson River snake its way through the countryside. I returned to Montana to descend into the Valley of Flowers where the Gallatin River feeds the landscape as it flows north to join two other rivers to become the Missouri. The river of my own life drastically changed course with the packet of coat orders stashed in my travel bag. Though the outcome of the show had provided me with a modicum of success in ways beyond my wildest dreams, I felt in my gut the fear of what the orders represented. While the handful of orders was my step into the future, my new world was a territory wholly unfamiliar, filled with unforeseen navigational obstacles.

The New York orders represented 25 coats that needed to be made, and soon. I sent no fireworks into the Big Sky to celebrate, but Maya was one happy little kid upon hearing the news. She was always my most steadfast fan. Just like standing with a mound of luggage on a New York sidewalk to hail a taxi, the production of so many coats felt daunting. With only one straight-stitch sewing machine and no room at the Peach Street studio to set up a true production room, with sewing and cutting equipment, I had to find a larger, more appropriate space. We needed large amounts of fabric. There were two of us, at the time, myself and my one employee, to sew the coats.

The list of to-dos, though long and complicated, didn't seem insurmountable, at least until I visited my local banker to ask for a modest loan of $3,000 to help pay for fabric, an industrial straight-stitch sewing machine, and an electric fabric cutter.

In Montana, during the 1980s, woman-owned clothing manufacturing businesses did not abound. Our state was rich with cattle and wheat ranches, guided wild game hunts, fly fishing outfitters, downhill ski resorts, and timber businesses, but no fashionable clothing manufacturing. COD didn't exactly fit. While I believed in my business, I felt great uncertainty. Faced with the prospect of borrowing money to buy the machinery and supplies, I turned to my trusty local bank. I had banked at this bank for more than 10 years as the wife of an MSU professor. I had bought a house and a car. They knew me. This should be easy, I thought. I was known in the Bozeman community.

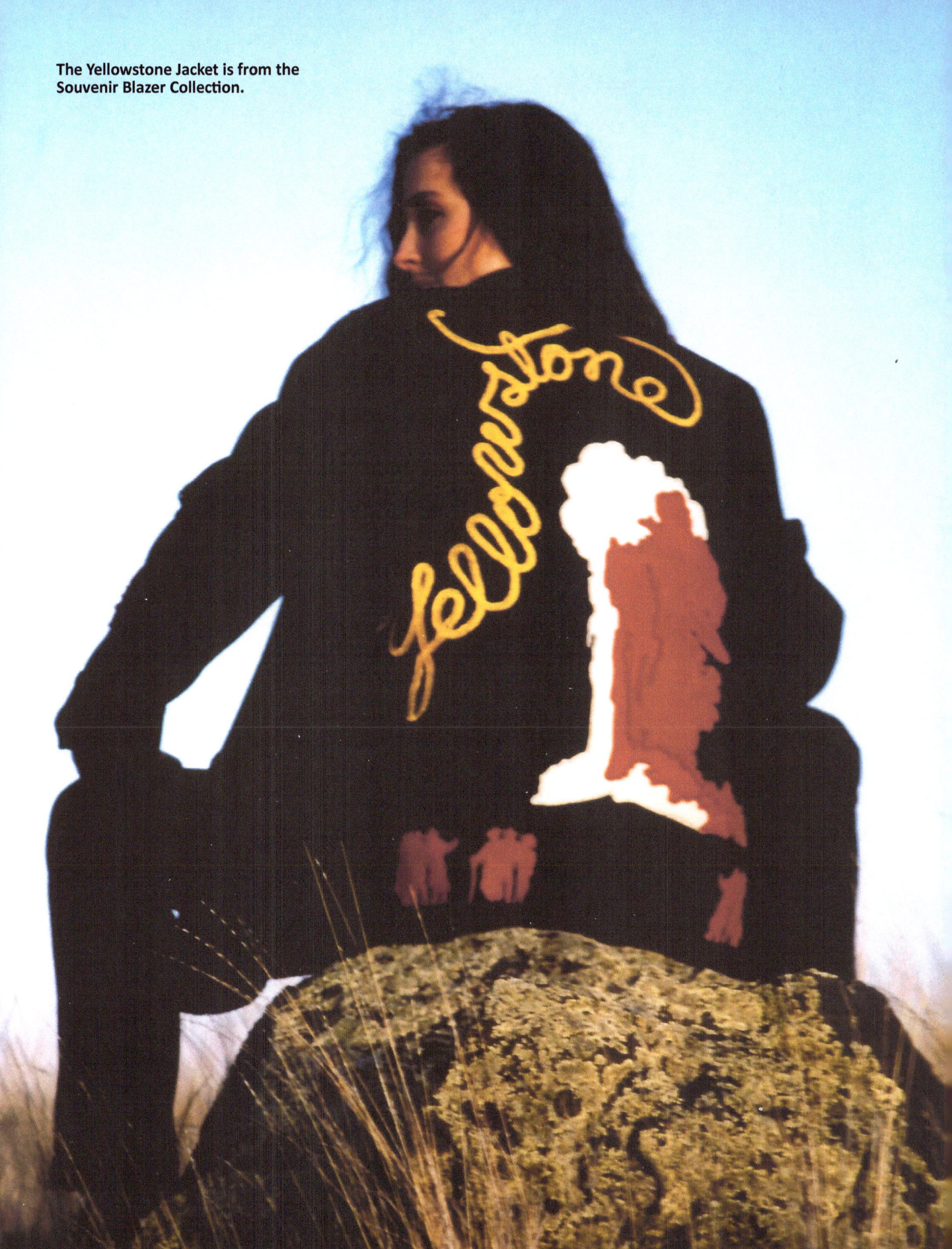

The Yellowstone Jacket is from the Souvenir Blazer Collection.

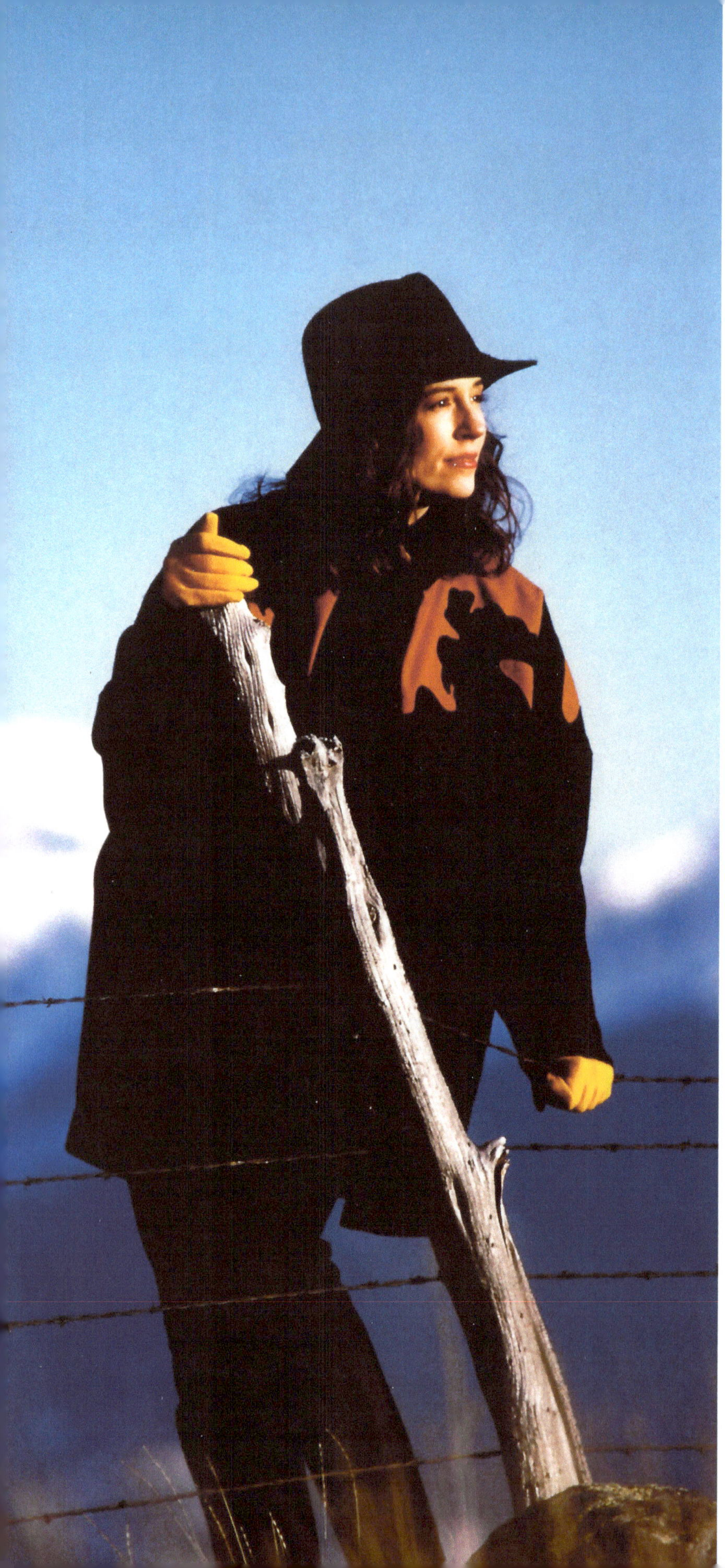

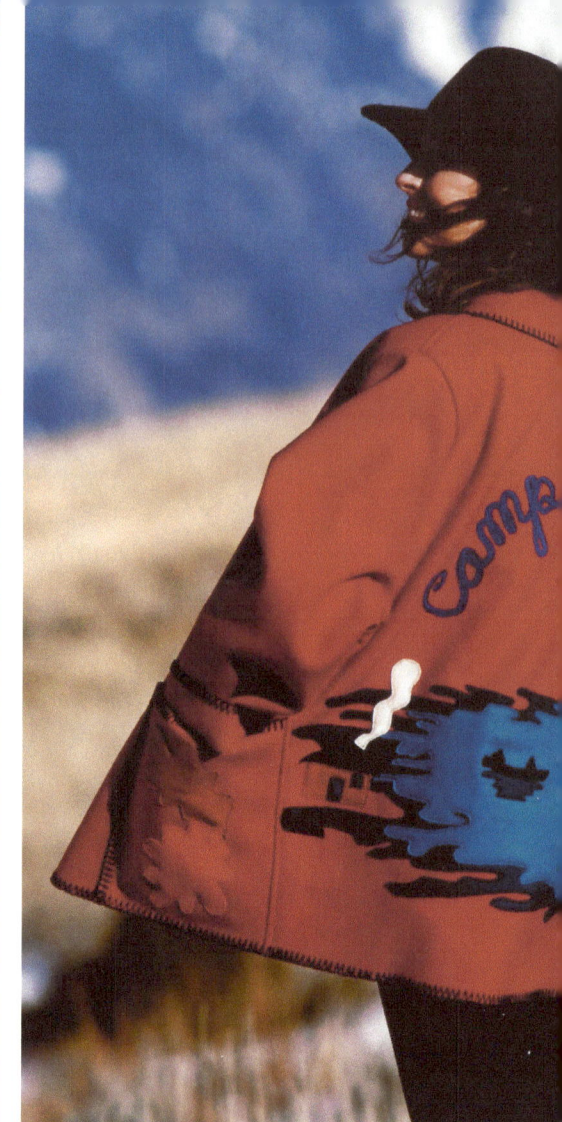
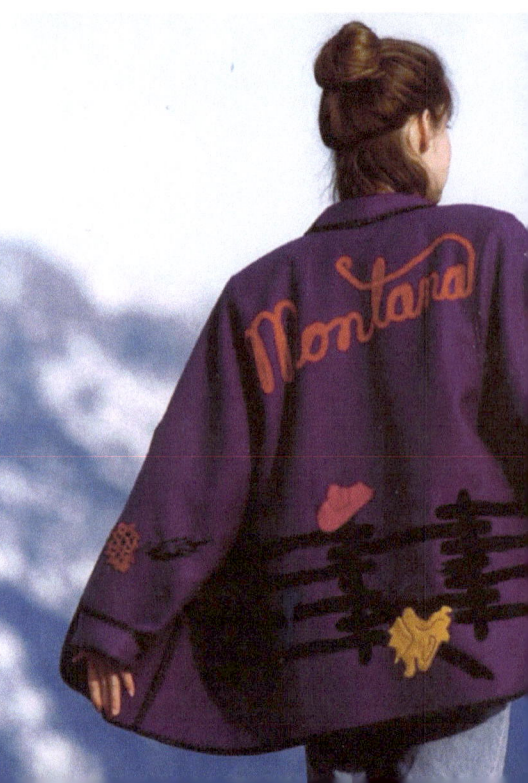

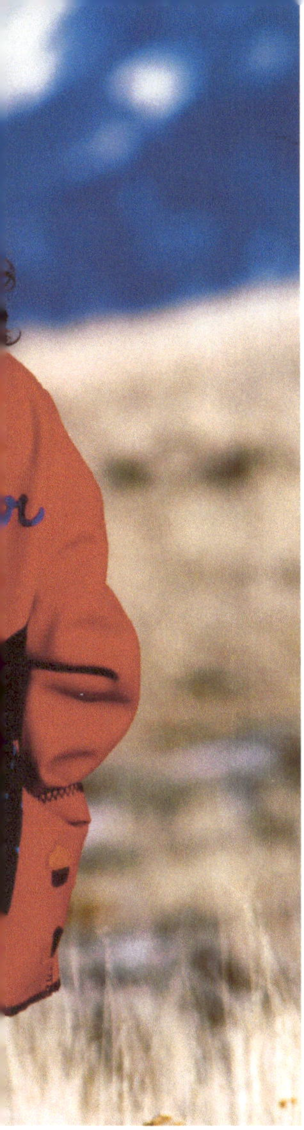

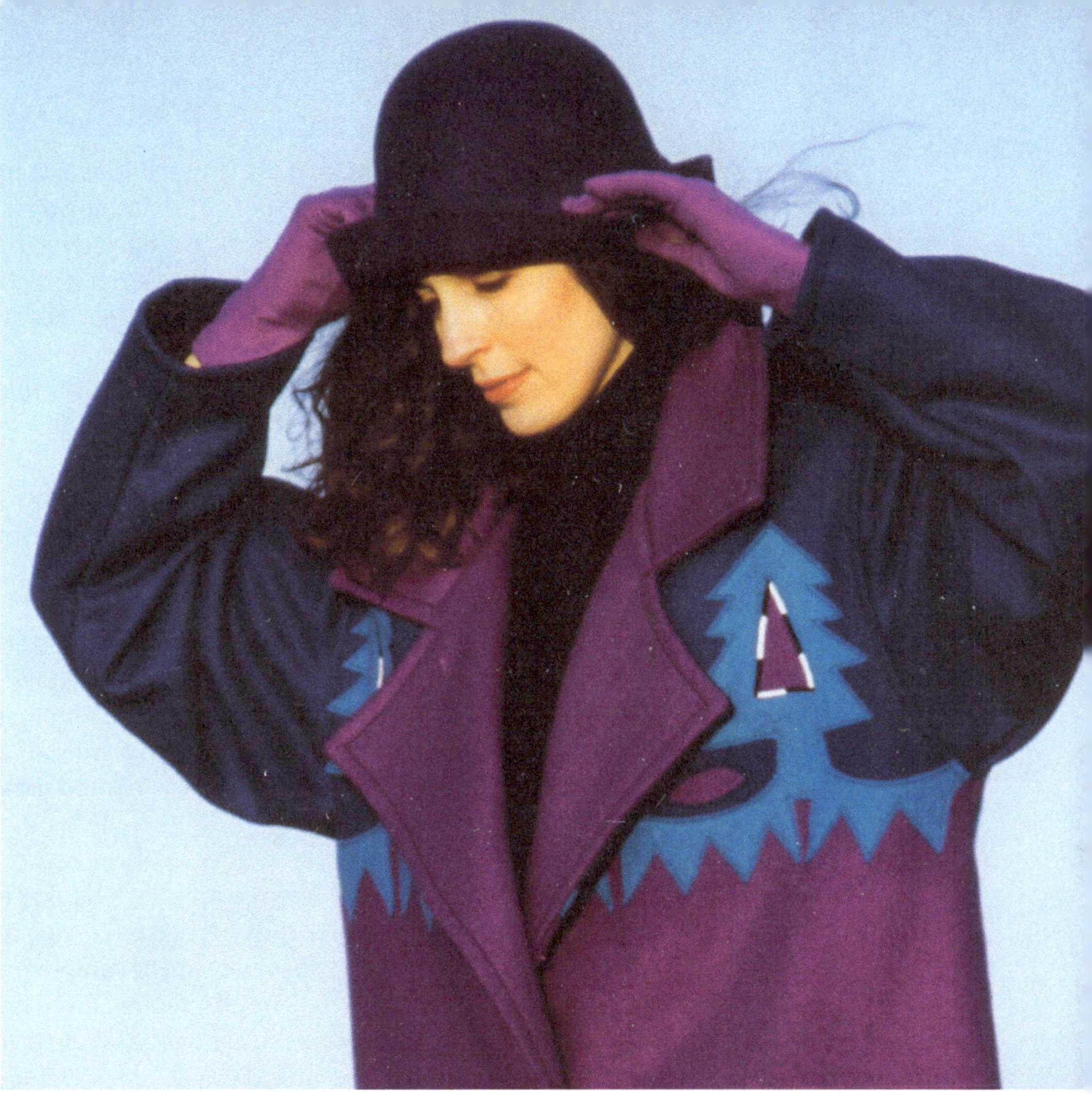

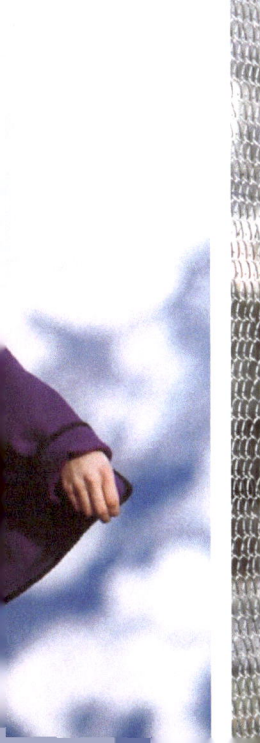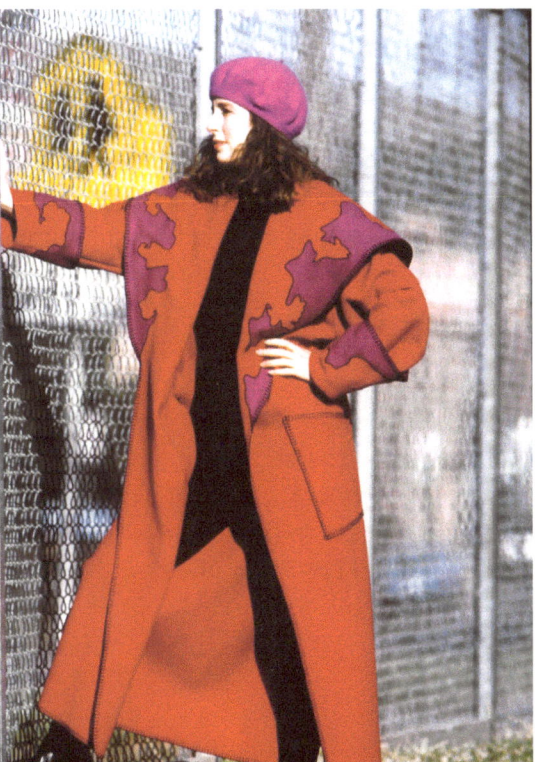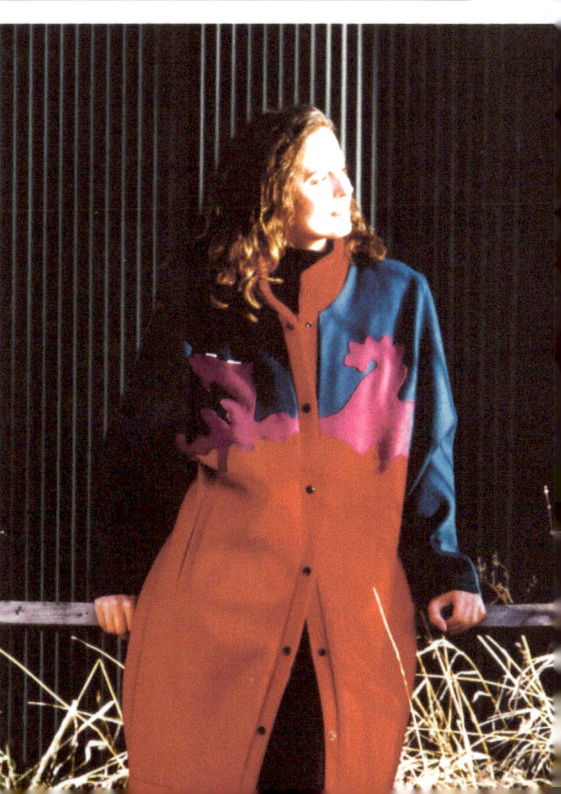

However, the banker saw me as just a single mom, dressed in bright patterned clothing, with a head of fuchsia-pink hair. I dressed the part of a clothing designer. While my appearance would be acceptable on the streets of New York, particularly in the East Village, here I stood out as an eccentric. The banker likely considered me a fly-by-night artistic type, who, in his opinion, did not fit the mold of an acceptable safe customer. Had I walked into the bank dressed like a woman rancher, my reception might have been more positive. When the banker opened his mouth to explain his refusal to grant me a loan, his first words told me it was the woman part that troubled him the most.

He said, "I cannot give you, a single woman and an artist, a loan. The only way we will give you a loan is if you have two co-signers, your former husband and your parents, for example."

No discussion. He did not see me as a viable prospect. It didn't matter that I had orders with payment promises from well-known fashion boutiques outside of Montana. It didn't matter that orders meant the potential to hire sewers whose employment would boost our local economy. Speechless, I marched out of the bank in a whirl of anger. At home, fighting back the tears, I pounded my bed with clenched fists. I screamed. How would I move forward with my business without money?

My choices were not choices. Being backed into a corner by a banker left me no alternative. I called my former husband and parents. They agreed to co-sign a loan for the $3,000. Asking for help from family and my former husband was beyond humbling. It made me feel like a downed tree or worse. I told myself to keep this money issue private. Don't tell a soul, I repeated to myself. The coats had to get made, or I might as well have walked away from my newfound success.

With the loaned money, plus my own savings, I began production on the coat orders. Overcome with conflicting feelings, my only salvation was to sit and sew. And sew we did.

I moved the Peach Street studio temporarily to a large building on Valley Center Road near Belgrade, 10 miles from Bozeman. The large open space had room for a cutting table, three industrial sewing machines, a table that acted as a desk, hanging racks for patterns, and shelving for fabric storage.

COD's one employee began to work on new patterns for the coats based on changes suggested by Peach Gilbert. I played with surface design using the Bernina embroidery sewing machine. I surrounded pieces of colorful wool fabric with contrasting satin stitching. I invented an easy way to stitch the black-and-white line that embellished each coat. We worked long hours existing on Taco John's greasy tacos, tater-tots, and coffee. It took just over a month of nonstop work to finish all the coats to fill the New York orders. When all the coats were finished, we stood back and looked at them. It was a sight to behold and a harbinger for what was to come.

I hired other workers and this brought our staff number to five. I moved COD yet again to a basement space in Bozeman because I needed to be closer to town. Large open space was hard to come by, so this space seemed viable. Above our new workroom was a Greek short-order joint and next door a cake bakery. The aromas from both food businesses were at times overwhelming. The smell of sweet cake frosting mixed with roasted lamb permeated our wool fabrics. There was no alternative. We aired the coats out by hanging them outside behind the building and only then packed for shipping. We couldn't have customers open boxes of expensive coats to be greeted by a cloud of food aromas.

With success comes the flip side, unexpected obstacles. It seemed that every time I took leaps forward I had to first take backward steps. One day we walked into the workroom to slosh through a foot of sewage that had flooded the basement from a broken pipe. The stench was overwhelming. We surveyed the damage and held our noses. The smell was pretty awful. Luckily, we had made sure to store fabrics and finished coats well above the flood level.

"We have to get out of here now!" I screamed.

I scanned the *Bozeman Daily Chronicle* and drove the streets of Northeast Bozeman where rents might be affordable. The historic Coco-Cola Bottling Building at 802 North Wallace in Bozeman was available. I jumped at the chance to move just two blocks north of my former Peach Street studio. COD took over the entire two-floor building. When I walked into the new space, I saw rickety floors, no basement stairs, and high ceilings, and bees had taken up residence in the southeast corner. We spent a lot of money and elbow grease to make this old building functional. We set up cutting and fabric storage plus offices upstairs. The staff break room was set up downstairs. We flung open the large double back doors in the basement in the summers to let in the sweet fresh air and bird songs. The sewing workroom soon became the coolest place in the factory. I felt right at home in this historical Bozeman building. Every red brick breathed stability and longevity. COD would be taken seriously. I would too.

When word got out that COD had experienced success at a Boutique Show in New York City, a reporter from the *Bozeman Daily Chronicle* knocked on my office door. My old chair squeaked as I got up to open the door. He introduced himself and asked if he might write a story about my coat business, and I agreed. When he asked me questions about the financial end of my business, I shared an edited version of my difficulties acquiring money through a local bank. The article ran in the paper a week later. The day the story came out, I was going through coat orders, to make sure we were on track, when my office assistant buzzed me with a phone call.

"Governor Schwinden is on the line," she said.

I nearly dropped the phone when his booming voice came across the wire. "I hear

SOUVENIR WOOL JACKETS

STYLE #	STYLE NAME
SVT215	Tepee Souvenir Jacket
SVF215	Fence Souvenir Jacket
SVH215	Horse Shoe Souvenir Jacket
	Bucking Bronco: select white, red, **or** jade plaid
SVS215	Sheriff Star Souvenir Jacket
SVP215	Plaid Yoke Souvenir Jacket
	Plaid Yoke: select white, red, **or** jade plaid
SVN215	New Orleans Souvenir Jacket
SVE215	New England Souvenir Jacket
SVG215	San Francisco Souvenir Jacket

All souvenir jacket are available in the following colors:

COMBO	COLOR
A)	Paprika
B)	Fuchsia
C)	Jade
D)	Teal
E)	Dark Red
F)	Scarlet
G)	Royal Blue
H)	Purple
I)	Yellow
J)	Black

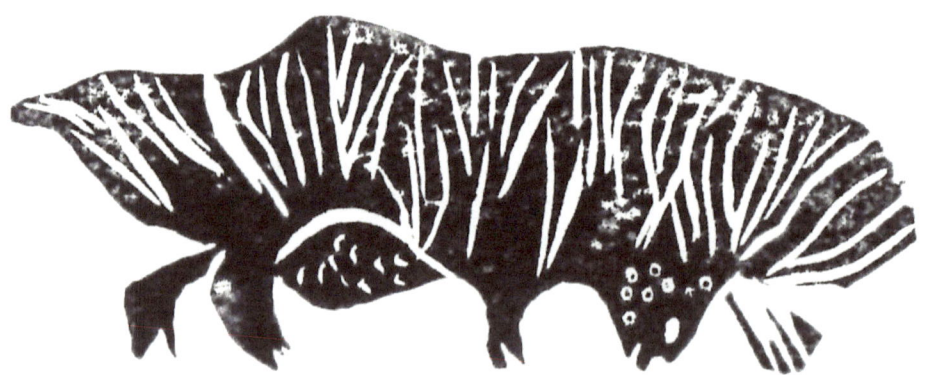

Cindy Owings hand carved this porcupine rubber stamp for handmade embroidery and print items.

you might need some help," he declared.

"Well, that depends on what you're talking about," I replied.

He told me he had read the article in the *Chronicle,* and it sounded like, as a new business owner, I might need help putting together a business plan that could help a bank consider my financial needs.

"Help would be most welcome," I said, taken aback.

"I have just the person who can help you with this. His name is Barry Roose and he works in the Montana State Commerce Department. I will connect the two of you. He is the Department's small business financial advisor," the governor explained.

Although Montana is the third-largest state in our country, few people live here. One million inhabitants are spread over huge sweeps of space and clustered in a handful of large and small towns. Many Montana residents look at our state as one large "small town." It's not too difficult to know what's happening here or there, down one dusty gravel road after another, or in a small town in the middle of nowhere.

Everyone knows everyone else's business, and that can be hard. But, on the other hand, COD got noticed. People could be judgmental. But also people were starting to take me seriously as a designer and business owner. I chose to stay in Montana when it could certainly have been more lucrative to live and work in a more densely populated place. So, when the state's governor called me personally to offer help, his phone call probably wasn't all that unusual in our state.

Working with Barry Roose over a series of weeks, our business manager and accountant created one spreadsheet after another. Out of the pile came a slew of scenarios detailing sales projections, a budget, and narratives explaining COD's financial situation in relation to what we thought the business could do in the near future. After finalizing the spreadsheets into a cohesive business plan, the financial wizards asked me to present the story to the bank. I called the event a real dog and pony show—numbers and coats go together "like love and marriage; you can't have one without the other," as Sinatra sang.

The bank seemed pleased enough to loan COD 10 times what I had initially asked for months before, $30,000. It's always good to have a governor in your back pocket.

COD was off and running. The business had taken on its second pile of debt (and there would be more down the line). COD's business manager and accountant questioned the veracity of carrying debt. The situation would keep me awake late into the night. How would we pay the loan back or even make the interest payments? But keeping my own counsel, I buried my worries in my favorite sketchbook and forged ahead.

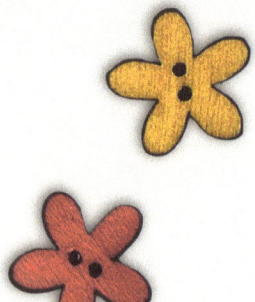

CHAPTER 8

A Blanket Becomes a Coat

The story I am about to tell you must be explained. I had a dream on a train early in my coat journey. I cannot remember where the train ride took place. The dream remains vivid. In the mid-1990s, I had the pleasure of working in the Republic of Georgia. I chose to place the train ride in Georgia because it was a place with people and events close to my heart. The train ride did not take place in Georgia. However, I have woven in aspects of my visit to give my mysterious dream experience a context.

The train lurched forward as seated passengers were jostled by the tilting sway of the cars. I strolled through the narrow passage in the train to find my private compartment, number 203. Finally locating my reserved spot, I pulled the door latch back and the door swung inward, revealing a tiny room with two leather-covered benches with padded backs facing each other. The cubicle, while tiny, was not as claustrophobic as it could seem because a large window opened onto the passing Georgian landscape. I could see all along the Caucasus Mountains. The green rolling foothills moved by below sharp snow-covered peaks. The rich, dark-wood-paneled interior creaked and groaned with each jostle of the train. After stowing my belongings in the storage area above me, I collapsed on the right bench facing forward in order to watch the scenery out the window. I covered myself with a blanket I had brought along. Even inside the heated train, chilly drafts of the high mountain air would seep through the window.

On assignment with a USAID (United States Agency for International Development) project, I was traveling with a group of Georgian women textile artists who wanted to expose me to the varied and exquisite handwork found in remote villages across their country. We had just returned from the Tusheti mountainous region high in the Caucasus near the Georgian border with Chechnya.

We visited a felted wool coat maker in a tiny village. Her primitive workspace was a crumbling stone farm building. A cavernous storage room held piles of shorn sheep's wool piled on the floor. We were invited into the fiber artist's felting room, where we spent an afternoon making felted slippers. As we formed wet wool around our feet, we chatted in Georgian and broken English about felt being a universal language.

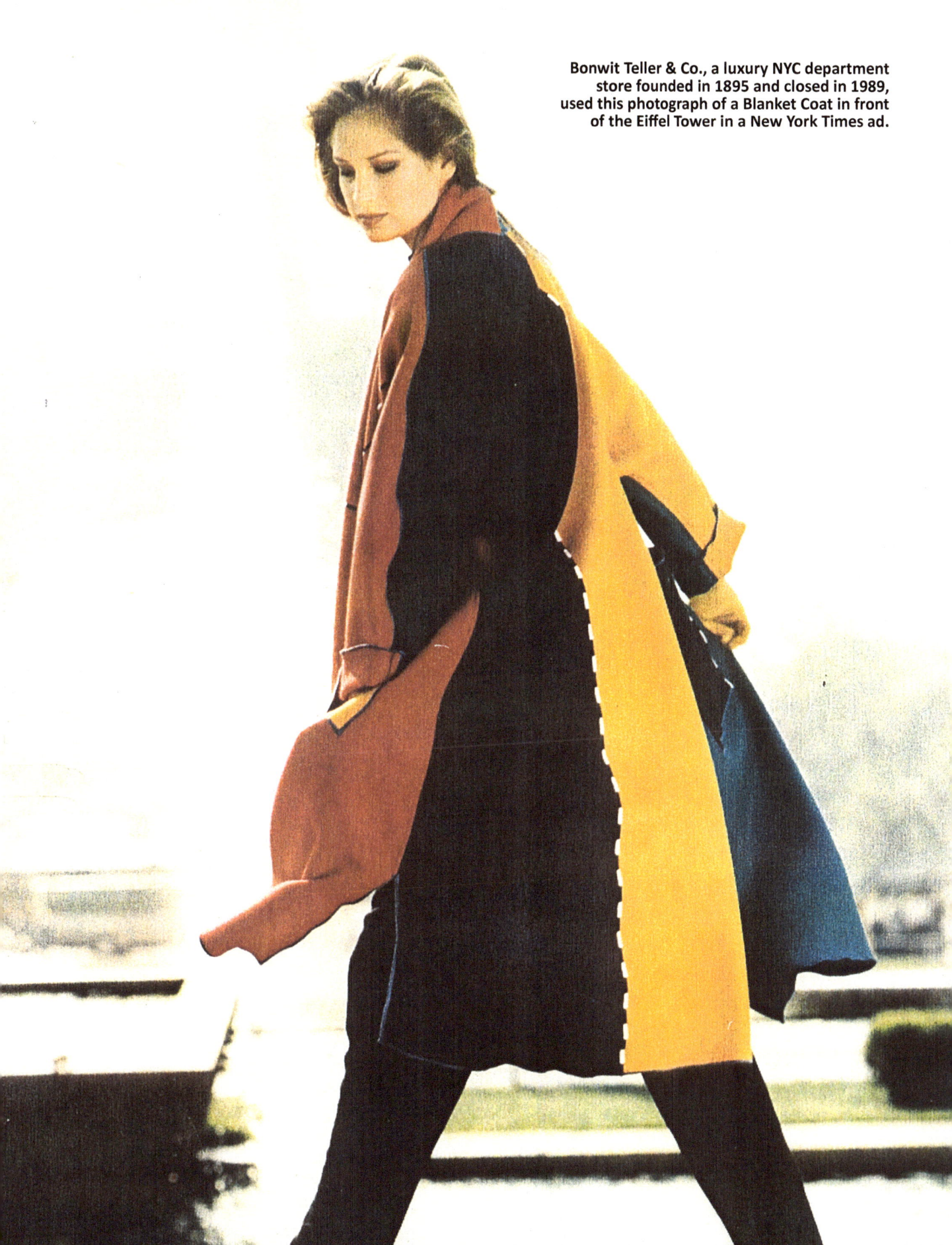

Bonwit Teller & Co., a luxury NYC department store founded in 1895 and closed in 1989, used this photograph of a Blanket Coat in front of the Eiffel Tower in a New York Times ad.

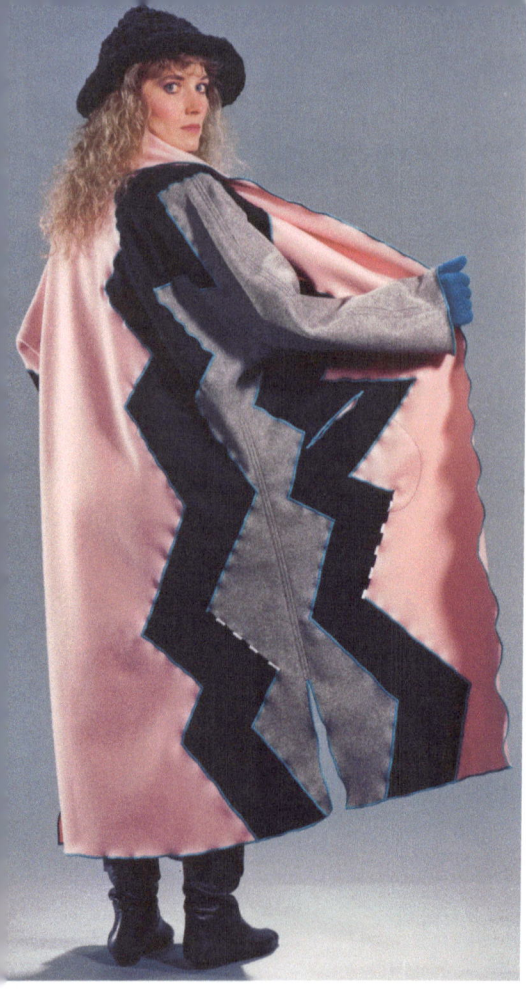

After many hours of driving through traffic on unpaved roads, avoiding potholes that could swallow a tiny Fiat, my Georgian friends dropped me off at the Tbilisi train station for the next leg of my journey toward the Black Sea for my second consulting assignment. As I relaxed into the train's easy rhythm, I was overcome by fatigue, falling into a deep sleep.

That night, the thick patterned blanket keeping my body warm swirled into a vivid dream. In the dream, the blanket sailed and flowed on Tusheti mountainous breezes, as I played with it against a clear blue sky. I was pulled into the folds and valleys, as the blanket landscape magically turned into a coat. Folds became sleeves, and a fluttery edge, the front opening to the chilly mountainous air. The coat wrapped over itself, as I held it together. The colors of the coat were many. It was pieced to mimic the woven patterns of a Navajo chief blanket or a Pendleton wool blanket. Down the center back, a seam became a stitched black-and-white-checked snake. A solid-stitched colorful line followed the folds. Hand-embroidered blips interrupted the bright line. The line provided an escape for the eye. The coat was made of sheep's wool, felted to a fine dense-surfaced fabric.

My dream skipped around. My own hands smoothly glided over the coat in order to feel the rough wool fabric against my skin. I liked the feel and stability of the fabric. I could see that over time the blanket coat could take on the rhythm of the seasons. The skin of the coat emulated the hides of an elk or a whitetail deer when their fur grows thick in the coldest part of the winter—in summer, it is thinner.

When I woke up, my train dream became a clear vision of transformation. A blanket becomes a coat. I was amazed at the vivid message of this dream. Where did this coat image come from? Even I was surprised by the dream. This had never happened to me. I knew in my heart of hearts that the dream coat had to become a real coat somehow.

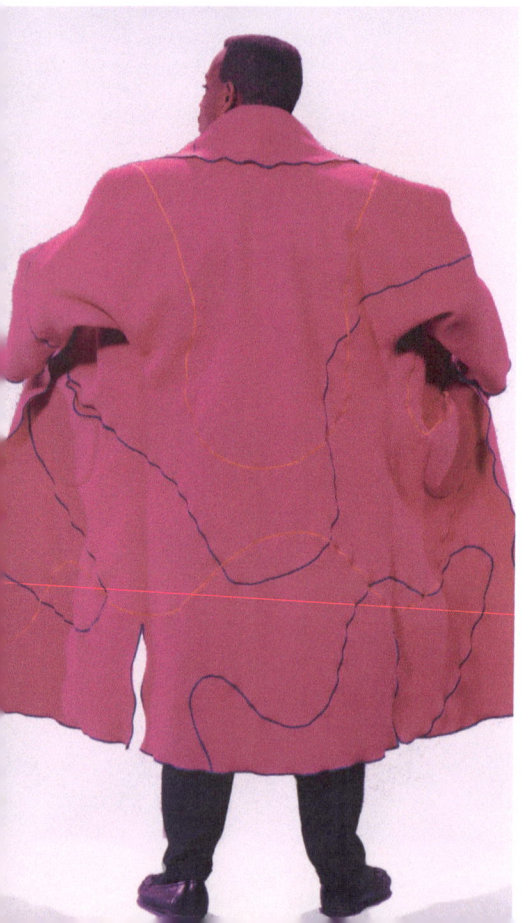

Top: COD made this Zig-Zag Blanket Coat, called Sunset Strip, with 18 oz, unlined wool.

I visualized the blanket coat adorning women. The coat did not immediately reveal to the wearer its deep origin. I intended that when the wearer was draped in this coat she would discover a clue to the coat's history and her own connection to the American West. Buried in the stitches of this coat are canyons, forests, and prairies. A blanket coat has no closures. It wraps. The flowing coat provides a shield against cold much as a Navajo woman drapes a wool blanket around her body for warmth.

I conceived of the blanket coat in the late 1980s. The four-color-blocked original suggested by my friend, Signa Schuster, became a COD classic. The coat would be added to our collection of more structured styles. The blanket coat exemplified a risky but fresh departure from the norm of coat designs in general. Unto itself, the multicolored blanket coat was an inspired design, steeped in functional simplicity. The black-and-white-checked stitched seams hold the wearer in sacred warmth, as the coat's high-fashion elegance belies its historical and cultural origins.

The ultimate blanket coat sailed into the world from its home in the mountains of Montana. A four-color version of the coat adorned a model as she twirled in front of the Eiffel Tower for a Bonwit Teller *New York Times* advertisement. The photo reminded me of the images created by R. C. Gorman, an American painter who portrayed women wearing blankets as ceremonial regalia. A few versions of the blanket coat ended up as characters on TV sitcoms. With each new design, the blanket coat took on a unique name. The "Zig Zag" pale-pink, gray, white, and black blanket coat adorned movie stars and Montanans alike. For a decade during the 1990s, the COD blanket coat was famous, traveling a path from dream to the backs of women the world over.

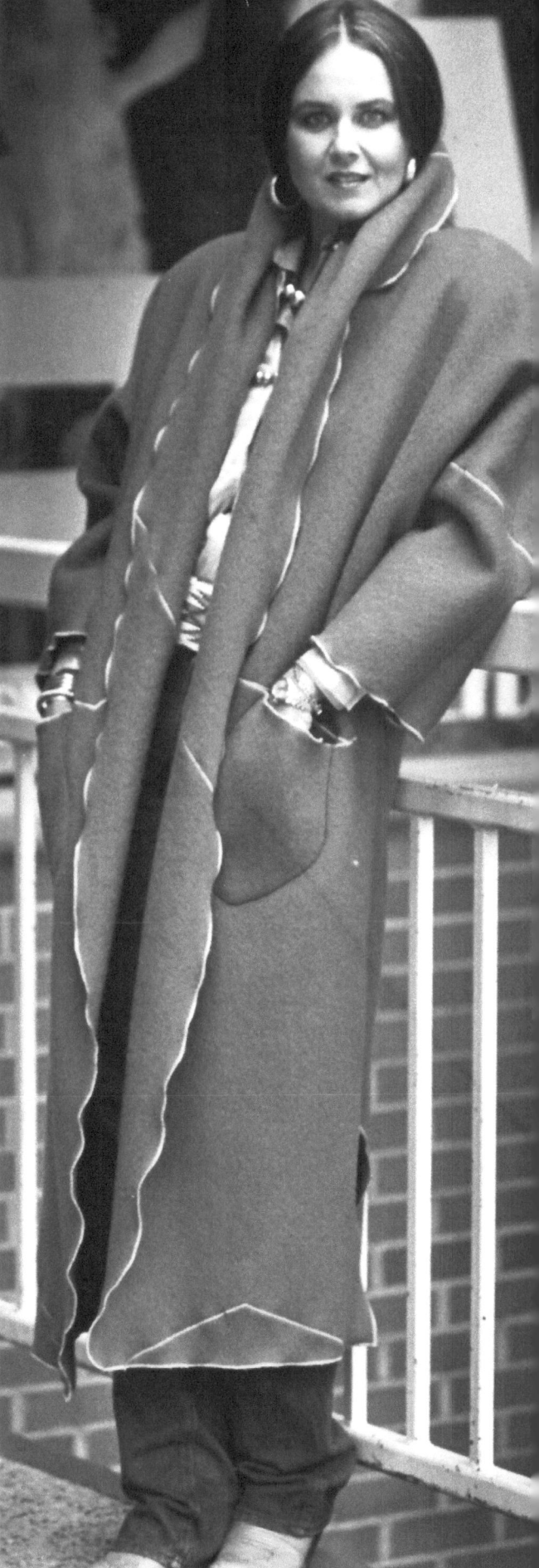

Blanket Coat photographed in front of Jones & Co. in Bozeman, Montana.

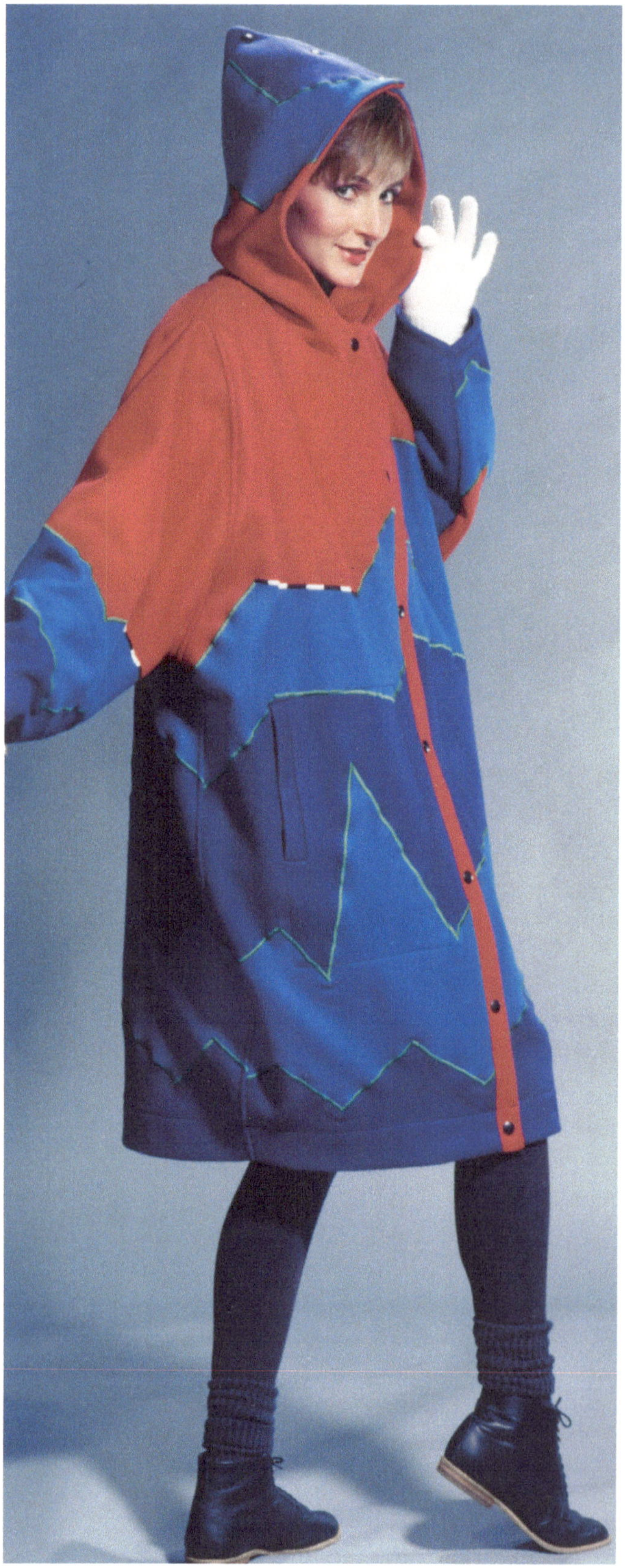

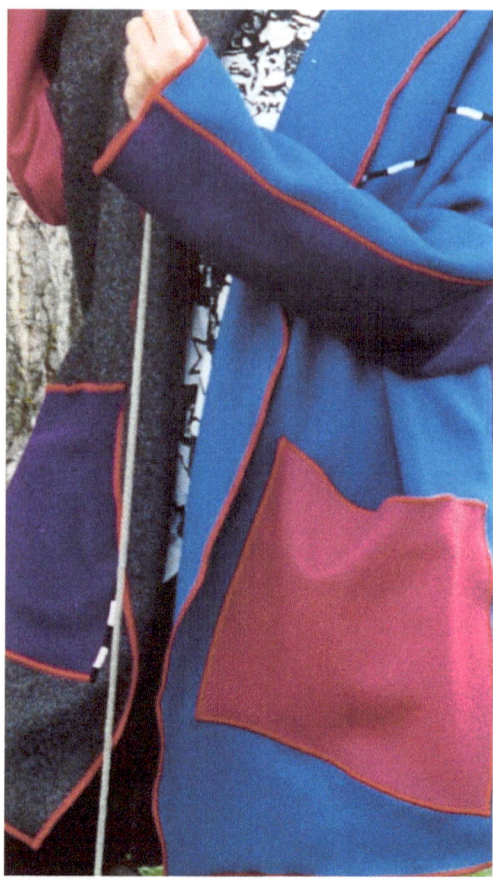
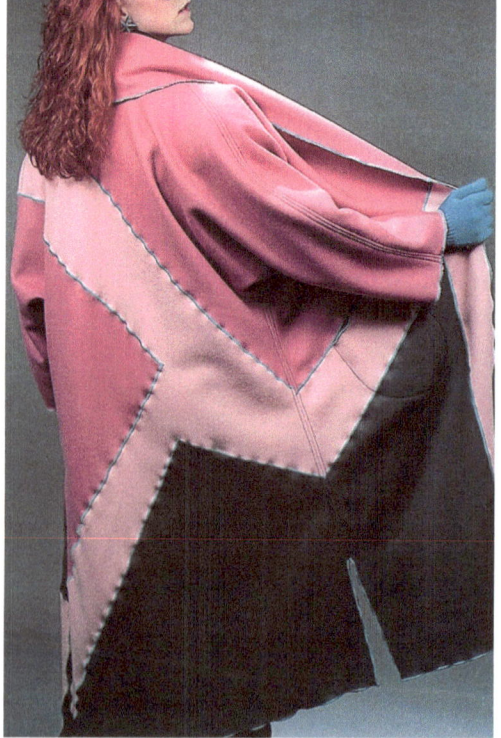

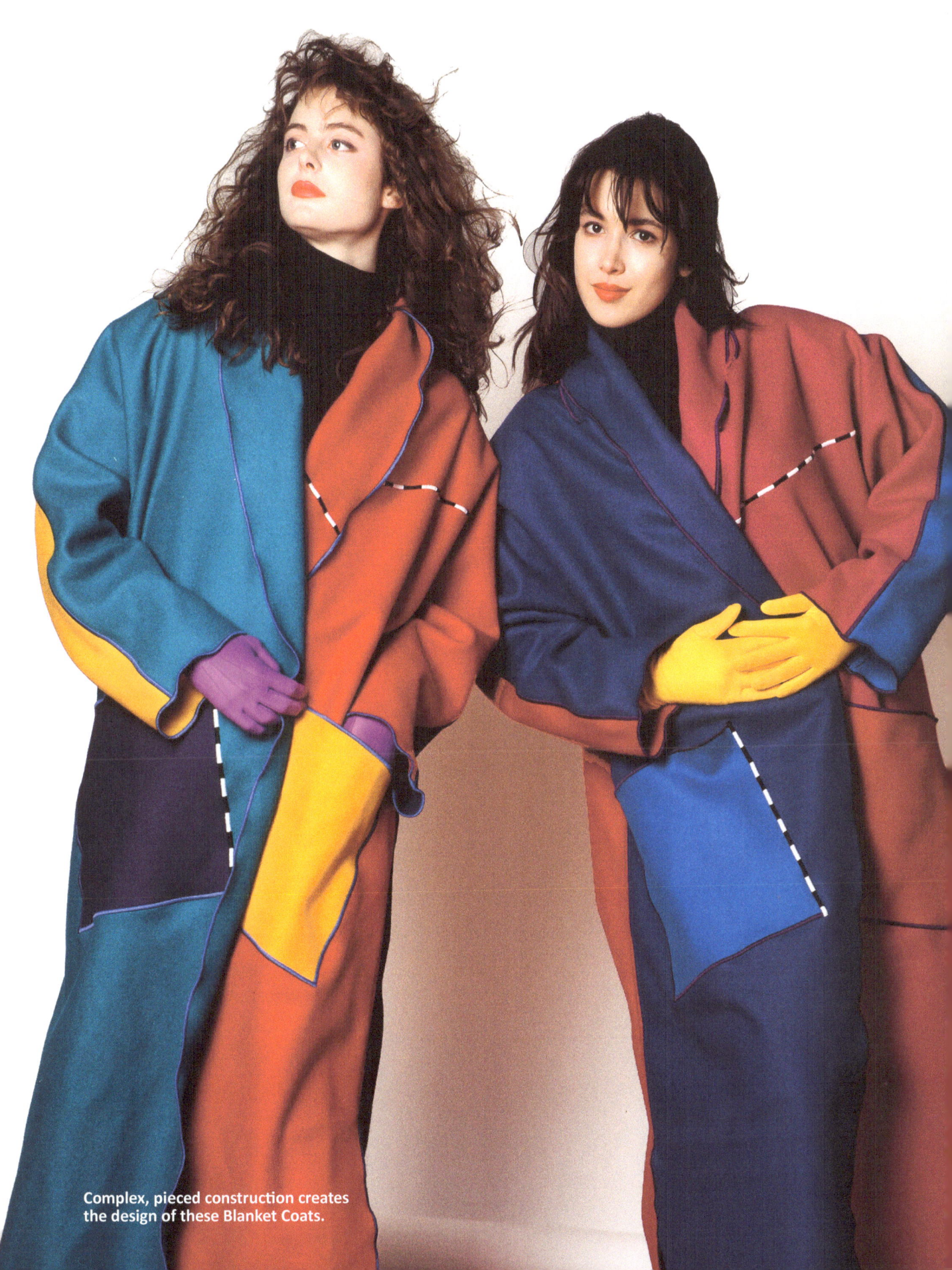

Complex, pieced construction creates the design of these Blanket Coats.

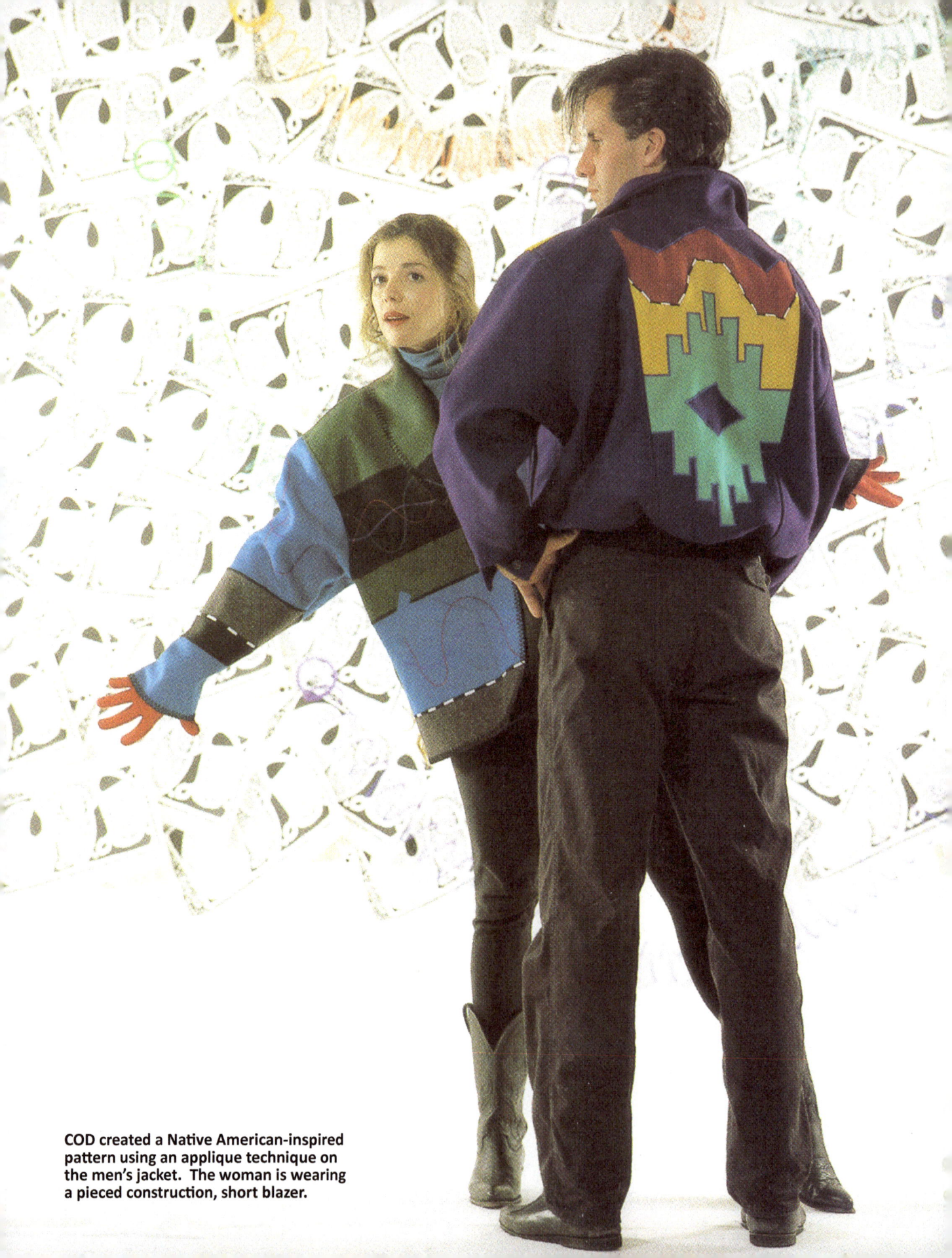

COD created a Native American-inspired pattern using an applique technique on the men's jacket. The woman is wearing a pieced construction, short blazer.

CHAPTER 9

Heady Times

"Hmm, isn't Montana part of Canada?" asked a fabric supplier from Los Angeles, an all-too-familiar refrain.

I hung up the phone and wondered, again, what I was doing trying to run this coat business in such a remote unknown place.

Living near three world-class fly-fishing rivers, mountains that invite a wanderer, and crisp, fresh air might hold enough sparkle for outdoor enthusiasts, but for a clothing designer our state could be just plain backward. While I drew inspiration from Montana's wildness, mountain beauty had its limitations. As the saying goes, you can't eat the scenery. I often wondered if I would be doing mainstream fashion, gray overcoats, boring blazers, or sports jackets, if I lived in Los Angeles or New York. But, after all, I was an artist first, who just happened to design coats. Living remotely was a bonus. My influences were the expansive spaces out the back door, down gravel roads, up forest trails, and beside clear, flowing, ice-cold rivers. However, in order to grow and survive, COD had to find new markets. Up to this point, and for the past two years, I had been selling in a few Montana and New York stores and galleries.

Again, I called my Denver sales rep friend, who put me in touch with a sales rep at the Minneapolis Mart, located in a multistory building filled with wholesale showrooms. Red-haired, with a hot, no-nonsense personality, Carol Curry took one look at the coat samples I sent and said, "I can't sell these, but I know someone who loves quirky and colorful." She then hung the coats on a rolling rack and pushed it down the hall to the Leah Cook Showroom.

Leah loved the coats upon first sight. She examined them closely and knew on the spot that they would sell well in her territory and beyond. As the industry saying goes, "These (coats) are my customer." Here was yet another woman who knew what I didn't know—that quality, style, whimsy, and color would attract the attention of many customers. Mrs. Cook signed on as COD's first sales rep.

Leah Cook, whom I came to call Mrs. Cook, was the picture of old-world style and elegance. She was attracted to the exquisite stitching and attention to detail maintained by COD's seamstresses. At that time, quality sewing was found only in the world of high fashion houses and unexpected elsewhere. Mrs. Cook committed a hundred percent to selling my coats, and like others, dedicated herself to making sure I, as the designer, heard her every whim. She was the third person in the history of COD who believed in my work, putting her stamp on many decisions I made regarding style, color, and design.

For many years, she wore a three-quarter-length baby-blue blanket coat that accentuated her natural elegance and, not incidentally, showed older women that they too could wear a coat of many colors. At the time Mrs. Cook took on COD's coat collection, she was approaching her eightieth year!

Eventually, Mrs. Cook's daughter, Deborah Cook, moved from Chicago to help her mother in the rep business. Deborah became one of COD's most stalwart advocates. She covered their territory—Minnesota, Illinois, Iowa, North and South Dakota, and Wisconsin—by driving her jam-packed minivan to shows and stores, where she sang the praises of COD coats. Both Mrs. Cook and Deborah loved the special feature of COD that customers could buy coats in colors of their own choosing. It was unheard of to sell wool coats in summer. For instance, the Cooks were able to offer COD coat delivery to a store in White Bear Lake, Minnesota, to be sold during summer temps of 80-plus degrees and 100 percent humidity. The storeowner could depend on COD coats selling then because a customer could pick her own colors. With freezing weather just around the corner, a custom wool coat saved the day.

COD coats may have come from remote and unheard-of Montana, but the Cooks were instrumental in COD's coats making the scene nationally. Deborah recently told me, "Those were heady times." Yes, I thought, and the giddy, capricious tempo continued into the mid-1990s.

Back at the COD factory, I knew that one sales rep couldn't possibly do the kind of business we needed to stay afloat. So I signed up to do wholesale shows again in New York City, as well as in Denver, Dallas, Atlanta, Los Angeles, Gatlinburg, Las Vegas, and Seattle. From these shows, we signed on more sales reps, until we reached a total of six, who covered different regions of the country.

COD extended its range by offering a home collection. I was crazed trying to keep up with the coat collection, so it was a welcome diversion to think about designing home items. And it was fun. I not only designed coats—I also designed blankets, Christmas stockings, and pillows. New products expanded our offering, so we could sign on to do wholesale home accessories shows. Our catalog business, spurred on by Deborah Cook, would be significant. We contracted with catalogs such as *Land of Nod* and *Crow's Nest Trading*, and the "Kissing Moose" coat graced the centerfold of an early *Sundance Catalog*. Our "Paint-by-Number" pillows were featured in *Country Living Magazine*. The "Welcome to the Cabin" pillows were included in *O, The Oprah Magazine. Cowboys & Indians Magazine* featured one of COD's blanket coats in a western setting. We even sold coats to Hamilton Stores in Yellowstone Park, known for western historical tourist trinkets.

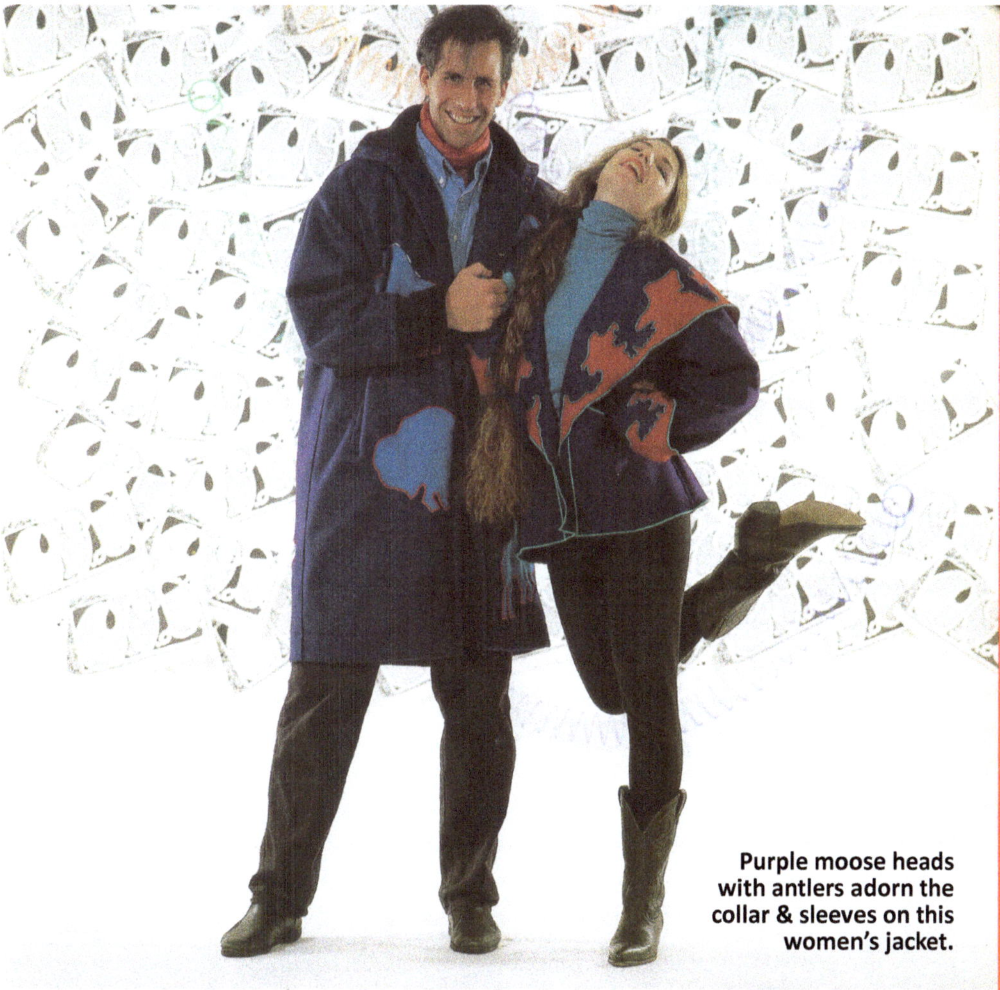

Purple moose heads with antlers adorn the collar & sleeves on this women's jacket.

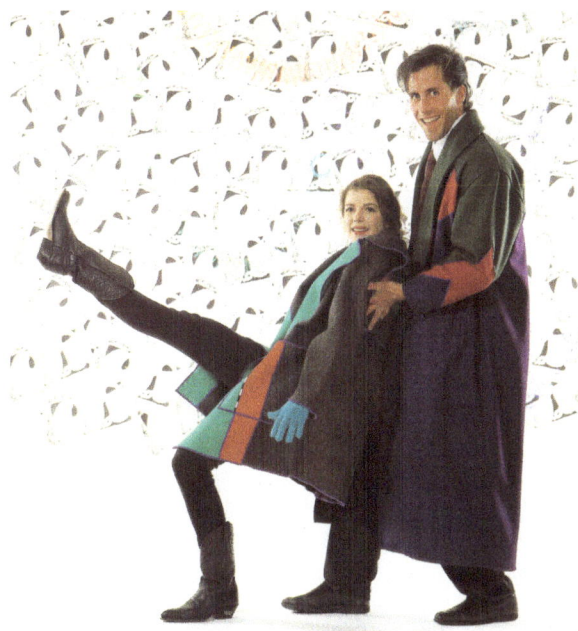
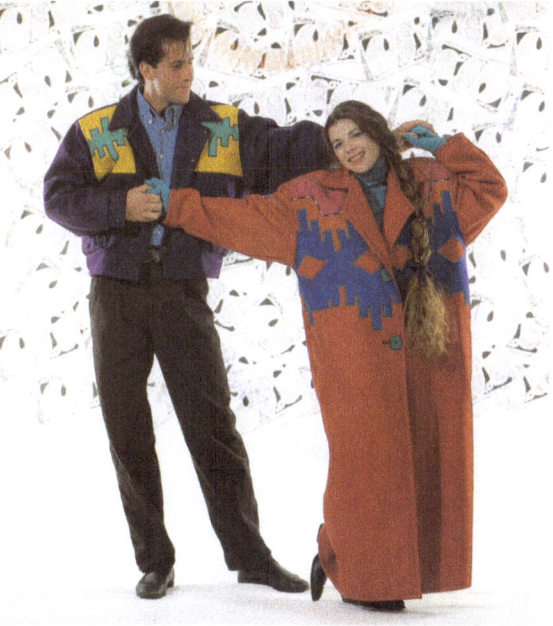

Some of the most well-known top-end women's clothing and department stores sold COD coats, including Gorsuch in Vail, Colorado, Santa Fe Dry Goods, Great Garb in Park City, Utah, Jackie Chalkley in Washington, D.C., Tanglewood in Lenox, Massachusetts, Wyoming Outfitters, in Jackson, Wyoming, Nordstrom's, Bonwit Teller, and Rising Sun Leather, in Bozeman, Montana. We sold to more than 500 accounts in the United States. Bob Haedt, owner of Great Garb, started out as a COD nonbeliever. Bob sat in our New York Pret Show sales booth for more than an hour scratching his head and voicing concerns about price and color combinations. Losing patience, I pushed him into ordering just five coats as a trial run. During the height of Great Garb's winter season, Bob called our office to order a dozen more coats, delivered immediately. Haedt's ski resort store sold hundreds of coats, much to his delight...and COD's.

When our sales team attended shows, we all wore a different COD coat. Before the New York Pret Show, in the early 1990s, four of us walked through Central Park. It was wonderful to be in the middle of a huge city and still be able to breathe fresh air and hear leaves crunch underfoot. As we strolled toward the lake, an attractive woman walking her dog came up to us and asked us to stop for a moment.

"Excuse me, but is the designer of these coats here?" she inquired.

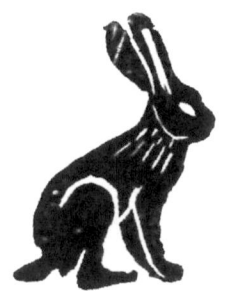

"Yes, that would be me," I said.

"I need these coats on my show. They are smashing. How can we make this happen?" she asked.

"Well, sure," I said, "but what is your show?"

The Cosby Show," she replied.

I nearly fainted. My voice came out shaky. I could hardly contain myself. I just wanted to jump with joy. I thought, wow, here in the middle of New York's Central Park, where people enjoy anonymity, a famous person noticed COD. Sarah LeMire, as she introduced herself, turned out to be the costume designer for the popular iconic *Cosby Show.* She, ironically, had grown up in Miles City, Montana, of all places. COD provided coats for Phylicia Rashad, the actress who played the mother on the show. Rashad wore different COD coats on three Cosby episodes. Back at the factory, we cheered to see our coats on national TV.

Every year COD held a sample sale at my Wallace Street factory in Bozeman. The first year we offered the sale, we sold maybe five coats. I was bereft. All of the money we spent on samples had to be recouped somehow. My stomach turned over in disappointment. Where were the locals? As time went on and people saw our coats on women in big cities, airports, and snazzy ski resorts, our sample sales became over-the-top affairs with well over 300 people in attendance. People lined up outside the factory early in the morning holding their cups of coffee with a muffin. When the doors opened at 9:00 a.m. sharp, crowds rushed in to grab coats off the racks. Shoppers didn't even care if a particular coat fit. It was intense but humorous when people pulled coats away from others, fighting to lay claim to a particular coat.

"Bozemanites" recognized COD's success. COD had finally arrived on the local scene. COD became a local phenomenon. We were asked to donate a coat for auction at many nonprofit fetes, where coats brought in far more than retail prices. For instance, the Museum of the Rockies offered a COD coat at a fundraising auction for many years during the early 1990s. I didn't consciously think about my success as a designer except when walking the streets of Bozeman and someone stopped me to ask about coats. I had arrived at a publically perceived pinnacle of success, and although I took it seriously, I was also having fun. I felt grateful that I could play with ideas, put the outcomes into the marketplace, and wait to see what happened. I looked at my successes and my failures as opportunities to discover where I stood.

I suppose because of all the exposure showered on COD's coats, the Lifetime network sniffed out my personal story. The show producer invited me to tell my story on the morning show, *The Balancing Act,* featuring women business owners. I was terrified but also excited to appear on national TV.

Right before my time slot, there was an interview with my favorite clothing designer, whom I had admired for years, Betsey Johnson. As she came off the set, she walked over to me and introduced herself. She stood right in front of me in one of her crazy tulle can-can skirts, sparkling high heels, and bright-orange frizzed hair with a giant bow. She smiled and tried to engage in a brief conversation. Good grief, here I was standing in front of my most admired of clothing designers. I wore a conservative green suit with strawberry earrings (harkening back to my teen strawberry dress) that matched my bright-pink hair. My one regret? I wasn't wearing my favorite long Betsey Johnson symphony director coat over mesh stockings and net underskirt. Words escaped me. My jaw dropped. I was more delighted to meet her than I was to be interviewed on the show.

As I sat before the bright lights and TV camera, my confidence flagged. How could I possibly have something to say that would measure up to well-known designers? It wasn't until the interviewer asked me about my business that I reached my stride. I talked from my heart about my Northern Rocky Mountains home, my factory, the people I worked with, and my daughter. At the end of the interview, I wanted it to go on.

Heady times, these, as Deborah Cook so aptly put it. None of us could guess what was around the next corner for COD. Even national news predictions were vague. Who could know the impact on business of the Gulf War, a national recession, or an ownership dispute? In the larger scheme of things, we were just a tiny clothing business in a remote Rocky Mountains town. COD's "sewists" just wanted to make beautiful coats to send out into the world, but the world came to us, heedless and beyond our control.

CHAPTER 10

COD's Underbelly

All was not what it seemed. Over the 20-plus years COD existed in the minds of the public as a fantasy of success, there were also times of strife, betrayal, and heartbreak. COD's underbelly could be described like the spaghetti western, *The Good, the Bad, and the Ugly,* where three gunmen set out to find a hidden fortune. I came to suspect that within my own endeavor there lurked an unforeseen dynamic associated with a woman-owned business.

Much of what became negative in my business likely grew out of my own naiveté or innocence about the intentions of others. I judged and trusted others when I could have been more discerning and professional in my choice of people who were hired or invited in to handle vital aspects of my business. While COD's staff of 25 performed tasks around the production, finances and accounting, and marketing of outerwear, each of these individuals wore her or his own coat of many colors. I describe these events as just that, events with no attachment to the precise time they occurred.

I fell into a personal relationship with a charismatic man who offered to become involved in my business. He had no experience in the fashion world. However, he came across as an astute businessperson and I was also in love with him. I accepted his offer to become COD's business manager. I could then do what I loved, work on new designs. He managed the finances of the business and oversaw the supervision of staff. For a while, his involvement in my business provided needed organizational policies and procedures. Due to his business expertise, my business soon rose from a home start-up to a nationally recognized source for unique and beautiful coats.

Within about a year of the arrangement, it became clear that the production staff had grown to have reservations about this guy's managing style. The way he communicated with women was gruff and rigid. He was also condescending and came across as knowing more than he did about sewing, which was nothing. The production manager informed me that the sewing staff intended to walk out if the business manager didn't leave. In tandem with this threat came a change in my own relationship with him. He had become involved with another woman. I found out that he had taken a "scouting trip" with her to Nebraska on COD's dime. The trip was made to visit her family. As soon as he told me that his new girlfriend had some good ideas for designs, I demanded he leave my life and business.

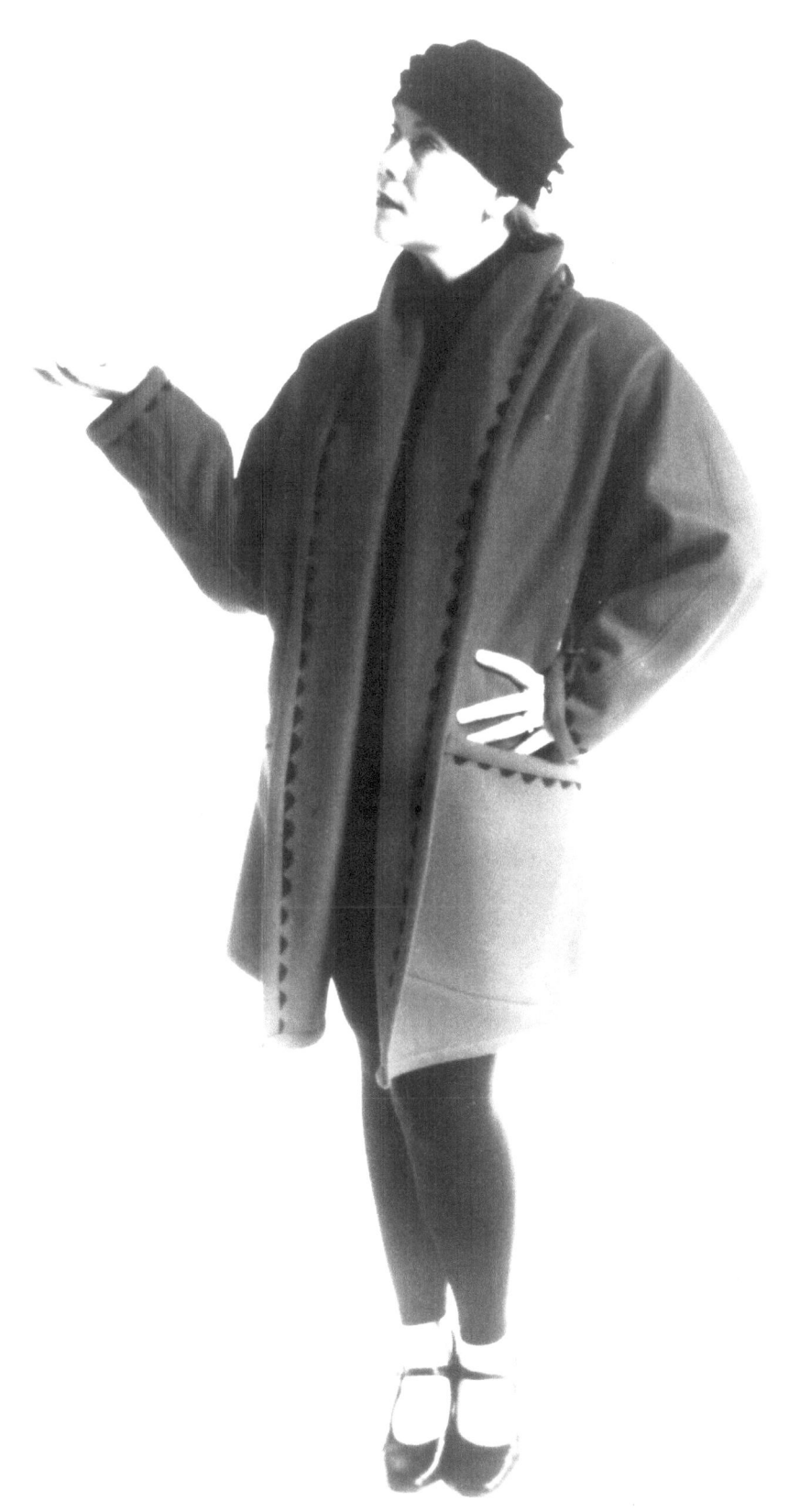

It wasn't long before I was served with a lawsuit. The day was gray. A messenger pulled up outside of COD's office, came in, and laid a packet on my desk. My former boyfriend and business manager claimed he owned one-half of COD. However, he had invested time but no money in the business. He was a paid employee. One day I went to the post office to collect COD's mail to find that the lock had been changed. I spun backwards in anger and amazement. My hand had been forced. I had to take action, soon.

I hired a lawyer. I spent hours and hours describing my business to the attorney so he could understand the gravity and scope of the situation. The lawsuit went to trial before a judge with a reputation for fairness. Meanwhile, I was worried, anxious, and jittery. It was difficult to think about anything else, let alone run my coat business. The trial experience was all-consuming, requiring constant strategizing, examining mundane details, and checking facts. The whole affair leading up to and including the trial was beyond nerve-racking. I stood in front of the design studio mirror to talk myself into projecting confidence each day of the proceedings.

During the testimony, I listened to unsubstantiated claims on the part of the other side, one after another. I had decided to wear my treasured Norma Kamali gray ankle-length sweatshirt dress through the entire three-day trial. This elegant understated dress was, for me, a strong statement of a woman who could stand on her own two feet. It carried Kamali's label, OMO (On My Own). I was familiar with Kamali's own business history and her dedication to women's rights in the fashion industry. The trial became my opportunity to move forward with grace, strength, and determination on my own terms.

The second morning of the three-day trial, I read in the *Bozeman Daily Chronicle* an article about my coat business ownership dispute in all its glorious gossipy detail. I was embarrassed. I refused to talk with anyone about the whole sordid affair, thinking, how could this be happening to me?

After days of testimony and heartache, the judge finally made his decision. The outcome of the trial was that I could keep ownership of the business if I agreed to pay my former partner $26,000, plus assume the Small Business Administration (SBA) debt of $120,000. I owed the attorney $50,000. How was this decision fair? I questioned. The decision was a hard nut to swallow.

Later, through my attorney, I found out that the judge had awarded my former partner money because the judge felt, based on how he testified, that he would hound and harass me otherwise. Also, through my attorney, I found out that the opposing attorney expressed regret at even taking the case against me. I wondered if this whole situation would have happened had I been a man. The outcome was unfair, but at least I was free to continue my design business. It was a welcome day when I could sit at my drawing board, to sketch designs for the fall collection, instead of wallowing in constant worry of losing my business and livelihood. I could fly again. The debt, however, eventually crippled the business in more ways than one.

Following the announcement of the trial's outcome, I walked into my office in the old Coco-Cola Bottling Building on North Wallace. Before me was a room filled with dozens of fresh red roses from my staff.

I returned to running COD, which meant I was responsible for finances, new designs, supervision of employees, communication with sales reps, and planning. The expenses mounted and staff confidence flagged. The debt loomed over our heads. It was a very difficult time. There were days when I didn't answer my phone for fear it would be a supplier or a sales rep asking to be paid. My time was spent juggling funds and worrying for COD's future.

We had signed up months ago to attend the sewing equipment show in Atlanta. I ended up not attending and instead sent COD's production manager. It wasn't long after her return that various members of my management staff met together outside of work hours. Then they approached me as a group—the office manager, marketing and promotion managers, and production manager—and asked me to attend a meeting.

At this meeting, they asked me to step down from running COD and turn over management to them. They implied I wasn't business-oriented enough. I wondered if it was a power struggle that grew out of my former partner's management style. Once again, I wondered, could this have happened had I been a man? To me, the underlying message was that I needed to be taken care of, that I wasn't capable of managing my business myself. I answered my trusted employees' request by saying unequivocally no. Then I quickly left my office to go home to become physically ill. I reached home in time to vomit in the toilet. Then I collapsed on my couch and sobbed.

In due course, the production manager departed COD. She started her own contract sewing business with a handful of COD's design and sewing staff. I suspected not only did I provide a wealth of production sewing experience over her time in my employ but she most likely outfitted her own new business at the Atlanta show. My long relationship with my first employee had ended. Feelings of betrayal do not soon disappear. My heart was heavy, as I had also lost a trusted friend.

One day I walked into my office to find COD's banker and a representative from the SBA. They were there to discuss me paying back the money I owed, $220,000. I said I could not in good conscience declare bankruptcy. The gray skies were raining down. What was I to do?

To raise money immediately, I laid off all my employees. The decision was my only alternative, but it was the most difficult decision I had ever made in my business. I also sold off all my sewing machines, except for what I needed to continue sewing myself: a blanket-stitch machine, a straight-stitch machine, an embroidery machine, and cutting tables and cutters. My sewing skills had always served me well, so I knew the remaining equipment was my life raft. I sublet the upstairs of my building to a nonprofit organization and a restaurant equipment start-up. I moved all of COD to the basement. It took all of my inner strength to move through this difficult period in my life.

Fallout from the roomful of roses was quirky. COD's handwork person was the man behind the gift of the bundles of roses. A handwork position within sewing production is critical. This person was responsible for sewing on buttons, final pressing of finished coats, and various seemingly tiny but important tasks. Handwork was the final station before a coat was sent out the door. Little did I know that the roses gift would come back to bite me. I believe that the partner of Mr. Handwork (as I'll call him), who worked at Patagonia's design facility, in Bozeman, took offense at the attention his lover paid me and invented a couple of ways to bring mischief and utter lunacy to COD.

Rather than provide paper towels to the staff, I had passed out small cotton towels that each worker kept to dry their hands. A commercial laundry laundered the towels weekly. One morning I arrived at my office with a notice posted on the door that OSHA would be coming that day. I had no other warning. Later in the morning, a man dressed head to toe in a HAZMAT suit walked into the office. He said he was responding to two complaints regarding the cotton towels and wool dust in our sewing room in the basement. A letter from the Billings OSHA office was handed to me. I escorted the man to the basement. Everyone looked up with shock to see the visitor. He proceeded to mount air-quality gauges on each sewing machine. The gauges could ostensibly calculate the amount of wool dust produced by sewing wool fabric.

I sent the Billings OSHA representative an actual towel. Apparently, the complaint indicated that I had not provided appropriate paper towels to my employees. The agent was taken aback. He called, saying, "The complaint was ridiculous and unfounded." He went on to say, "I have never received a towel in the mail." He also told me that when the results of the wool dust gauges came in, they read "0." He told me that he could not report a result with "0." The report had to stipulate "1." We both laughed. He revealed the source of the complaint. And, that was that. I didn't want to, but I had to fire Mr. Handwork. He must have been complicit with his partner on some level in the towel/wool dust scheme. He never denied involvement. Ironically, he had been the best handwork person I had ever employed. He was meticulous in his work and his attention to detail was unsurpassed.

Often I recognized a deep resilience within myself that rose to the surface when extreme measures were called for. I was reminded of the strength of women before me who spoke out for their rights. I thought about the isolation of my childhood and my own family's irrepressible choices to scratch out a life in tandem with the rivers of the West. COD flowed on in the face of despair and pitfalls, graced with frequent highs. I lived the three-year bumpy journey fully and with an undeniable singular presence. As proof positive, my own future attendance at the Atlanta Sewing Equipment Show opened a door of opportunity, and the direction of COD was once more on an upswing.

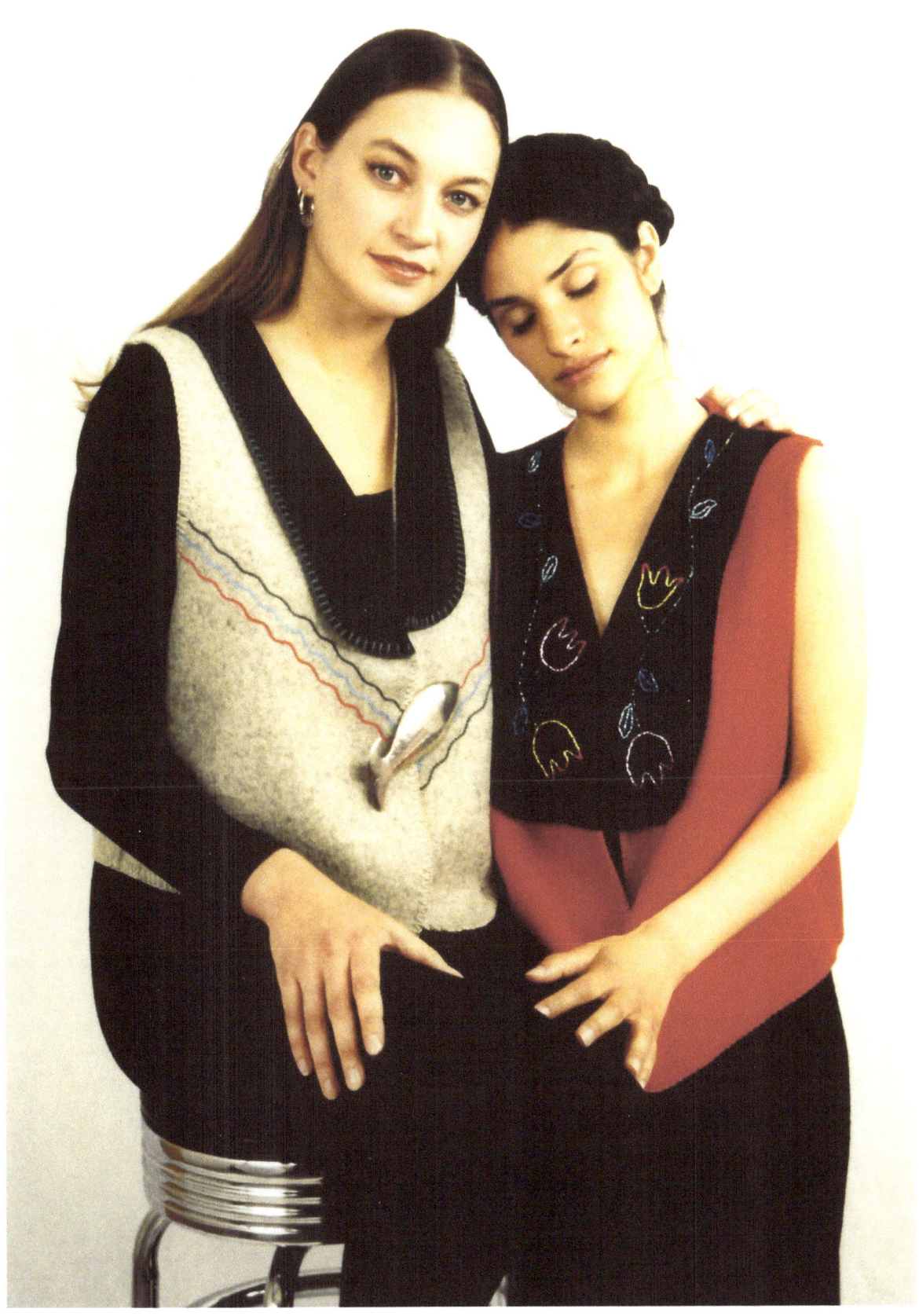

COD production staff embellished wool vests with stitching, beading, and pin closures.

CHAPTER 11

Coats and the People Who Made Them

A river of activity swirled around the creation of coats. Magpies swooped and screeched with advice for this and that. Coats twirled their own colors and patterns. Coats were like baby robins always demanding attention. "Zig Zags" and "Punk Navajos" sailed through each day and shrouded my every move. "Kissing Moose" and "Trout" appeared out of thin air. "City Scapes" with "Rocky Mountains" sweaters reigned. "Beaverheads" skipped to and fro with "Two Dots." "Camp Cedar," "Teton," and "Montana Souvenir Blazers" jumped into the fray. Eventually, black bears skied down the sides of Christmas stockings, autumn leaves fell around the edges of coats and blankets, and cowpokes rode bucking horses that leaped over jack fences across the back of blazers—all, COD "Wonders of the West." (This also was the name of COD's little sales booklet.)

We developed new collections of eight to ten coats and jackets every six months, spring and fall, fall and spring, each year. As the COD designer, inspired by ideas seemingly carried on the wind, I also surrounded myself with fashion magazines to discover current trends in style, color, and function in the greater fashion universe. For each coat collection, I assigned a theme such as "The Souvenir Blazer Series," "The Fruit Salad Fleece Collection," "The Kissing Wild Series," and "The Blanket Coat Collection." Themes were related to natural elements from my surroundings and included fall colors, wild animals, and flower or vegetable gardens. Other themes were cityscapes, well-known paintings, and vintage ski and western clothing.

I spent hours late into the night in search of inspiration from photos of wild animals, Japanese hand-woven fabrics, Indian saris, and African mud cloth. Beside my bed a 3-foot stack of favorite books became my go-to reading. My collection of books on the vast world of woven, painted, and embroidered fabrics, vintage and indigenous clothing, hand-carved furniture, and folk art influenced my imagination.

I penciled rudimentary drawings of garment ideas and then handed these over to the production manager for review. The two of us then discussed how the drawing would become a coat. Decisions had to be made about every tiny detail: type of sleeve, closure,

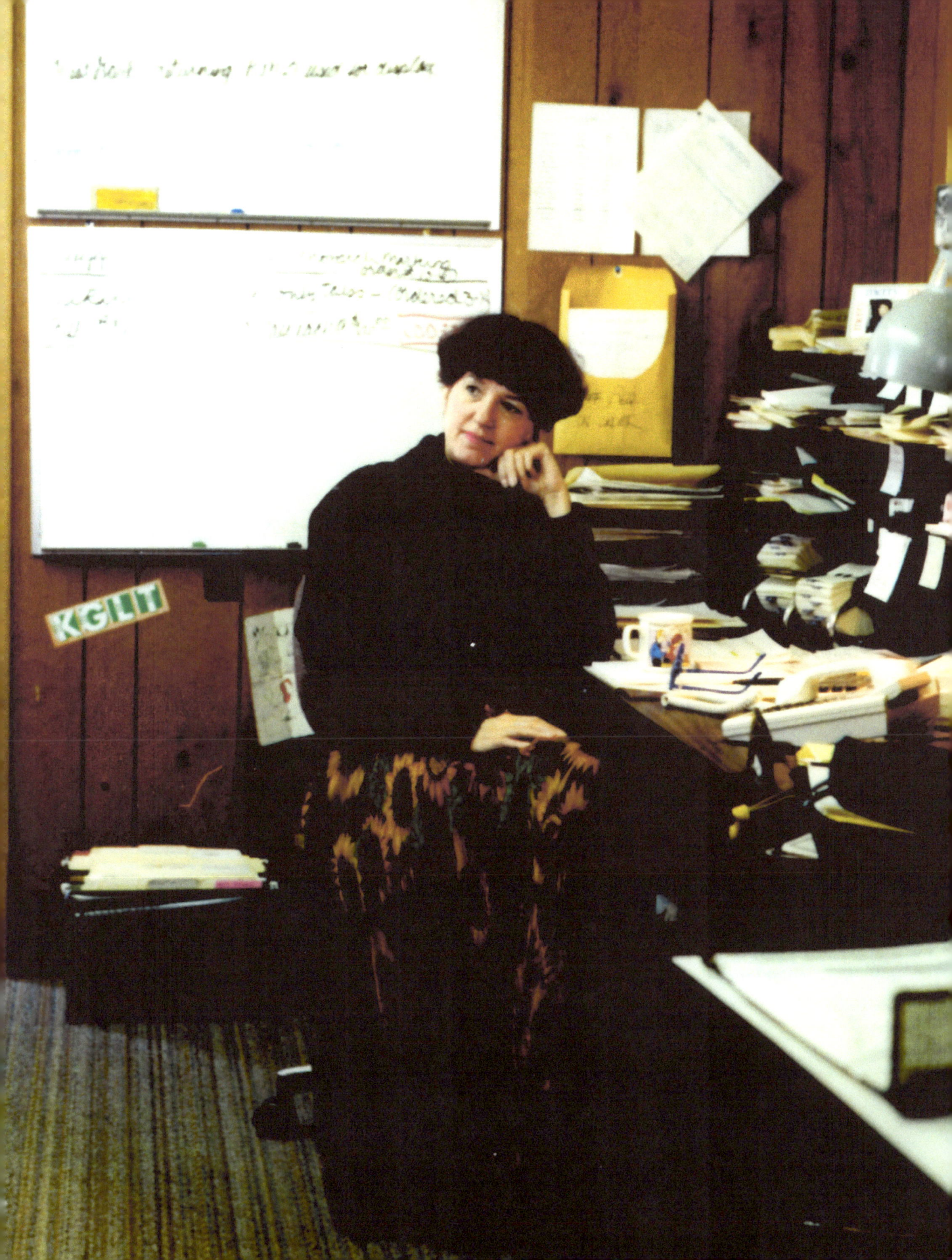

facing, collar details, pocket opening, length of coat body, flare of hem, tucks, seams, lining, and darts. Then came the coat's surface design that needed to be integrated with the construction of the overall garment. For many coat collections, I designed the wooden buttons used for closures. A good friend offered to cut and paint our multi-planed buttons that ended up being tiny works of art within themselves.

    When a design was finalized, the production staff set about making patterns for each size of each coat. COD's coat patterns hung along one entire wall of the downstairs sewing/cutting workroom. The patterns were like cardboard curtains. They swayed and rustled in backdoor breezes, seemingly alive. Next came sourcing fabric and notions for any unique additions to a coat sample. We tried to work within specific parameters, such as certain kinds of wool outerwear fabric that we had in stock, to cut down on costs. Waiting for a new on-order fabric could put our production schedule behind. Balancing all of these elements became a challenge for our design team. After all, we lived in the remote state of Montana with only a phone and a telephone book to track down unusual notions, buttons, zippers, thread, yarn, and pattern paper.

    I brimmed with ideas for new coats. I returned often to my love of the unknown. One idea sprang forth as another was dashed to the rubbish bin. Staff sometimes tore their hair out by the roots as they tried to keep up with my flights of fantasy. However, there were no guarantees that staff or customers would agree that a certain style or color combination could fly. Retail storeowners could be persnickety. Sometimes we had to repeat coat designs, especially the more popular ones. We also always added fresh designs. However, the trial-and-error process was excruciating. I presented to staff piles of design drawings, fabric swatches, notions, and color palettes. The presentation opened for discussion either rejection or acceptance. I spent many sleepless nights and long days drawing and re-drawing designs I hoped to be the year's best-selling coats. I was the sole designer, but I depended on a design assistant to offer suggestions and complete working drawings.

    The design process started at the beginning of September for the following year's fall collection. It took much research to be able to anticipate fashion trends a year out. Squeezed into regular coat production, we had to cut and sew coat samples for the January fall season shows. From September through December, we lived with uncertainty and were on edge and stressed as work piled up. But all deadlines had to be met. We all understood that the following year's sales depended on our work at this time. Sample sets were sewn for each of four sales reps plus our in-house samples. All samples were labeled, packed, and shipped by mid-January. All of us wanted to run away to warm lands, to relax, to wrap ourselves in the warmth of accomplishment.

    As new coat samples were finished, members of my staff and I gathered around our conference table at the Wallace Street factory to name each new coat. "The Naming Party," as we called it, could be a raucous affair fueled by wine and food. The moment we all anticipated with glee after many hours of hard work had arrived. It meant the newest line of coats was off the drawing board, hanging on hangers, and ready for their flight into

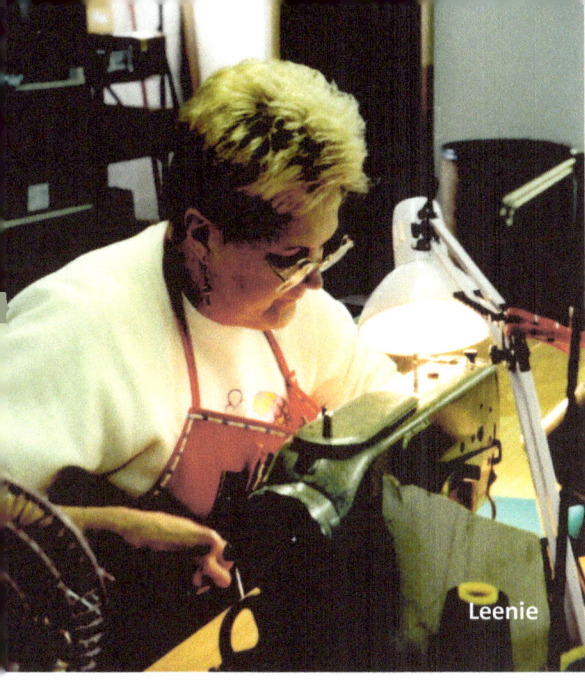
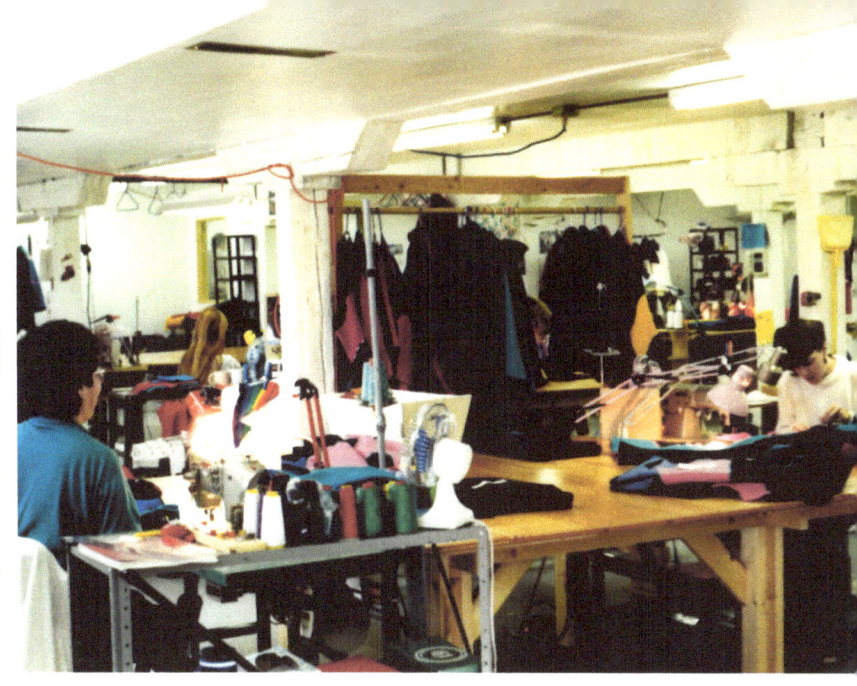
Leenie

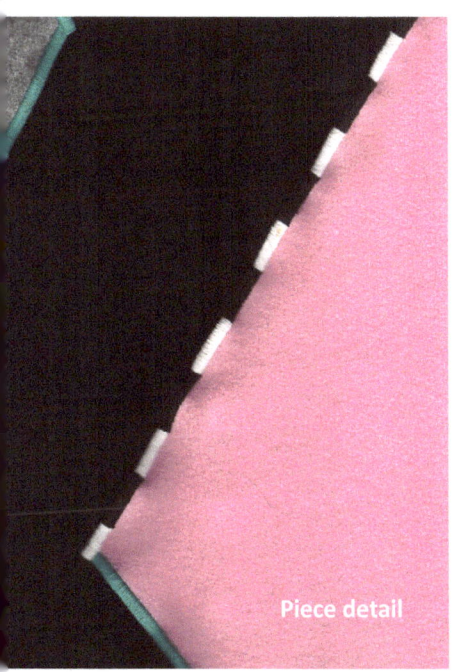
Piece detail
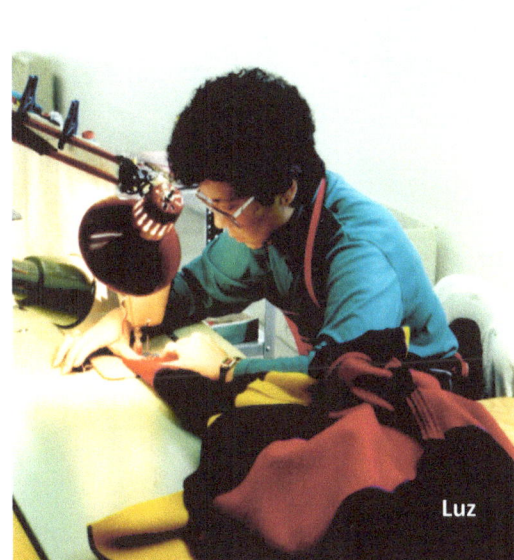
Luz
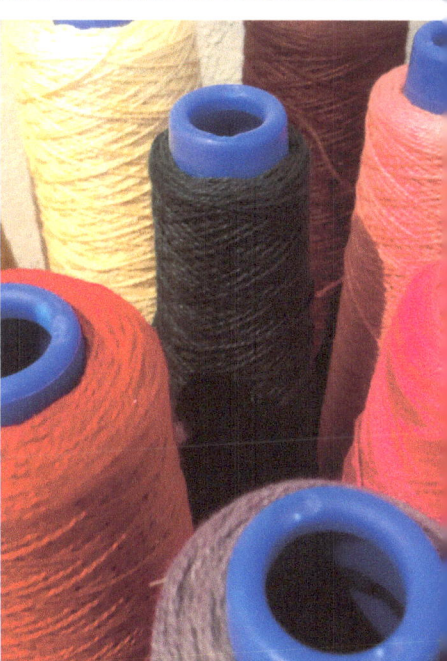

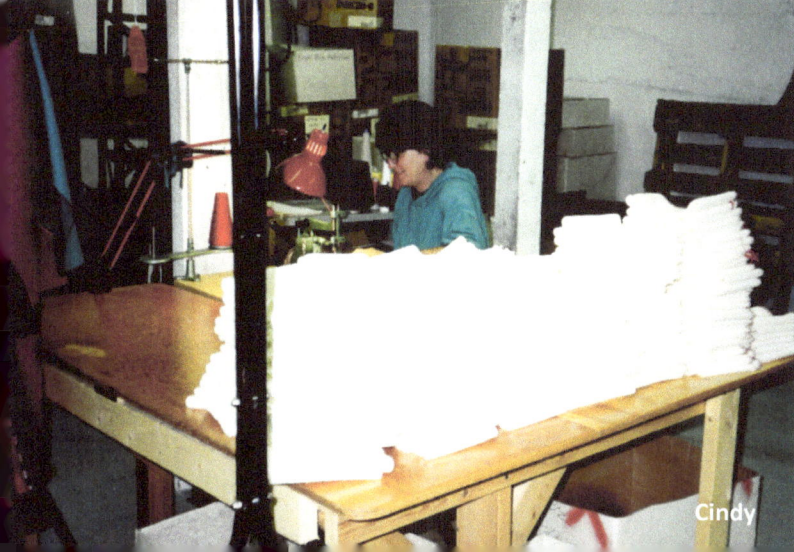
Cindy
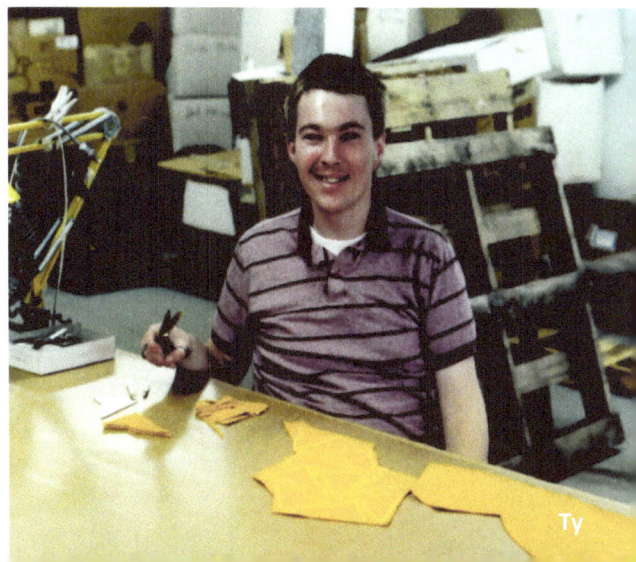
Ty

the world. As each coat was brought forward, possible names were shouted out. If a name seemed like it fit the coat, then the name stuck. "City Scape," for instance, was obviously named for its carefully detailed, outlined silhouettes of a city skyline that graced the upper coat's yoke. "The Kissing Animal Series" names sprang up at the conference table, along with names of blanket coats, elegant, long, structured coats, and short jackets. Because over the years we came to know our customers, staff would take a guess and say, "I think that coat fits Tanglewood and Great Garb. It's perfect for them." In the end, the staff would usually be correct in their predictions.

In order to turn out hundreds of coats per year, COD employed about 25 people off and on. One quarter of the staff handled office tasks, marketing, and supervision of production. The largest portion of people who worked at the factory was skilled in sewing, cutting, and handwork. Workers' lives were woven into the cloth of each coat that left our doors. These lives guided COD's canoe on a river of swales and calm. Most of COD's workers came to us as gems in the rough. They held a wealth of clothing construction knowledge and skills born of Montana rural childhoods spent with grandmothers and mothers who worked with their hands. Embroidery, crochet, knitting, and sewing machine skills were engrained passions. Training these workers to sew in a manner specific to our needs was seamless. These rural women became the backbone of COD's reputation for quality, creativity, and style. COD's fabric workers shared skills in common, rural backgrounds, and Montana, but not a lot else.

As factory life evolved, each morning workers arrived with personal stories to be slung from the workstation across the cutting table and back again. As raw fabric turned wearable with each cut of a scissor and stitch of brightly colored thread, personal life stories bubbled over. The river of lives seemed quiet on the surface, but as humanity meshes with itself in daily encounters, clashes, harsh words, and hurt feelings often peppered the work atmosphere.

Why did professional stitchers refuse to pass coats in a production line to the next worker because that person was of a different religion? The tiny communities of Manhattan, Amsterdam, and Churchill, west of Bozeman, are populated by people in two main religions, the Dutch Reformed Church and the Christian Reformed Church. The COD workers in both camps coalesced around their respective church. Unfamiliar with either religion, I couldn't fathom the depth of the disagreement among the seamstresses, nor did I much care. To bring these kinds of issues into a production line situation was beyond the pale. Many of these women from a rural culture, while valued highly for their sewing knowledge and skills, refused to do their assigned job because of personal or religious differences, creating an untenable situation for me. This state of affairs brought forth an unnecessary toxicity in the workplace, and the morale of the entire sewing workroom took a dive. In the end, the members of one church group actually resigned.

The roiling waters of worker relations remained a source of endless careful navigation and time spent in negotiation by management and staff. Sometimes if individuals didn't feel satisfied with our response to demands, they quit. For instance, two sewers

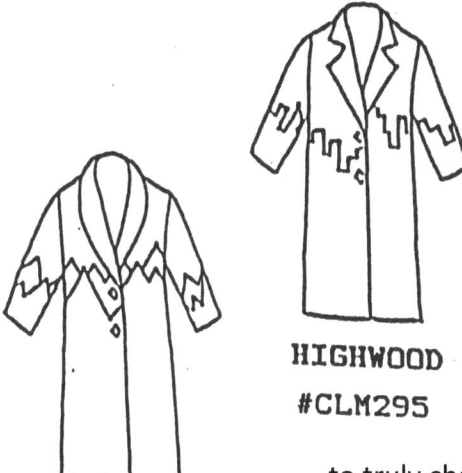

PLENTIWOOD
#CLM298

HIGHWOOD
#CLM295

decided they could run the production far better than the production manager. When we told them we had a different take on the situation, wanting to keep things as they were, they both gave up good jobs in the wink of an eye. Ironically, there was always someone new who knocked on COD's door to bring in a fresh spirit and positive attitude. Personally, I remained aloof from the fray. I depended on my production manager to handle most of the sewing personnel problems. Such negativity weighed on my emotions, but I felt powerless to truly change many employee-expressed grievances. I consulted outside help at times with varying results. Religious differences, sexual orientation, age diversity, and differing values were sewn into every coat, whether we liked it or not. Such was the workroom dynamic.

Odd events materialized at the factory for no known reason, a reflection possibly of hidden jealousies and personal inadequacies. I don't know. It remains a mystery why an employee chose to ruin completed buttonholes by slicing the opening beyond its perimeter into fabric on a finished coat. The coat was, of course, rendered useless. On one occasion, a longtime worker told me directly, "When I see your face each morning, I know I hate you." She offered no explanation as to why (nor did I particularly care to hear why). Without blowing up at this attack, I said goodbye and told her to please leave. One day, the basement workroom was filled with gas fumes. Upon investigation by authorities, it was found that someone had stuffed a rag in the outside furnace gas vent. I must say that my own trust and naiveté were my own blindside. I found in my own soul searching I couldn't see my own contribution to these matters. Yet others must have found fault with my leadership in ways that remained a mystery to me.

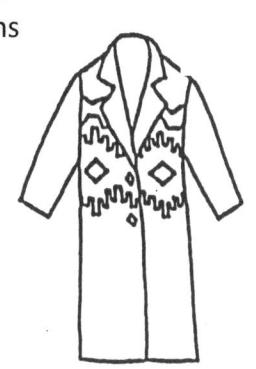

EKALAKA
#CLM330

I often wondered when it came to matters of employee relations, had I been a man with understood accepted power, would interactions within the staff have been different? Do workers view authority of men and women in different ways? Could COD have been a microcosm of rural family life, where positions and roles are understood from birth? The people who worked at our factory weren't professionals, per se, meaning our employees were not educated or trained in a vocational or higher education school setting to acquire production skills. They brought their own rural family upbringing to the sewing room to form a new family of sorts with all of its positives and negatives. COD was primarily a female business up and down the line, as the designing, production, and selling of garments were mainly done by women, to be mainly worn by women. I only knew that what my employees expressed, good or bad, needed to be respected.

BOULDER
#CLM290

The illustrations on this page are from the 1991 men's collection.

People, not machines, made our coats. Every person had the right to be heard and to make his or her own choices.

The bottom line, however, was that coats needed to be manufactured if COD's canoe could continue to float. Someone (and that would be me) must hold a steady unwavering vision, come what may.

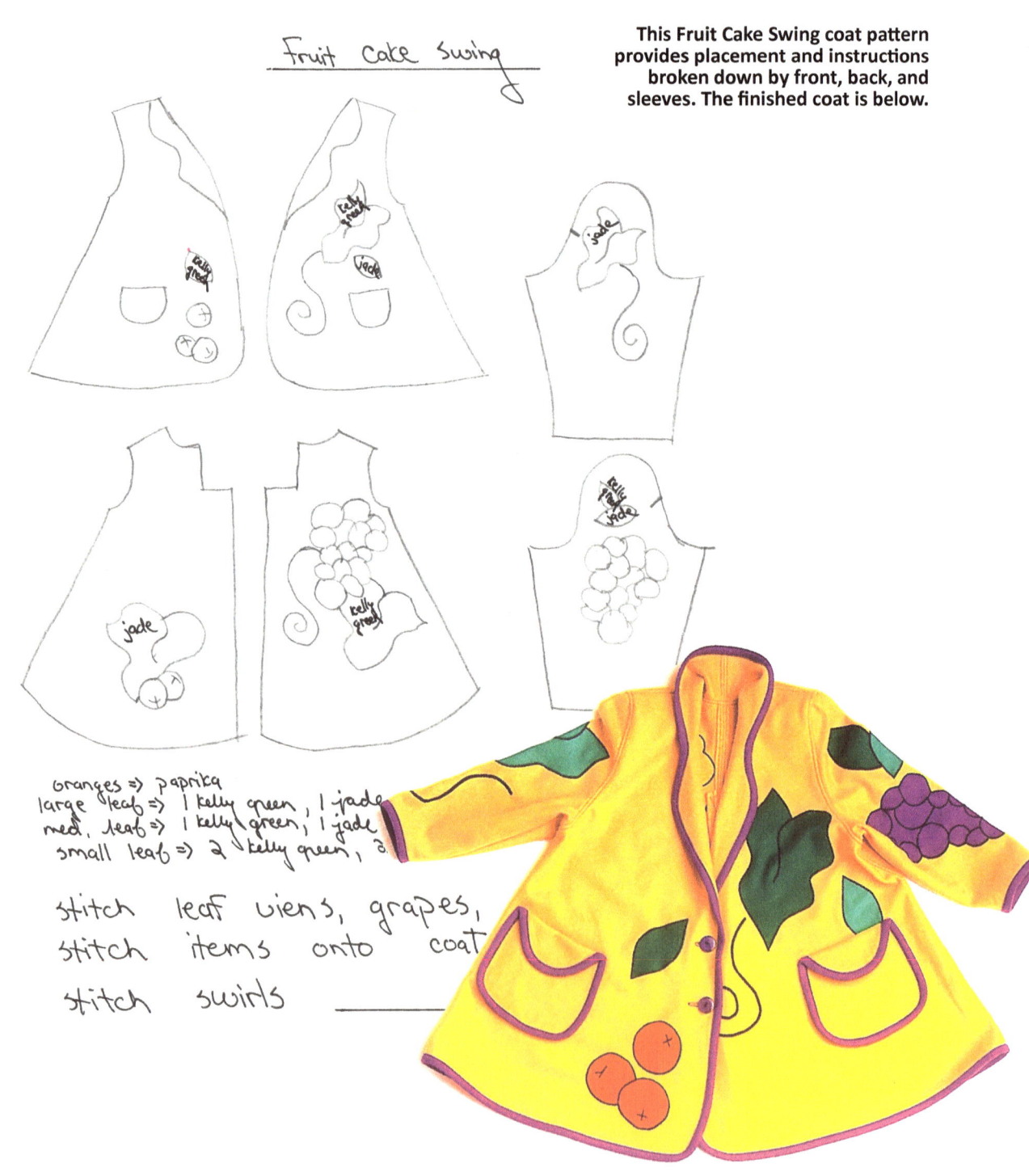

This Fruit Cake Swing coat pattern provides placement and instructions broken down by front, back, and sleeves. The finished coat is below.

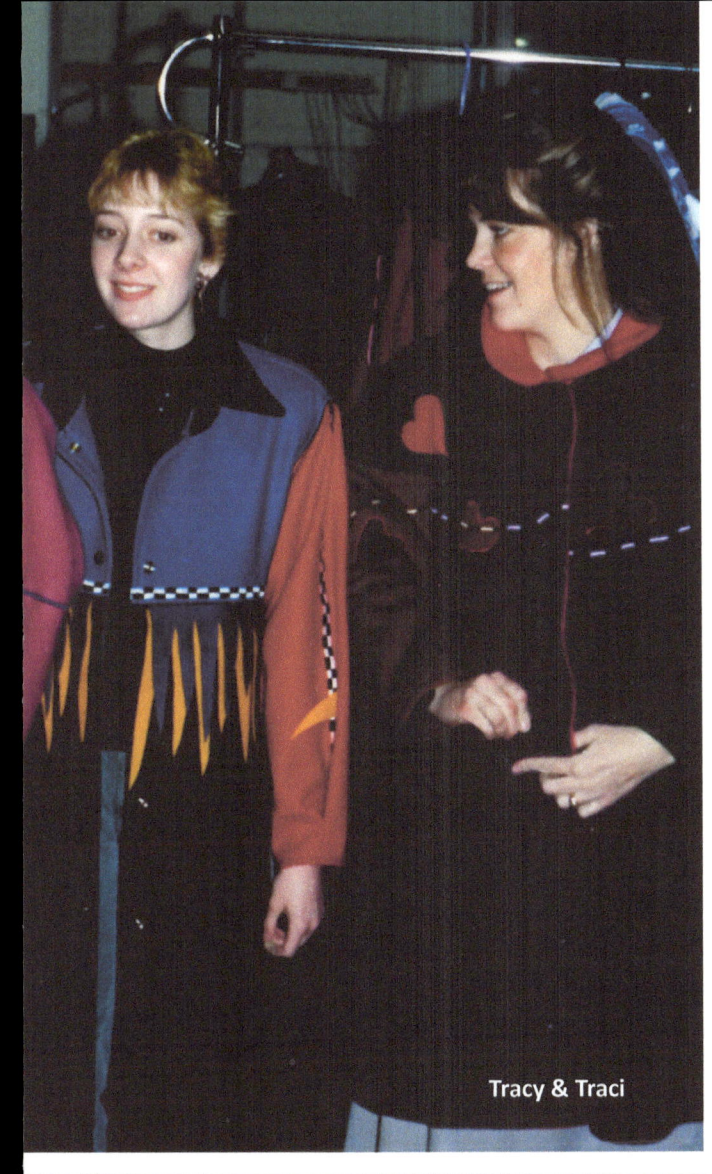
Tracy & Traci

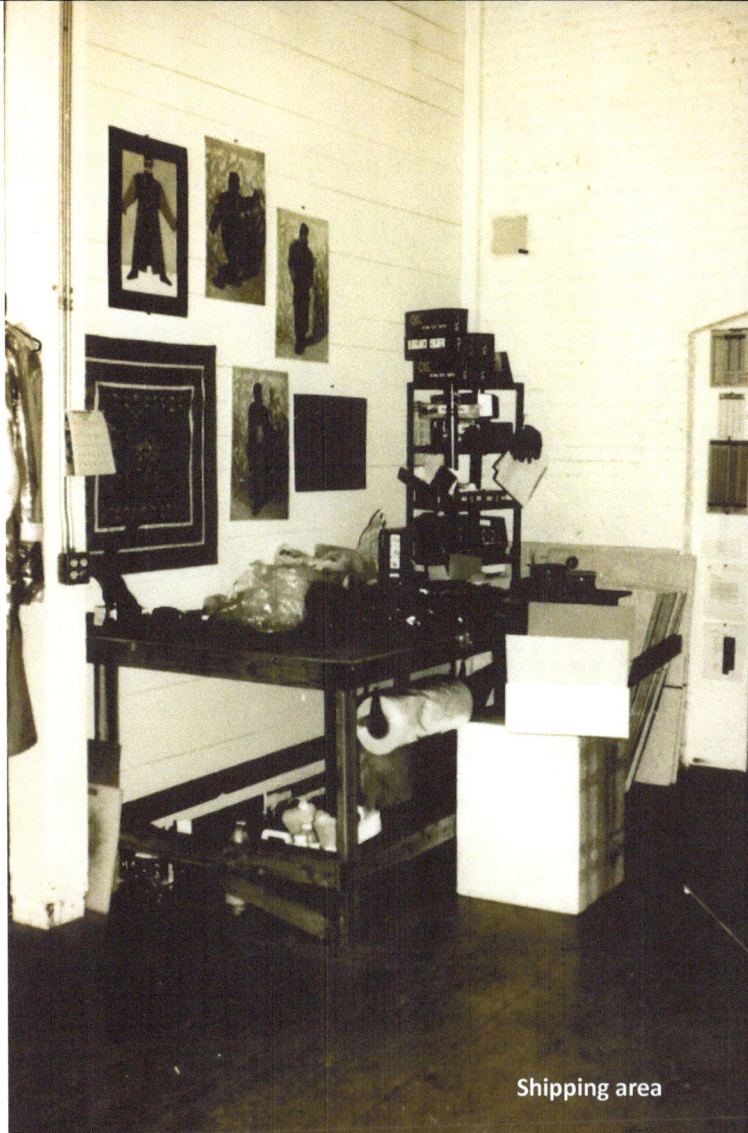
Shipping area

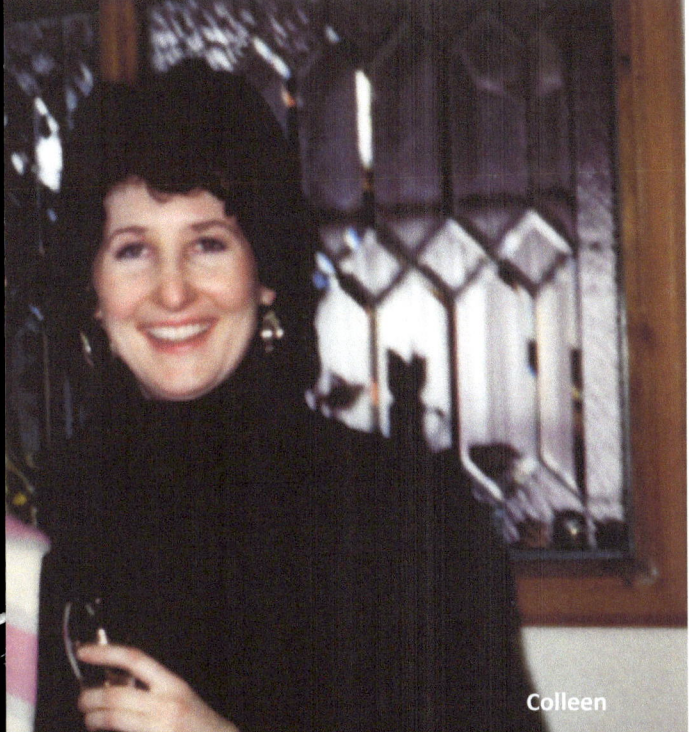
Colleen

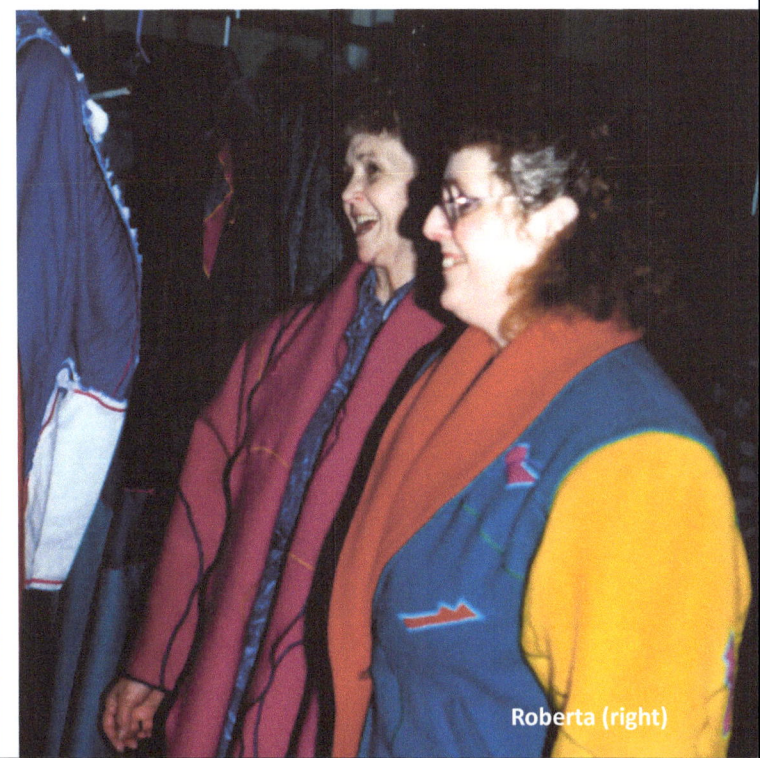
Roberta (right)

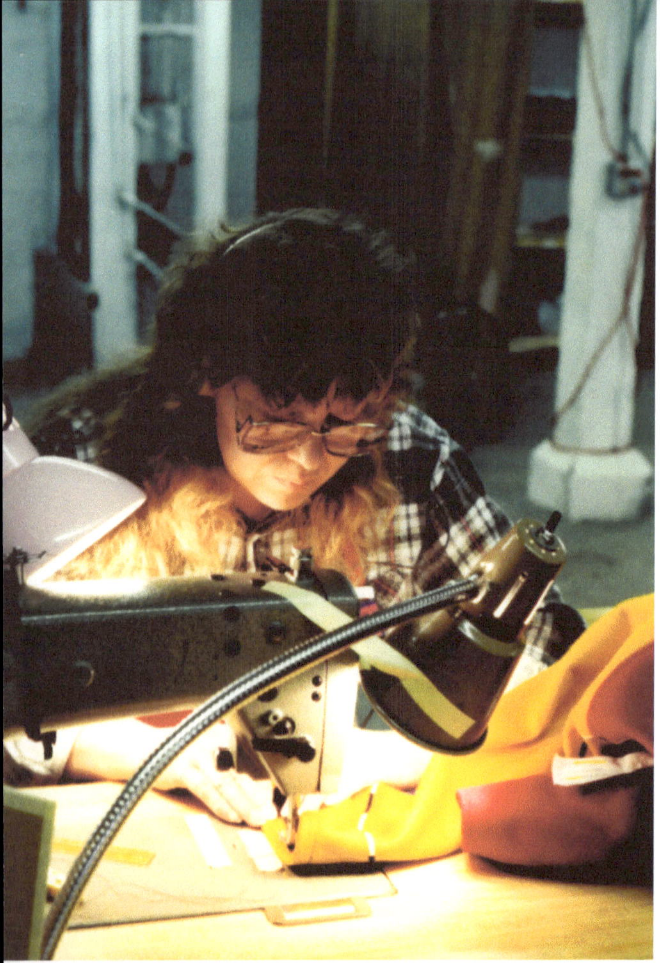

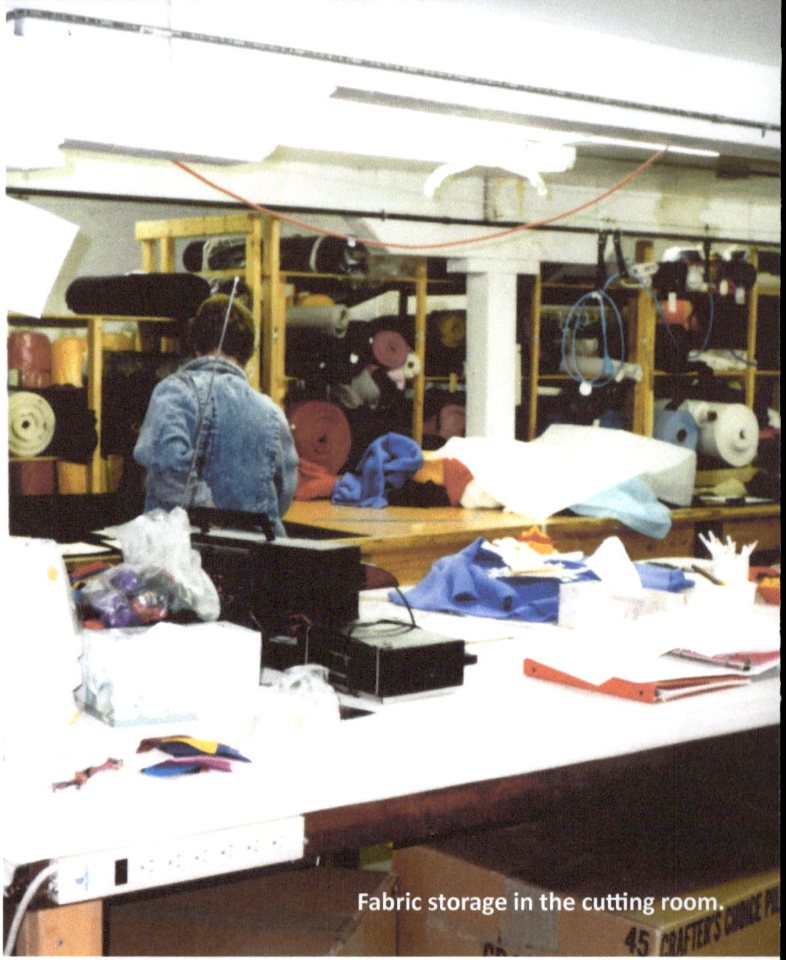

Fabric storage in the cutting room.

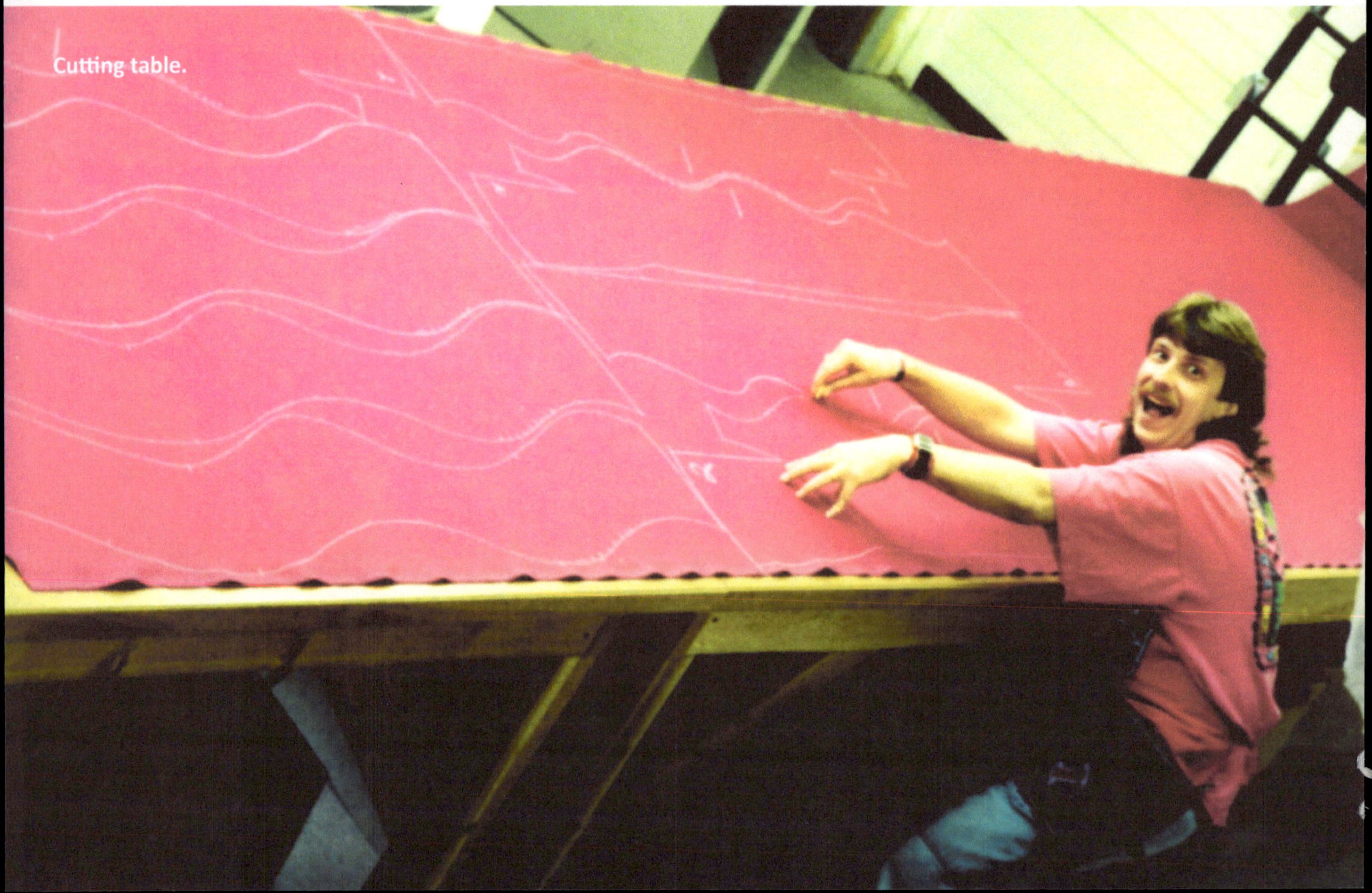

Cutting table.

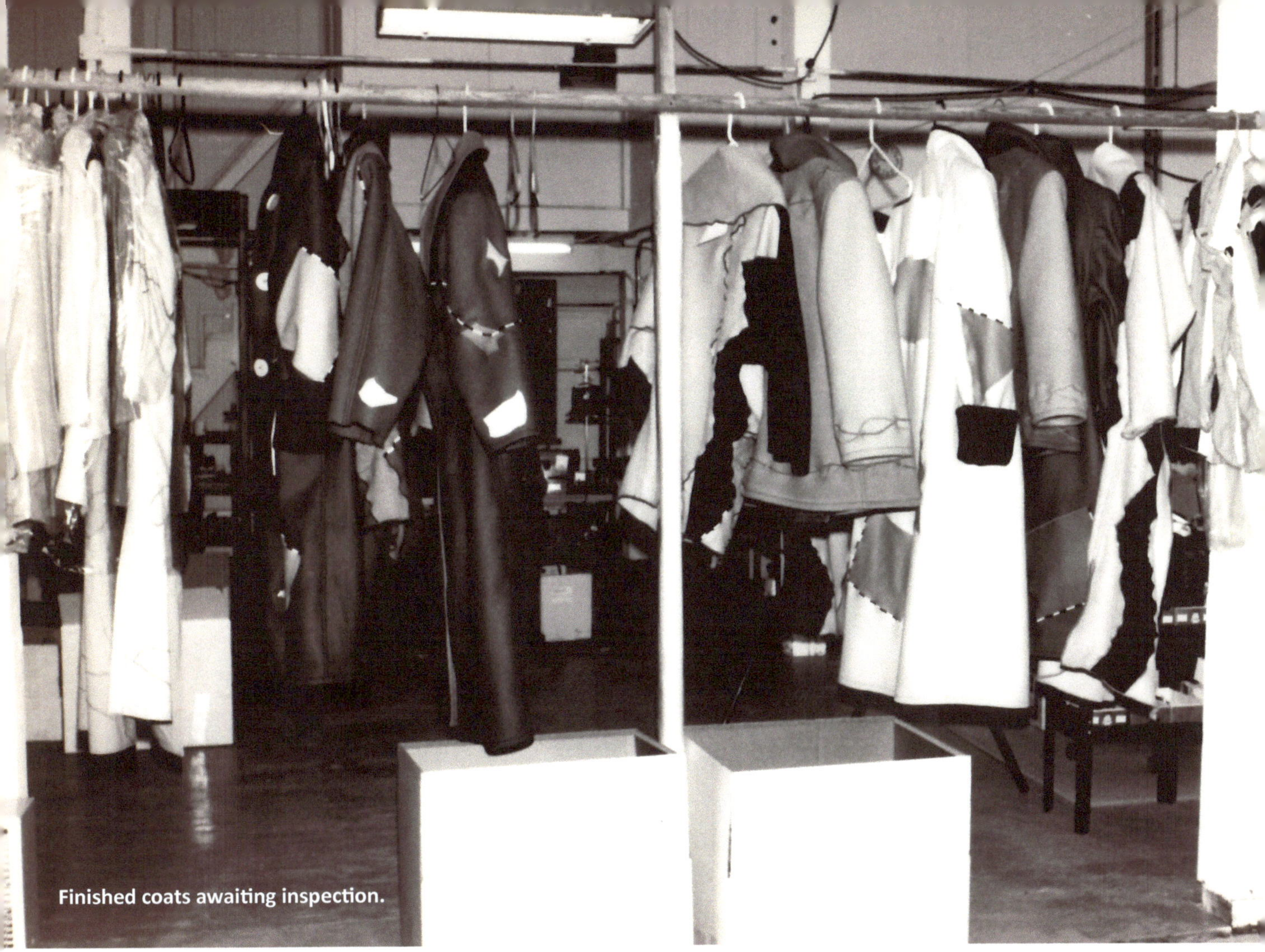

Finished coats awaiting inspection.

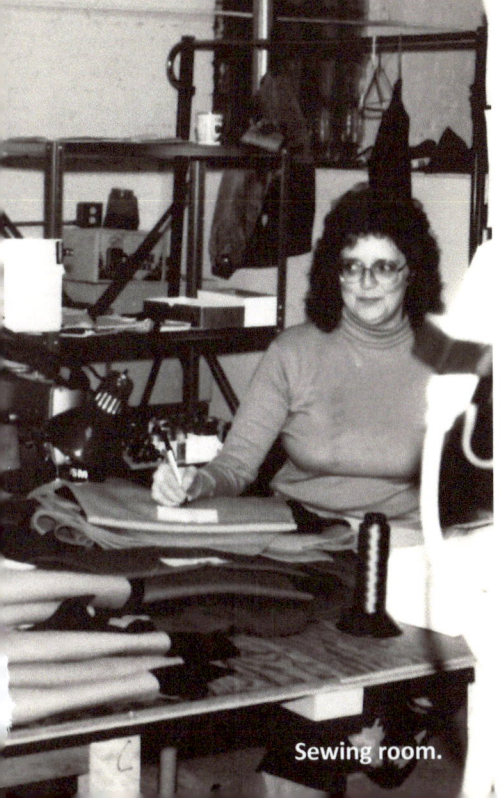
Sewing room.

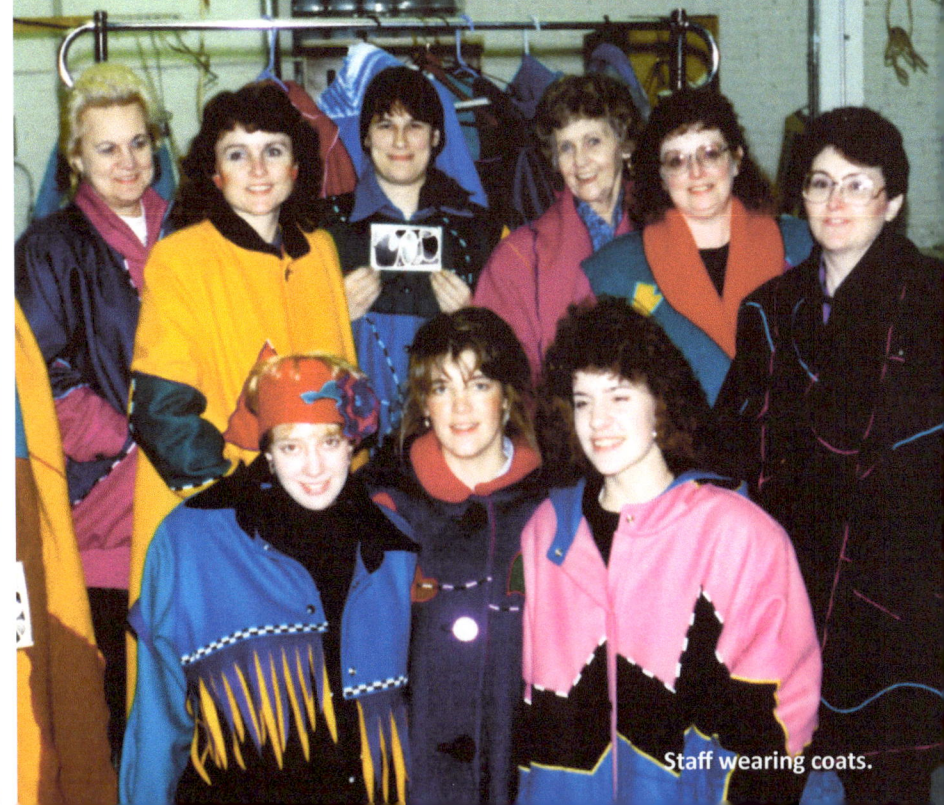
Staff wearing coats.

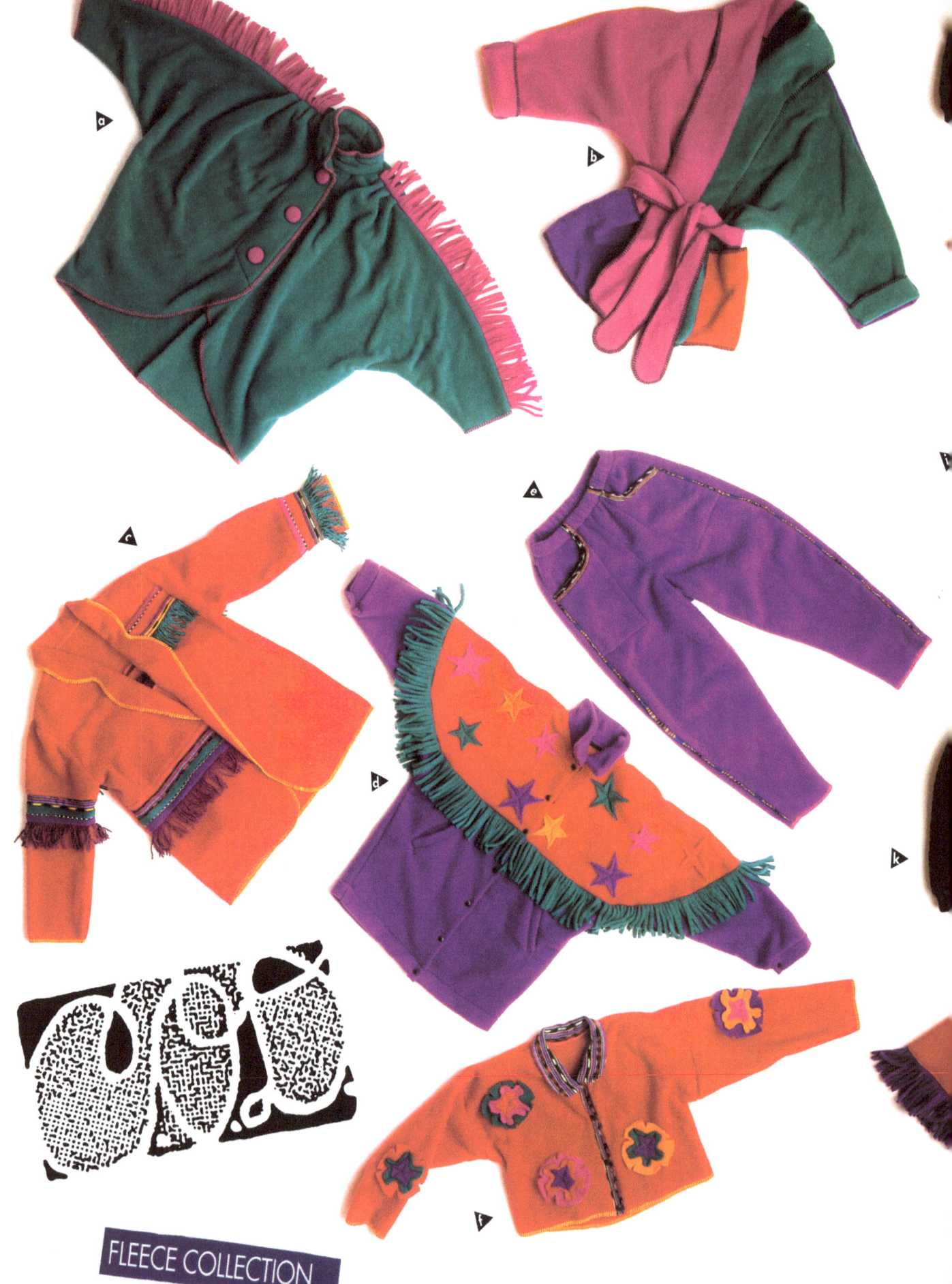

FLEECE COLLECTION

CHAPTER 12

Gifts of Discovery

COD's river of serendipity ran deep over the years, meaning almost everything positive, and negative, for that matter, that nudged my business along happened with a magical drift to it. There is no way to describe all of the charmed instants that buoyed COD's boat. Suffice it to say, the journey would have been far less fun or meaningful had I not recognized these occurrences for what they brought COD's staff, coats, and me. These moments were like meeting a long-lost friend who gave me a kiss on both cheeks with a warm hug. These gifts of discovery helped me know the universe was working in my favor.

On holiday in Oaxaca, Mexico, I stayed in a little guesthouse owned by an architect some 10 miles outside of the city. One morning I awoke to a thick web of daddy long legs spiders building a nest above my head. I slipped gently out from under the covers so as not to disturb the spiders, got dressed, and walked down the red dirt road to a bus stop about a mile away. It was hot and dusty. I hoped I was heading in the right direction, but it didn't really matter. After all, I was on vacation. I walked and walked, enjoying the desert vegetation and the aromas of distant village cooking. The smell of fresh fried tortillas and roasting chilies drifted in the morning air. The thought crossed my mind that I could sit down to breakfast along this road someplace. Just then I heard a car *putt-putting* up behind me. When I turned around, I saw an orange VW bug driven by a woman, who stopped her car beside me.

"Do you want a ride?" she asked in English.

"Sure, thanks," I replied, jumping in the front seat.

Bumping our way into Oaxaca on curving roads, the woman introduced herself, saying she was a textile designer and she was here to oversee cotton weavers for Smith & Hawken, the well-known garden lifestyle store and catalog, based in Novato, California. I could hardly believe my good fortune to meet a complete stranger in the middle of nowhere who spoke my language and was involved in the textile industry. We talked nonstop about the ins and outs of running a textile manufacturing business.

"I haven't heard of your coat business. Tell me about it," she began.

"COD is a tiny business, but for a Montana small business, we are big. We sell coats all over the United States in boutiques, catalogs, and department stores. My coats are colorful, whimsical, and artsy."

"Then you can understand what I do."

"I would love to do what you are doing," I replied, thinking my situation could be the perfect model for untrained textile workers.

"There are many opportunities to share your experience. You just have to open your heart to the idea," she explained.

The Volkswagen woman dropped me at the Zocolo. I wandered for the rest of the day in deep reflection. I was inspired by the designer's work with village women, their wonderful innate skills, and the lovely cotton fabric she said the weavers wove. My own designs had been influenced by the knitted, hand-woven, embroidered, and dyed fabrics from Central and South America. I was drawn to the vibrant colors and intricate patterns of these textiles. I felt in my bones this chance meeting would be significant, but I had no idea just how meaningful it would become.

I returned from Mexico to land in the Valley of the Flowers after two glorious weeks away. This was just the respite I needed, as COD had become more than stressful. A couple of months later, I flew to Atlanta to attend the sewing equipment show. I was in search of ways to further mechanize our workroom fleet of sewing machines to expand our design possibilities.

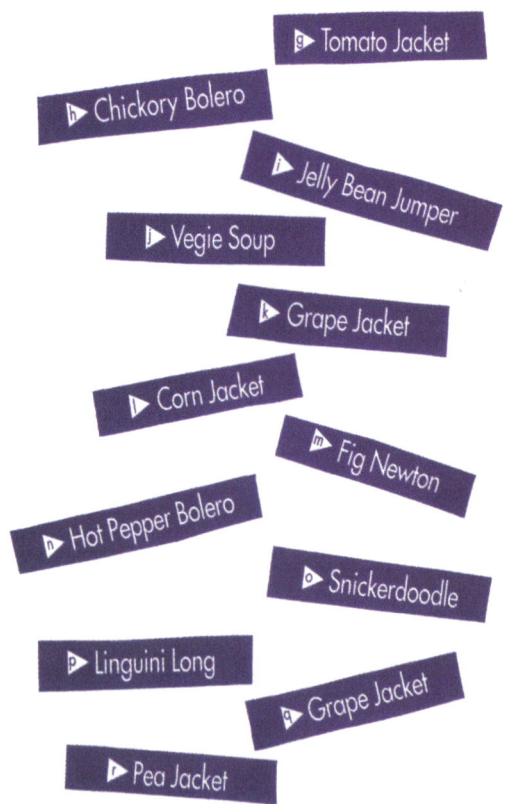

Just off the plane in Atlanta, I stood at an airport kiosk to wait for a ride to the convention center. I was tired and stressed from flying all day. I stared into traffic, trying not to breathe exhaust fumes. My thoughts wandered to the show, and what it would hold for COD. There is always something to learn and take away from walking the aisles of this gathering of the finest and most recent technologies in the sewing industry.

In fact, I found COD's first Omnistitch machine at this show. This sewing machine

**Opposite & Previous: COD dresses up these fleece jackets with applique flowers, fruits, vegetables, & fringe.
Above: The style names are as colorful as the jackets.**

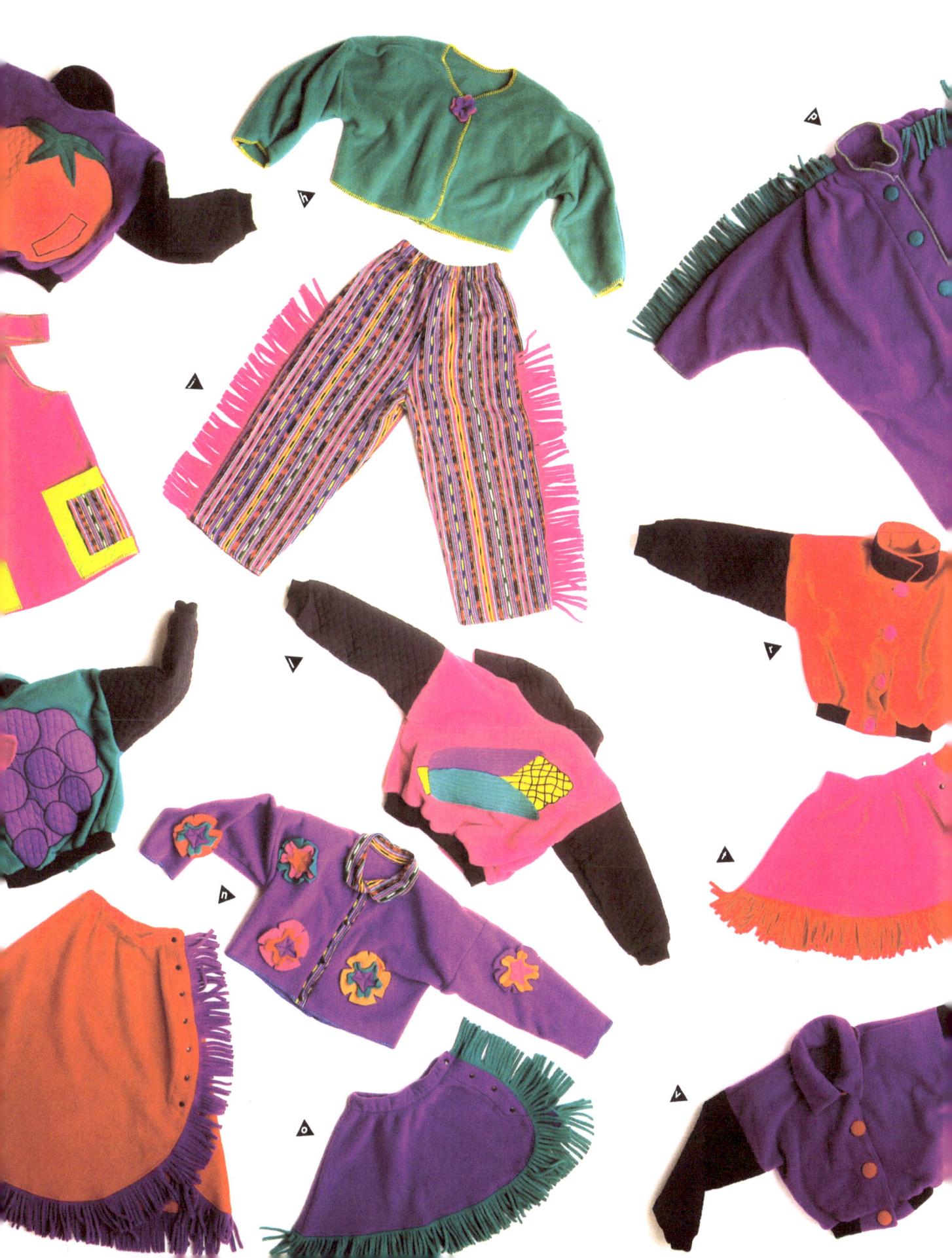

enabled the operator to literally draw with heavy cotton yarn that could create a nap on the surface of fabric. It made a tiny stitch that replicated hooked rugs. This machine, with its unusual technology, would transform our design process.

I was wearing a COD blanket coat that day. It was way too hot in Atlanta for this coat, but I felt comforted by wearing one of my own creations. As the sound of traffic blared, a woman walked up beside me and asked if I was the designer of the coat I was wearing. When I said yes, she went on to say, "Maybe you can come to the Northwest Territories to help us?"

Not really knowing where in the world the Northwest Territories was at the time, I just said, "Sure!"

The textile designer in Oaxaca, Mexico, sat on my shoulder as I visited with Kathy Weir, the director of an Inuit sewing project at the Rankin Inlet for the Canadian government. We ended up spending time at the show planning for my visit in the coming months.

Shortly following my trip to Atlanta, I arranged to attend the Los Angeles Gift Show, a huge wholesale show of great importance both to vendors and retail buyers alike. We were excited to present our new spring collection of fleece and cotton jackets. In addition, we would offer a home collection of whimsical animal pillows made from vintage drapery fabrics. Both collections would be a new look for COD, and both involved the use of the new Omnistitch machine.

For instance, the surface design on the pillows would be made of collages of vintage bark cloth fabrics with detailing made by a raised loop stitch from our new machine. I was so excited by the prospect of using this new machine that all kinds of new designs bubbled up in my imagination. The possibilities were endless. Magic again reigned. What a gift I thought, having found this machine when COD most needed a shot of fresh juice.

I attended the Los Angeles show alone. Hauling all of our show display items, plus our products, reminded me of the first show I did years ago in New York City. The memory was humbling and helped me have the confidence to set up for this large show alone. No problem. The three-day-long show started with great excitement as I presented COD's new styles and products. The morning a show opens is usually the busiest, as buyers walk the aisles to take note of what's new. About an hour into the morning, I looked down the aisle and thought I could have rolled a bowling ball to the far end without hitting one buyer. The silence was deafening and shocking.

The show turned out to be a disaster for all vendors, including COD. What could be wrong? Everyone began to wonder if the beginning of the Gulf War was keeping people at home. No one wanted to fly. Everyone was glued to their TVs. It was one of the oddest experiences I had had in a long time. We wrote no orders. People were worried and confused. It was very unusual to have such a slow show with so few buyers in attendance.

Generally, retailers were not buying. The economy had come to a screeching halt. It was also the beginning of the 1990 recession. The combination of the Gulf War and the recession colluded to be the perfect storm. Disposable income was scarce. COD's sales plummeted. We were dead in the water. Further downsizing was needed. I ended up moving our production workroom totally downstairs in the factory. I rented out the front space where my office had been plus the entire back of the first floor. I cut expenses even further by laying off office staff and the new production manager. These were depressing times. The big question was, how would I pay off what I owed?

At the end of COD's tunnel of debt would be a glimmer of hope with Kathy Weir's offer to work in the Canadian project. I ended up planted on a hard bench between huge boxes of fresh and packaged food, toilet paper, machinery, and motor oil in the back of the transport plane out of Winnipeg, Manitoba. I did this trip three times over a period of two years to work at the Rankin Inlet and Baker Lake near the Arctic Circle. I counted my lucky stars that a coat of many colors could awaken possibilities beyond my wildest dreams for business solutions, with adventure attached.

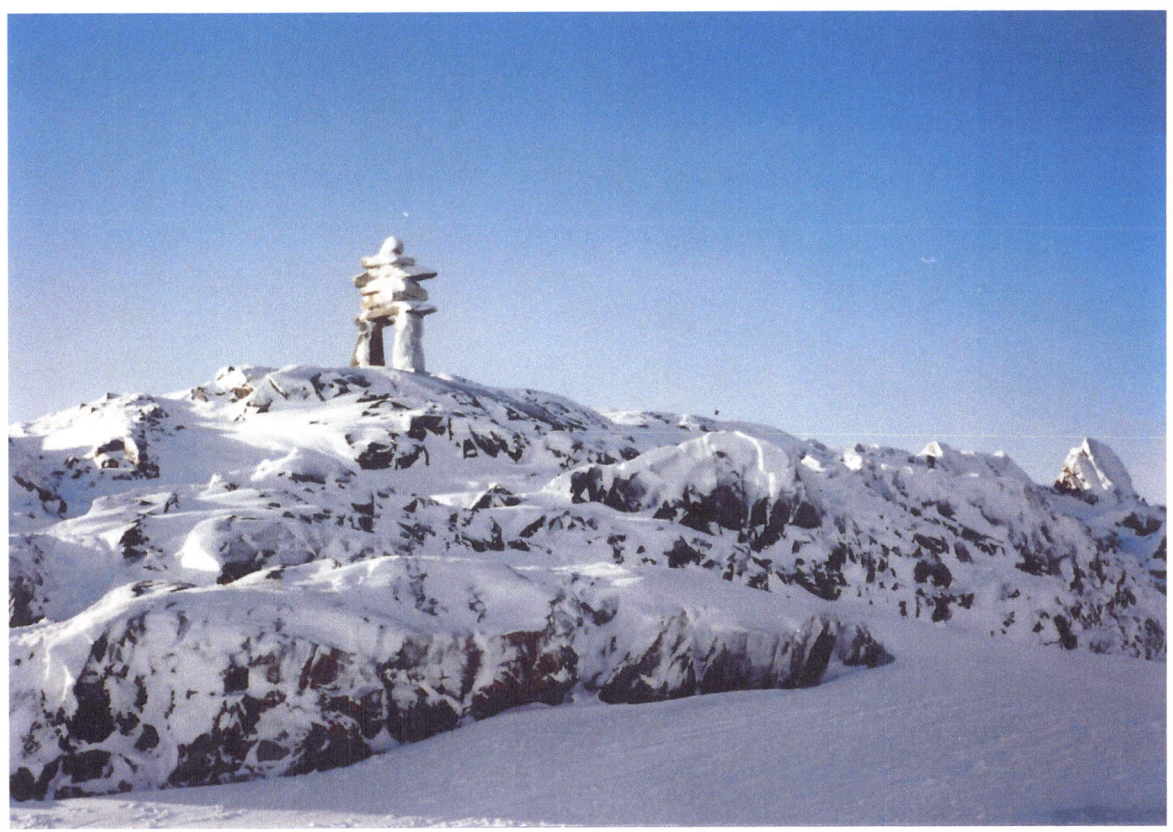

Cindy visits the Rankin Inlet, an Inuit hamlet known for high level craftmanship and artistry. The giant manmade cairn, also known as an inukshuk, is a stone landmark overlooking downtown.

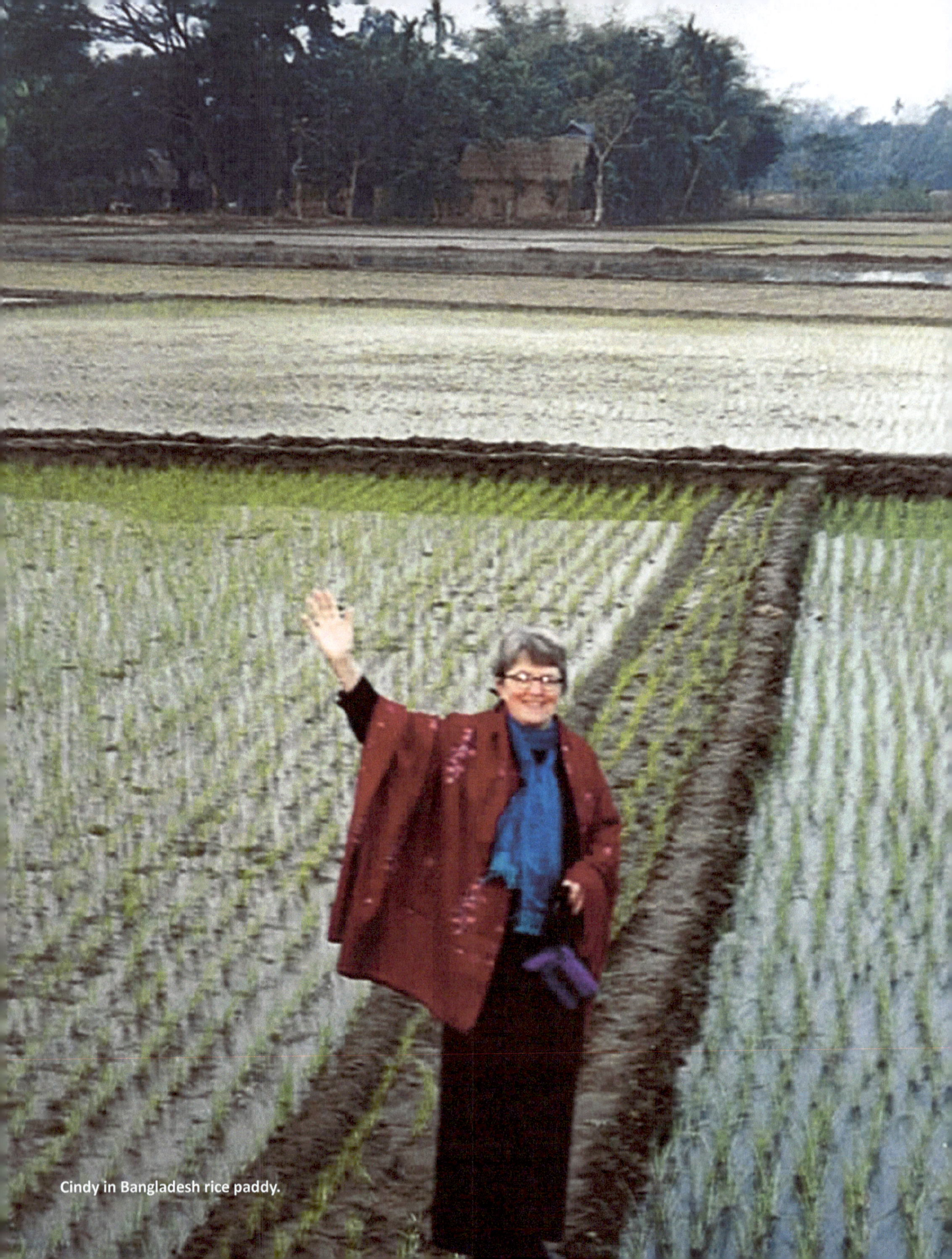
Cindy in Bangladesh rice paddy.

CHAPTER 13

Reaching Out to Share and Receive

A field of irrigated rice spread before me on a morning walkabout. A thick humid haze shrouded the field. I balanced gingerly on a raised path weaving its way through the sprouting rice. Luckily, the water wasn't deep yet. I looked up from my mud-caked feet to see three men, garbed in the traditional Muslim salwar kameez, emerge in a line from the dreamy mist. The soft breeze rustled their loose clothing as they approached. Each carried an open umbrella in anticipation of the expected rain, I assumed. The heavy air smelled of wet earth that never dried. As hard as it was to believe, I was standing in a rural northern province of Bangladesh near the city of Mymensingh. The languorous Brahmaputra River flowed nearby, bringing water from the Himalayas in India. A few more steps would put me inside India, a world away.

Yes, a long ways for sure, and the Bangladeshi village was even more rural than Bozeman. The creation and running of a textile business from a rural location far from needed resources, marketing potential, and available labor seemed like a slam-dunk opportunity for sharing my own experiences with others who could benefit from them. I could feel in my bones it was time to help others navigate the complexities of running a textile business with no money, no technical assistance, and far from the madding crowd. I knew I had a lot to offer, considering my own unique colorful history in product development, manufacturing setup, marketing, and sales.

My first consulting job was for the Canadian government in Inuit country, the contract I had accepted while attending the Atlanta Sewing Equipment Show. My task was to help redesign and freshen what the Inuit women were already sewing and selling in southern Canada. Transforming COD's own designs into far north images seemed pretty obvious. We made "Kissing Moose" into "Kissing Polar Bears," for instance. My own designs were similar to the appliqué work the women were already sewing. I brought a whimsical way of looking at the women's own northern culture. The Inuit designs were stylized and stiff. The same reindeer silhouette trotted repeatedly around a coat hem. In contrast, I suggested repeating only the intricate coral-shaped reindeer antlers. The antlers became beautiful appliquéd silhouettes around sweeping sailor-type collars and cuffs of a long unlined coat. As the new designs were sewn, big smiles appeared on the women's faces. They got it. They were excited. Since the wool fabric COD used happened to be the very same the Inuit used from Quebec, I felt right at home.

I ended up working at the Rankin Inlet once in the summer and once in the winter. Minus-70-degrees winter temps seared exposed skin and instantly froze a banana. I was amazed that people lived in these extremes, but the native women were unfazed by outside conditions. Tiny bundled kids played broomball on neighborhood ice in shadows of low sunlight. Beside dilapidated houses, freezers stood with doors open, often brimming with wild game meat. The landscape was a soft pastel patchwork quilt of pinks, grays, and blues, bordering Hudson Bay—breathtaking. And the Northern Lights were vividly bright as they streaked, swam, and played over hockey skaters on a circular ice pitch.

I also worked on a slipper project at Baker Lake, the only inland village in the Northwest Territories (now Nunavat). My assignment was to standardize the sizing of wool fur-lined slippers being made by the village women. These women had no way of measuring home-sewn slippers against a universal sizing chart. Their slippers ended up in Southern Canadian boutiques where shopkeepers could not depend on receiving a true size 7, for example. The slippers were exquisite, with embroidered Arctic flowers, animals, and native designs on the tops and lined with fluffy rabbit fur.

In my free time, I hiked the squishy tundra above the village. One step onto the tundra and I discovered my shallow boots were no kind of footwear for this ground. I needed rubber boots. One day, the village art center director took me on his ATV (all-terrain vehicle, also known as a quad bike) to locate the grave of Jessie Oonark, a well-known Baker Lake artist whom I had admired for a long time. Oonark's vivid Inuit images through stone prints and stitched hangings had brought her fame, and her work had influenced my own.

The project director took me to her grave, where I saw that her body was covered with heavy, lichen-covered rocks, her calcified bones barely visible. I was moved to tears. For spiritual reasons, burial is above ground for the Inuit people. The body is covered with rocks and sometimes ice. What a world, the Arctic and its people, I thought. My eyes and my heart had been opened to a culture struggling for survival in the face of dwindling natural resources and economic hard times.

Not only did the Inuit project introduce me to the world of consulting, but it also provided needed income for COD. I left my company in the capable hands of staff. I had no choice. I had to earn outside money to support COD and pay off its debt. The Inuit project gave me the confidence to accept other consulting job offers as well.

Months later, Aid to Artisans, a Connecticut nonprofit, called my office. Their mission was to work with indigenous artisans to develop products, provide networks in marketing,

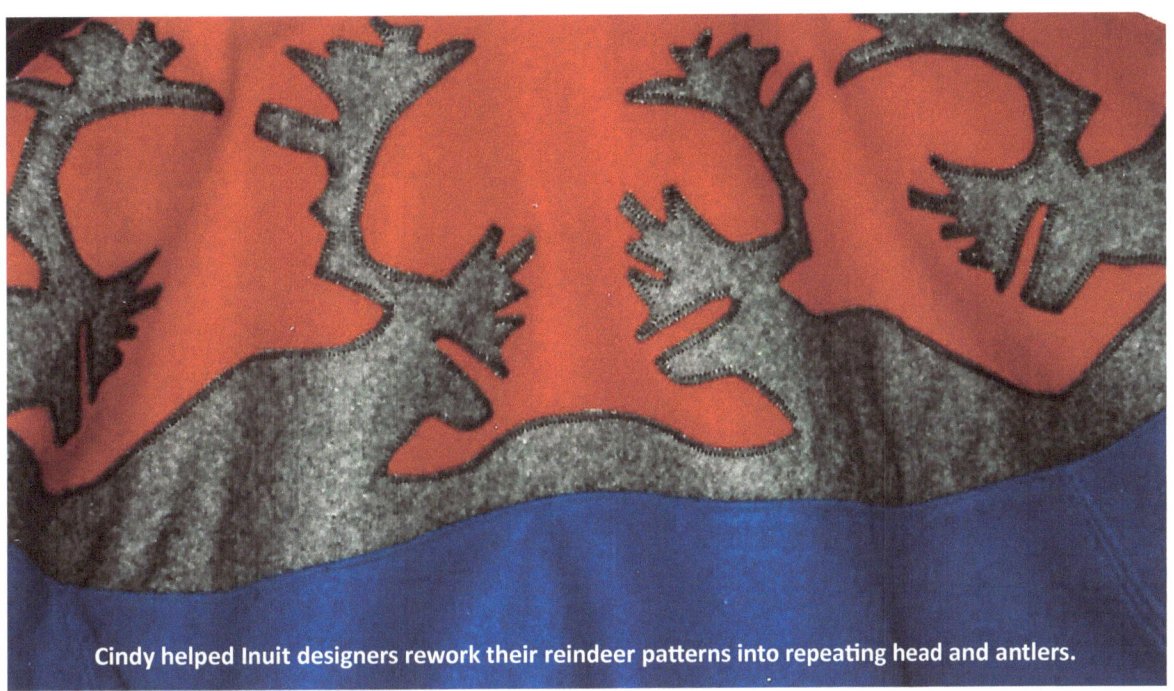
Cindy helped Inuit designers rework their reindeer patterns into repeating head and antlers.

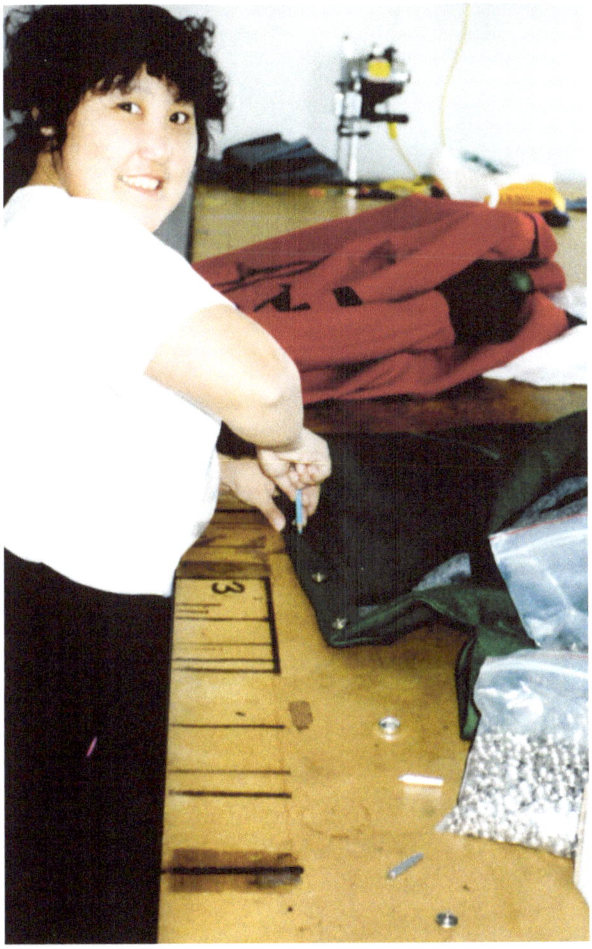

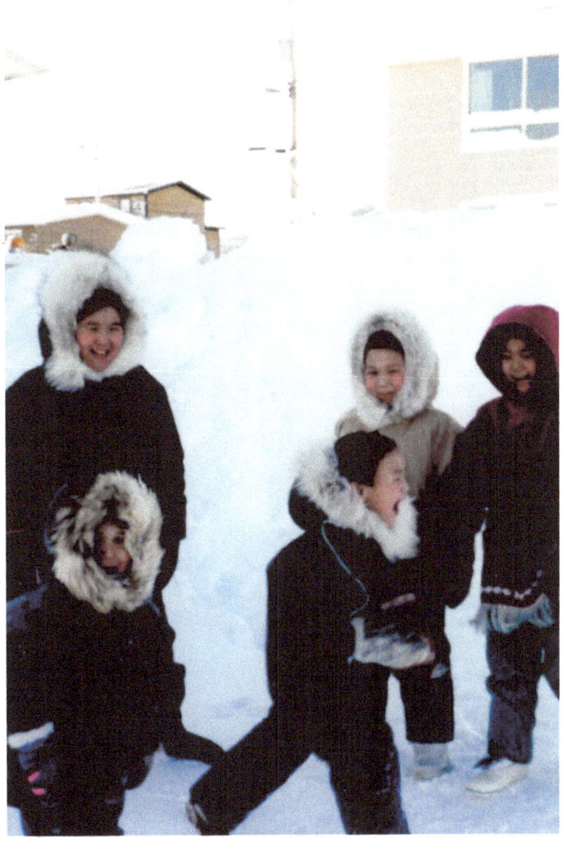

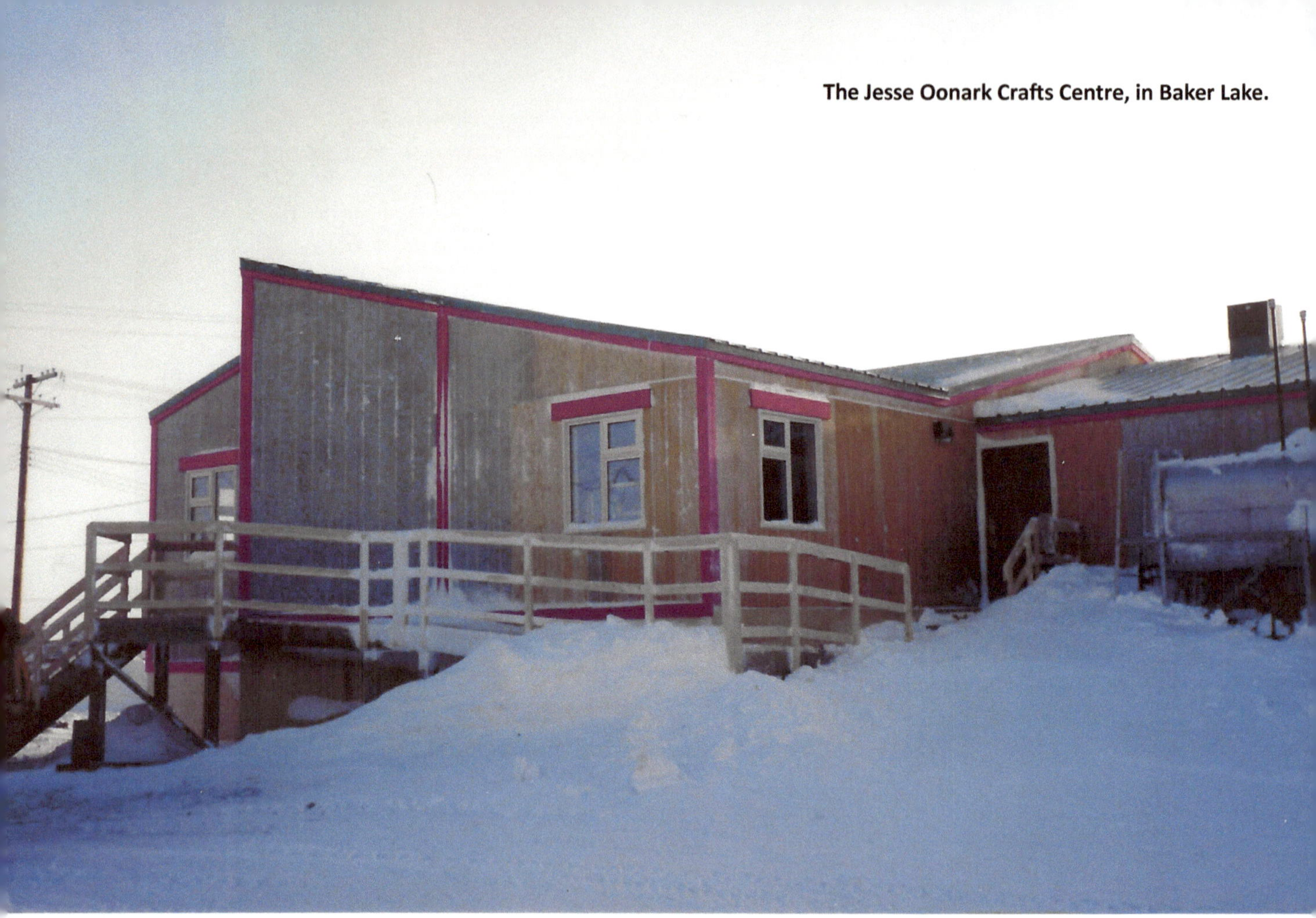

The Jesse Oonark Crafts Centre, in Baker Lake.

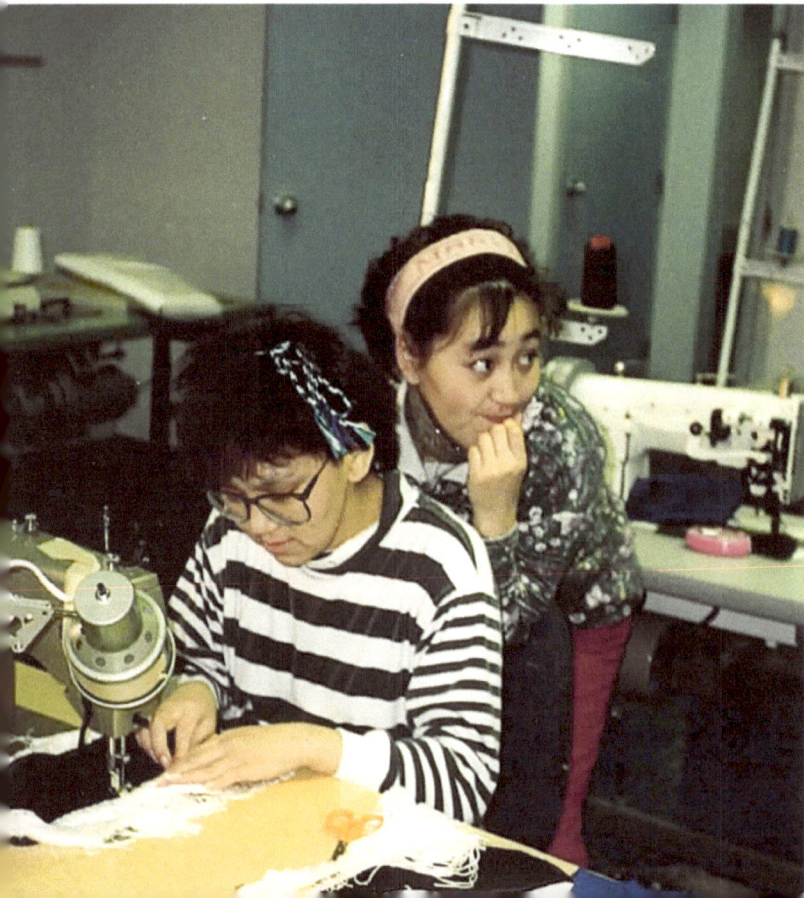
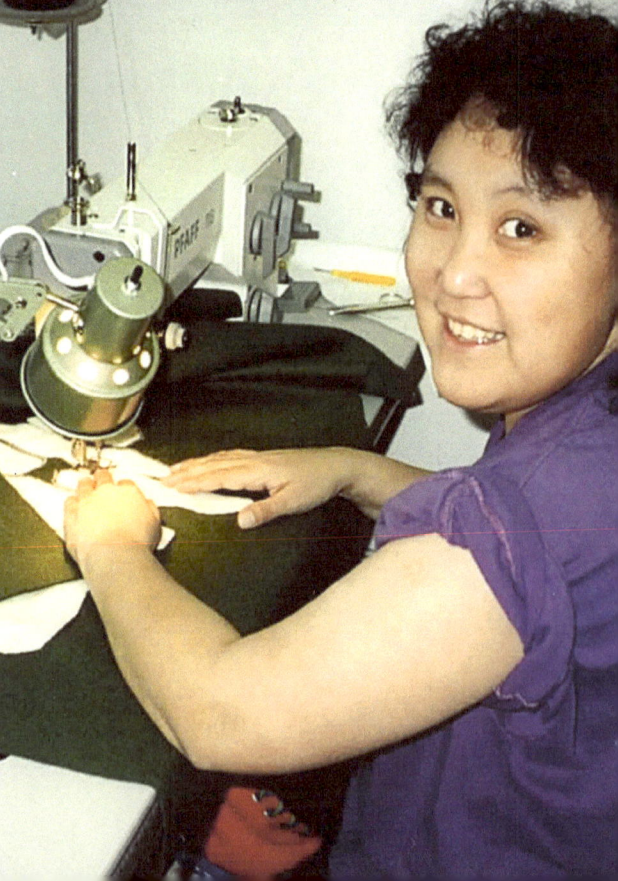

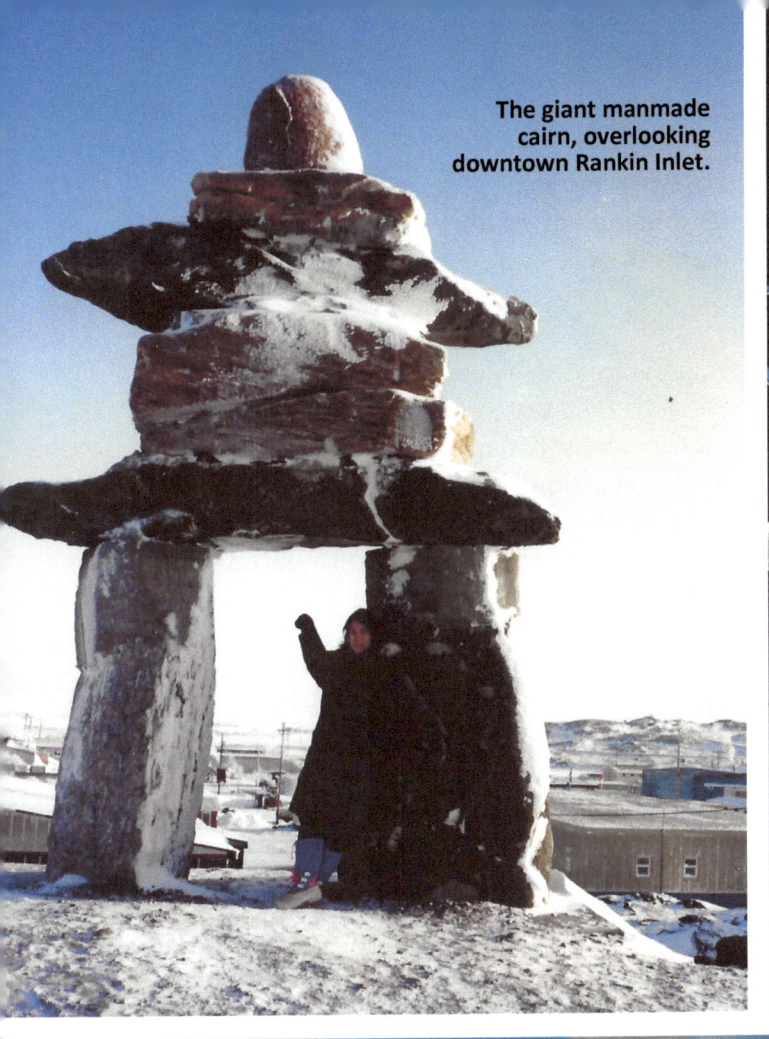
The giant manmade cairn, overlooking downtown Rankin Inlet.

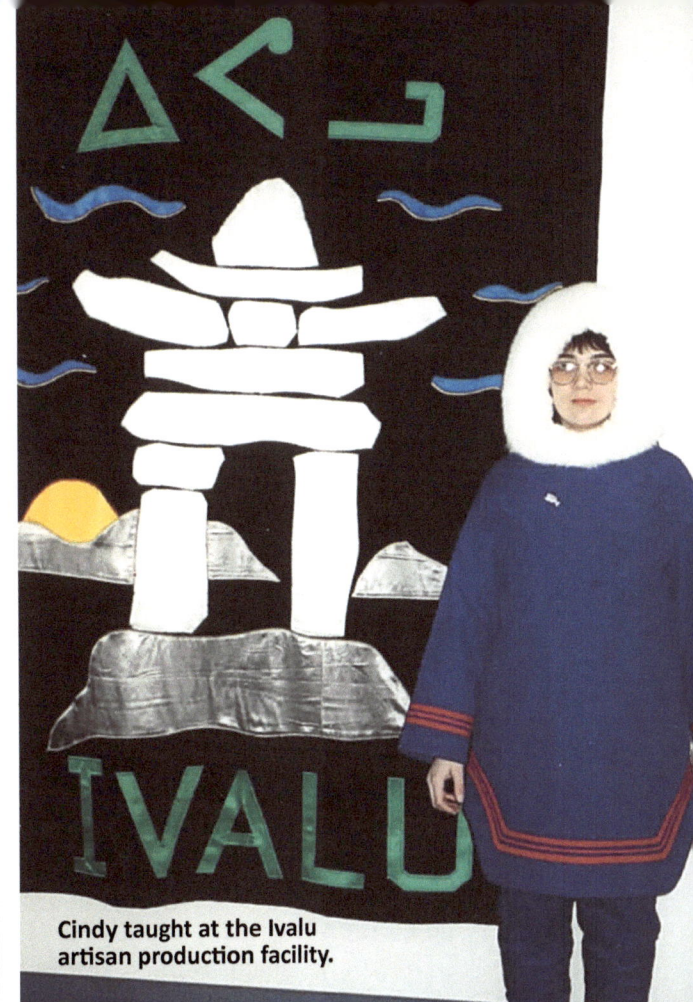
Cindy taught at the Ivalu artisan production facility.

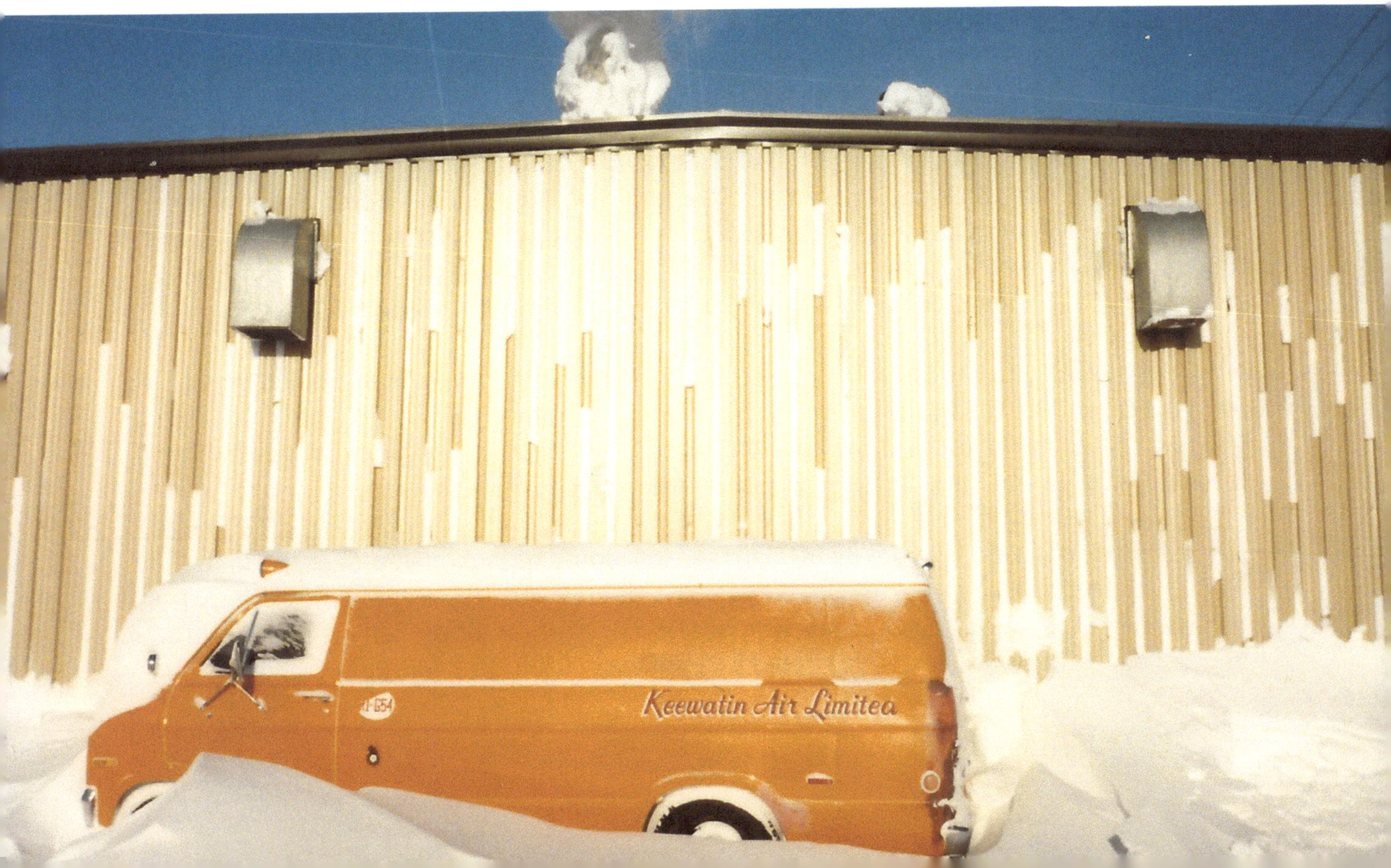

and foster economic sustainability. I was hired to work in two projects, one in West Africa and the second in Pakistan, places I never dreamed of visiting. Both projects were focused on economic development by utilizing artisan skills to help support families and communities.

In November of 1997, late one evening, at my Lahore, Pakistan, hotel, I heard the Muslim call to prayers. Outside my fifth-story room, I could watch as the mosque next door filled with worshippers. So foreign to my Southern Baptist upbringing, the sounds of Islamic religious practices did not prepare me for my reaction to the fax from the U.S. State Department that advised me "not to leave my hotel under any circumstance." On television, I learned that four Houston oil workers had been slain by terrorists in Karachi. I paced back and forth in my hotel room, alternating between heart palpitations and jags of weeping. I had no one to advise me on how to proceed.

Finally, I called one of the local women with whom I worked. She laughed off my reaction and deemed the incident of little importance, believing the situation posed little danger to an American visitor. I was even more confused. My Pakistani coworkers were so accustomed to unrest they had become inured to what I saw as terror. On the other hand, Aid to Artisans requested I leave Pakistan as soon as possible.

So I left on the next plane to Hamburg, Germany. The Lahore project would be put on hold. The young village women with whom I worked, who taught me how to dress in shalwar kameez and bangles stacked up my wrists, were set back in their progress toward gainful employment. Levi Strauss, which funded this training, had to reevaluate their commitment to the project. The true meaning of "collateral damage" sat heavy on my heart.

I travelled to Bangladesh three times, sent by an economic development program at the University of Virginia that partnered with USAID (United States Agency for International Development), the U.S. State Department aid arm. The village of Adivasi indigenous people, Christians known for their exquisite weaving of hemp, farmed the rice field where I walked that morning. I stayed in a tiny house in the village with a baby pig tied to a tree out front. I increased my knowledge of toilets when I was shown a hole in the ground.

Attempting to eat what was generously given to me in a large bowl, I pulled meat from the tiny mysterious bones that were slathered with a fiery chili sauce. I smiled and put my napkin over my mouth. My gag reflex motored full on, but I kept down the meal by some miracle. Tears flowed from my eyes for a lot of reasons, not the least being the chili sauce.

My work task was to design new images that could be woven into rugs and mats. The women had refurbished large upright wooden looms and were very proficient weavers. They had no market, however, for their lovely goods. We worked for more than a week to create a new collection of colorful mats that could be displayed at the New York Home Textile Show.

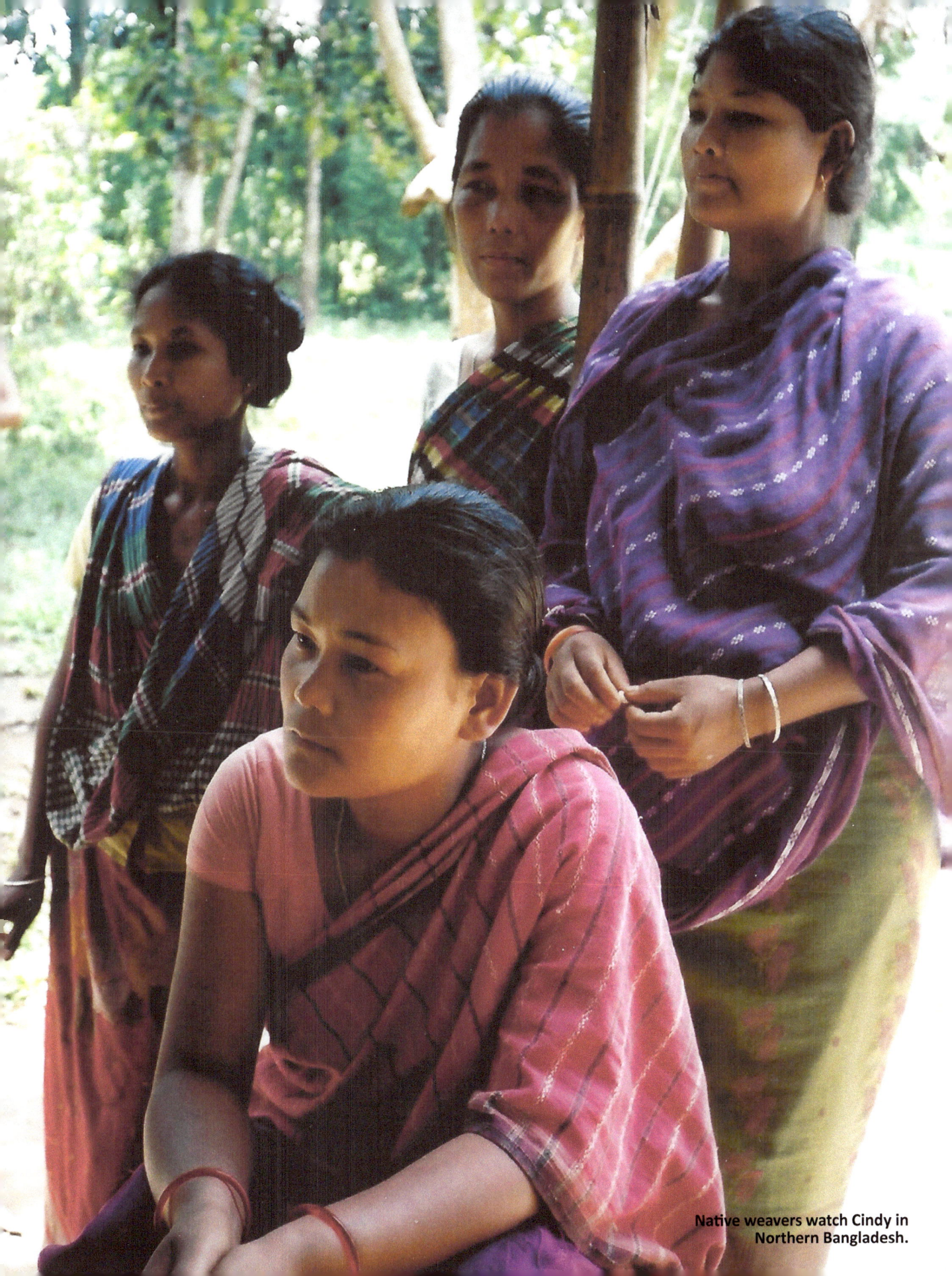

Native weavers watch Cindy in Northern Bangladesh.

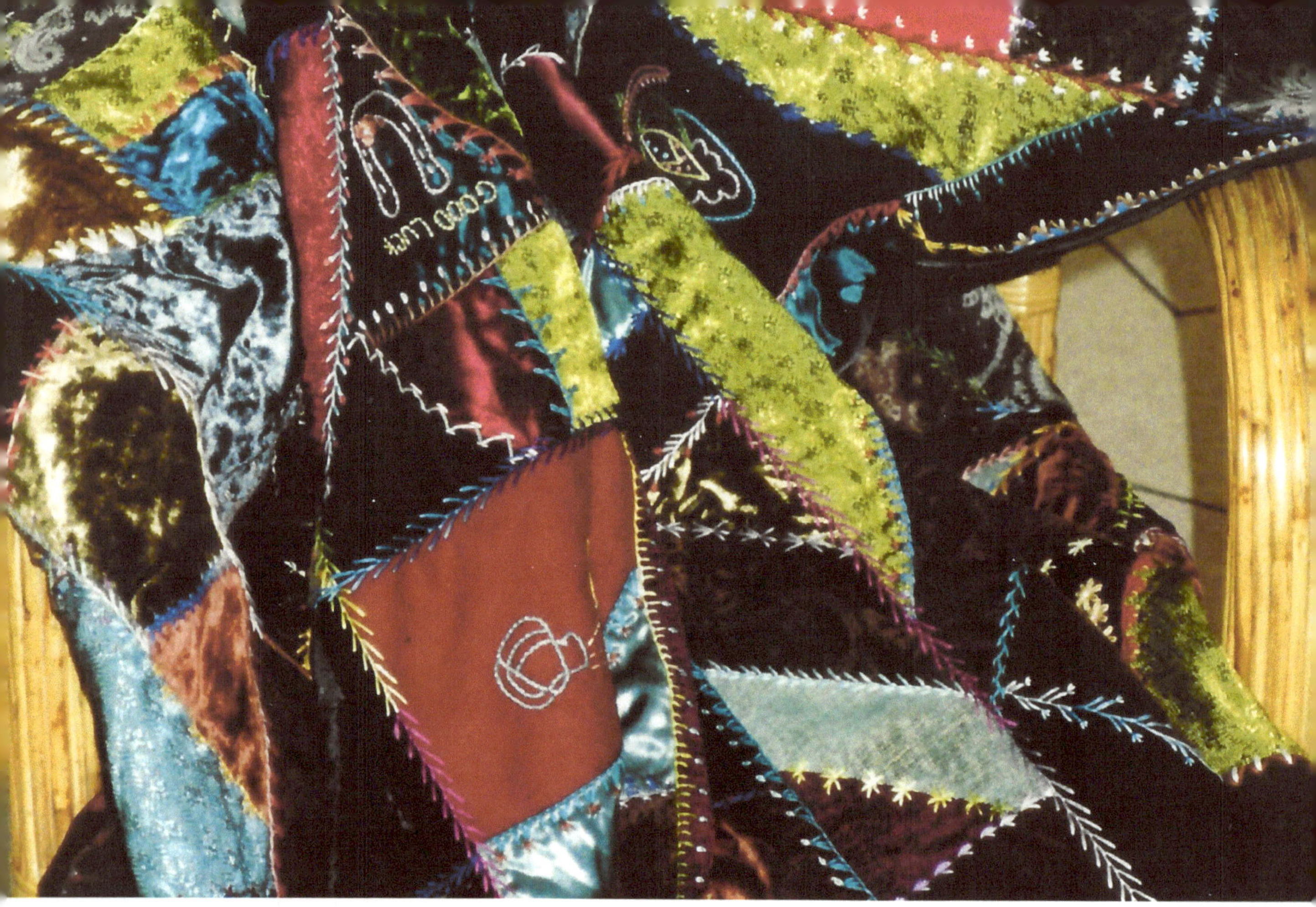

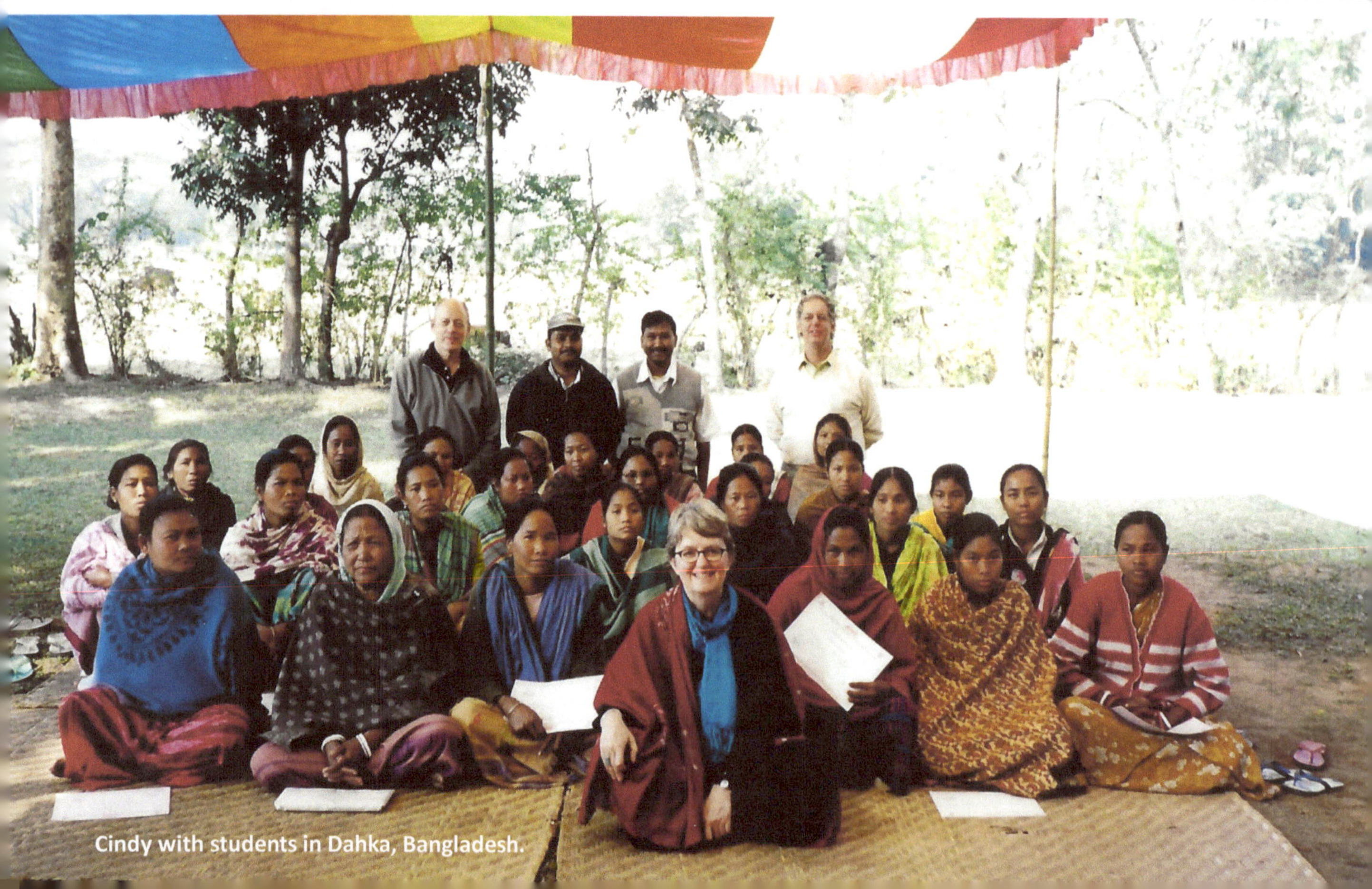

Cindy with students in Dahka, Bangladesh.

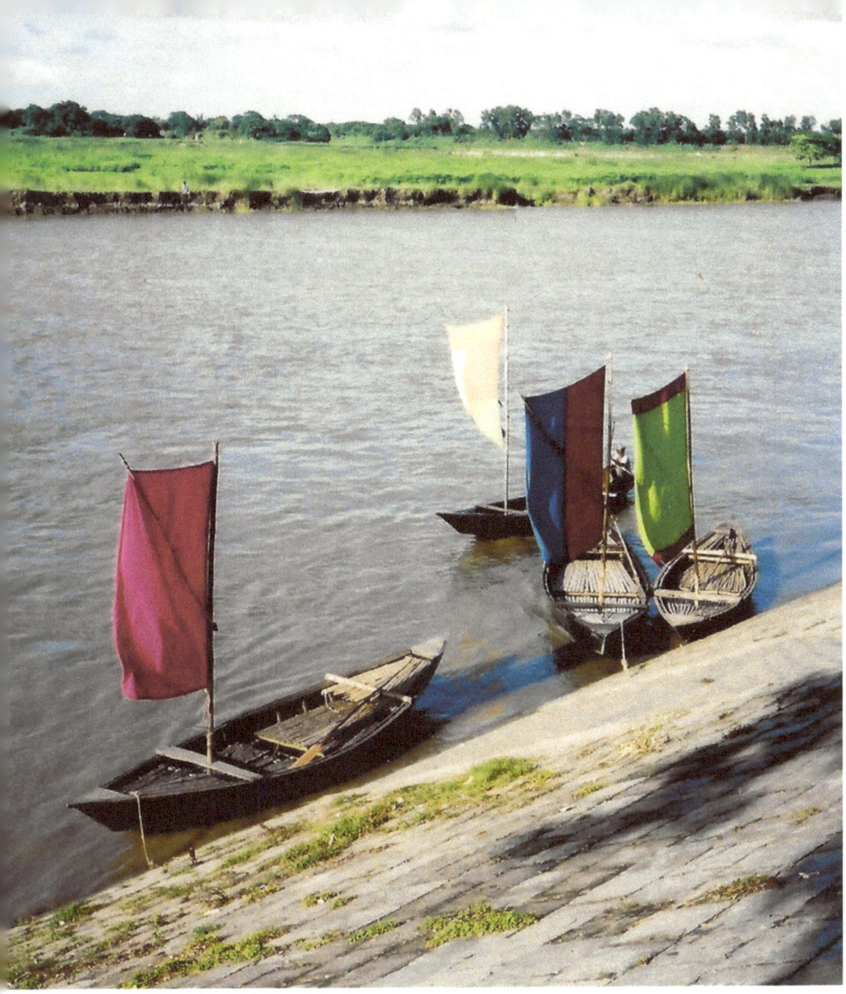

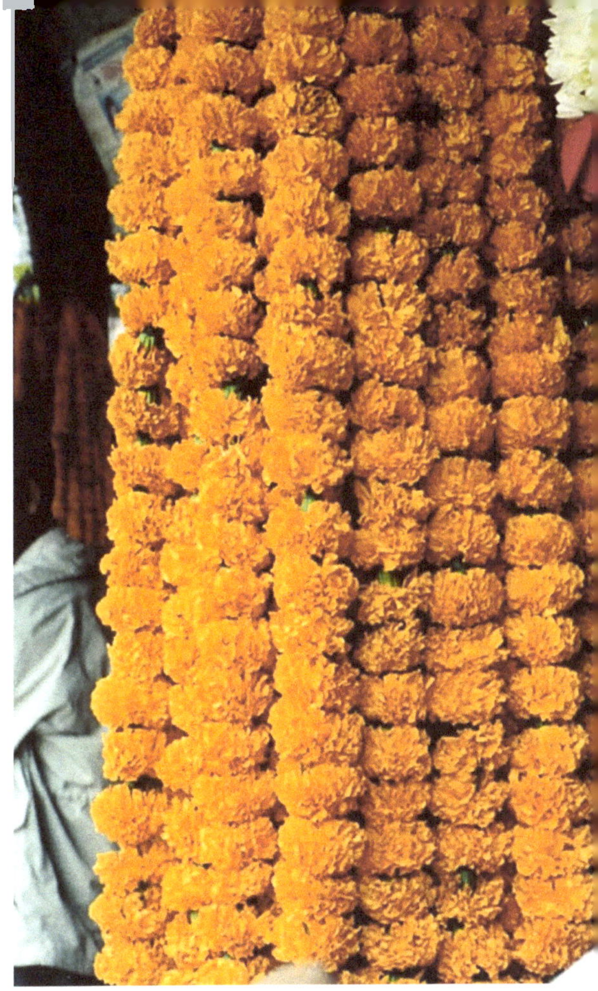

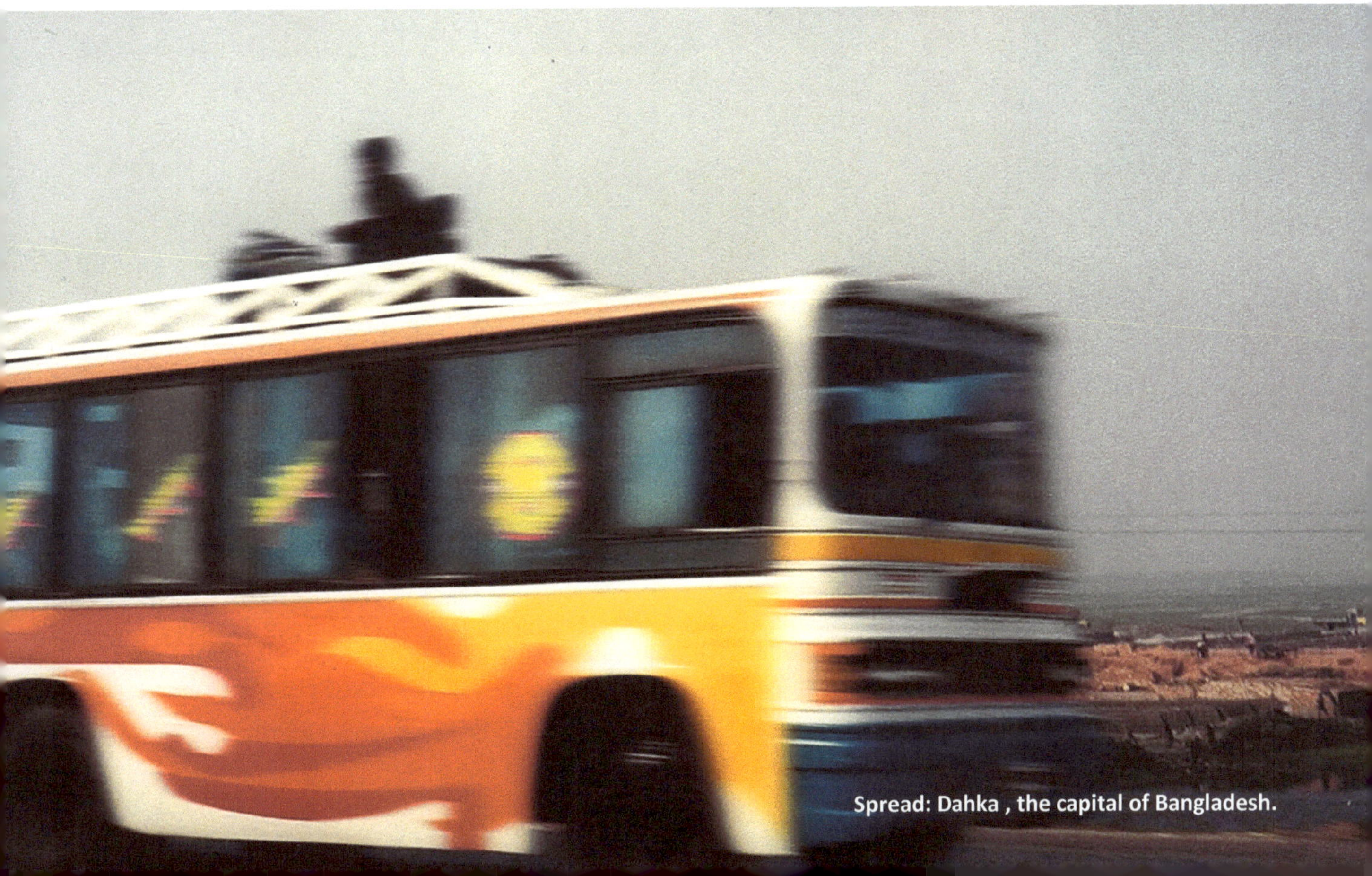

Spread: Dahka , the capital of Bangladesh.

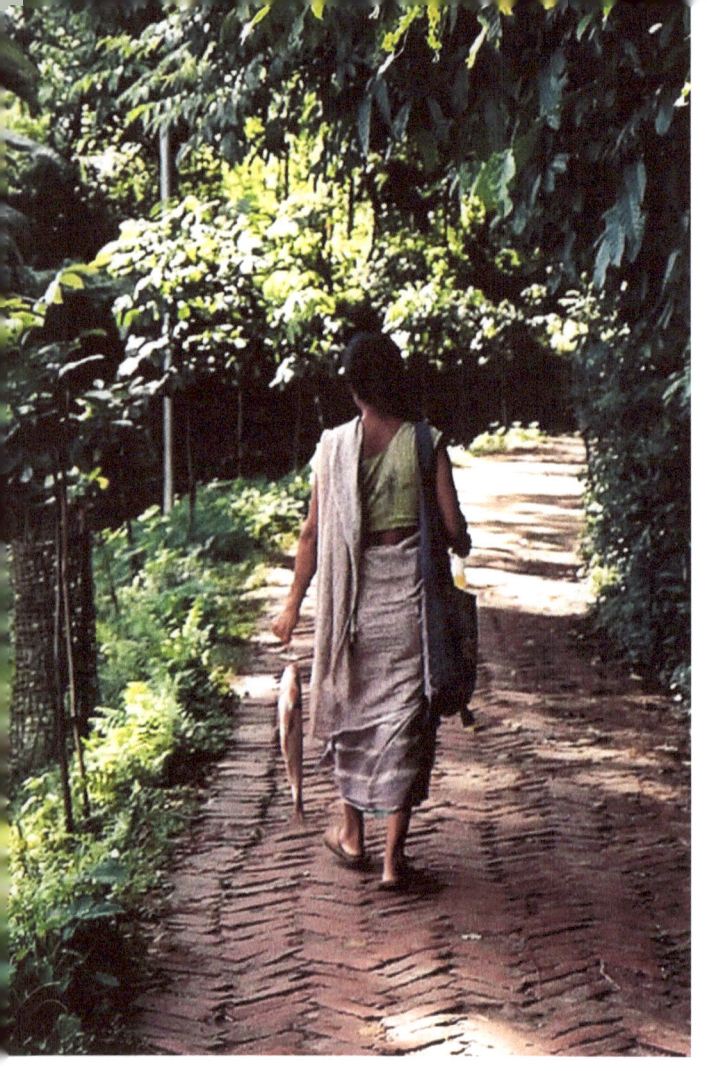
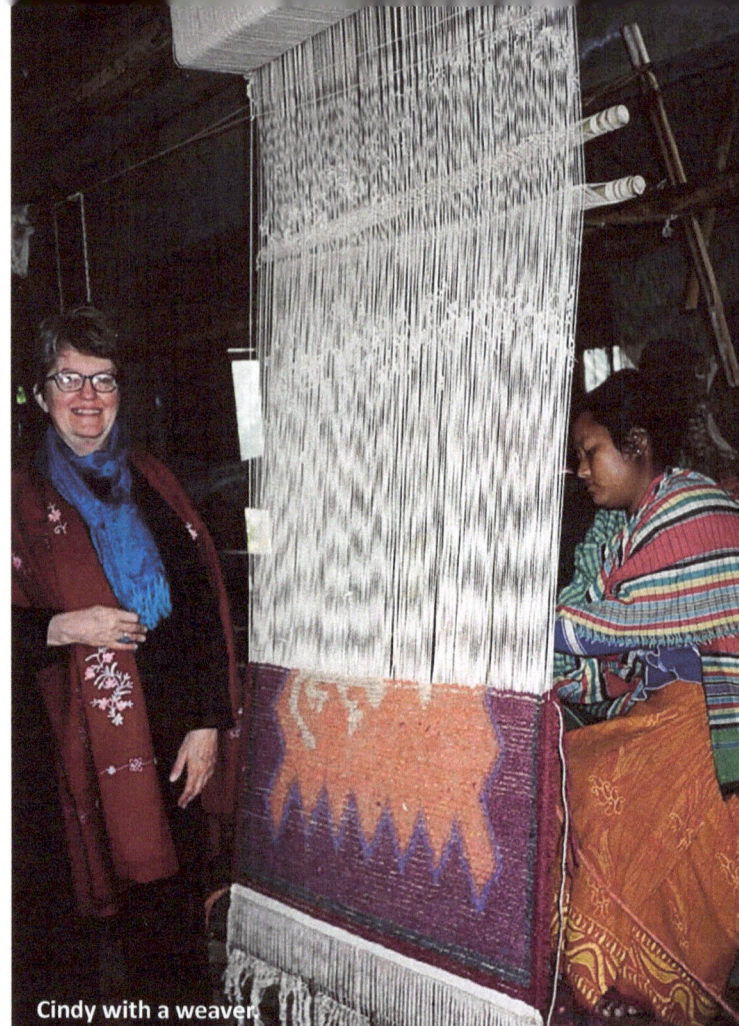
Cindy with a weaver

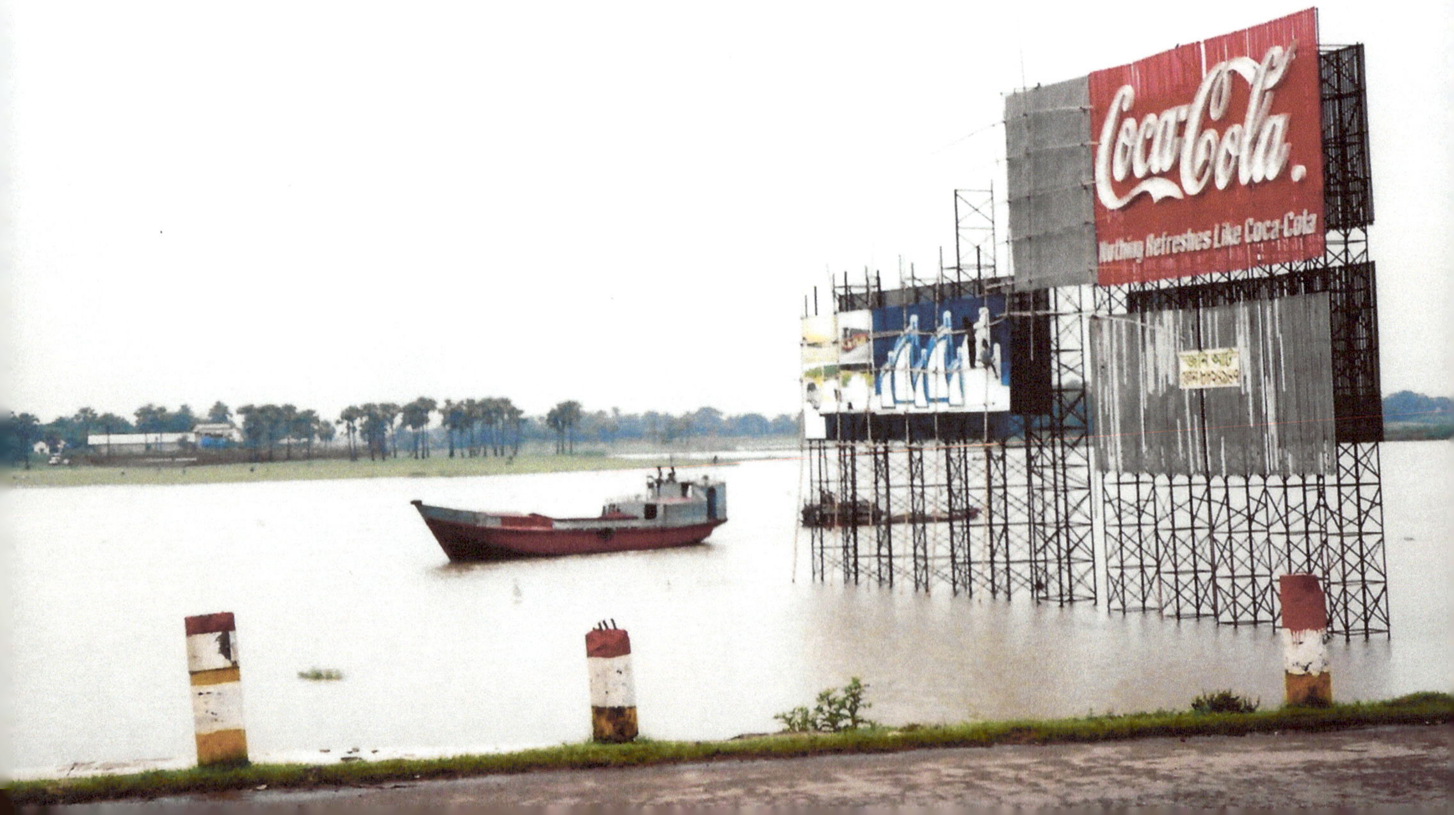

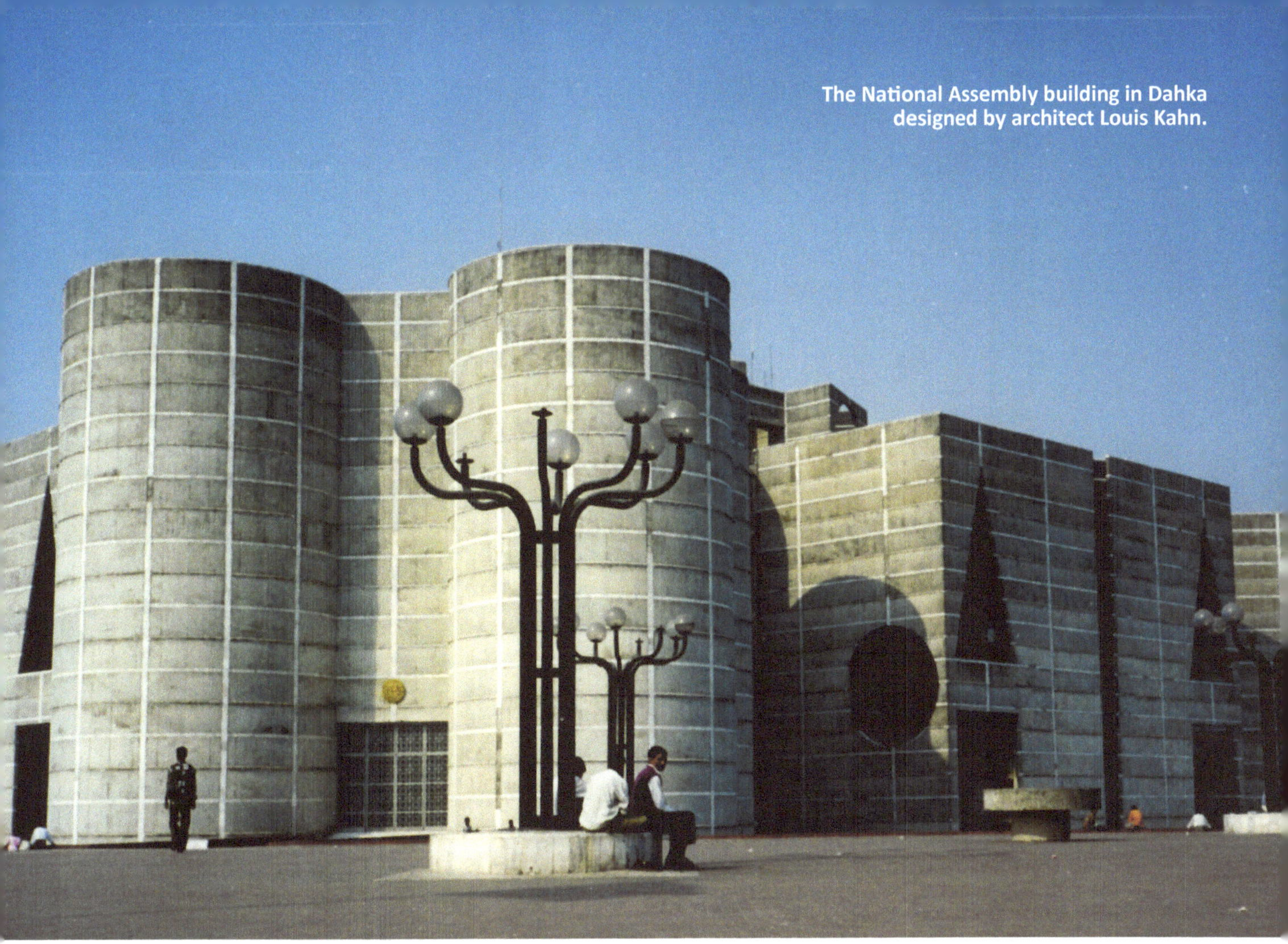

The National Assembly building in Dahka designed by architect Louis Kahn.

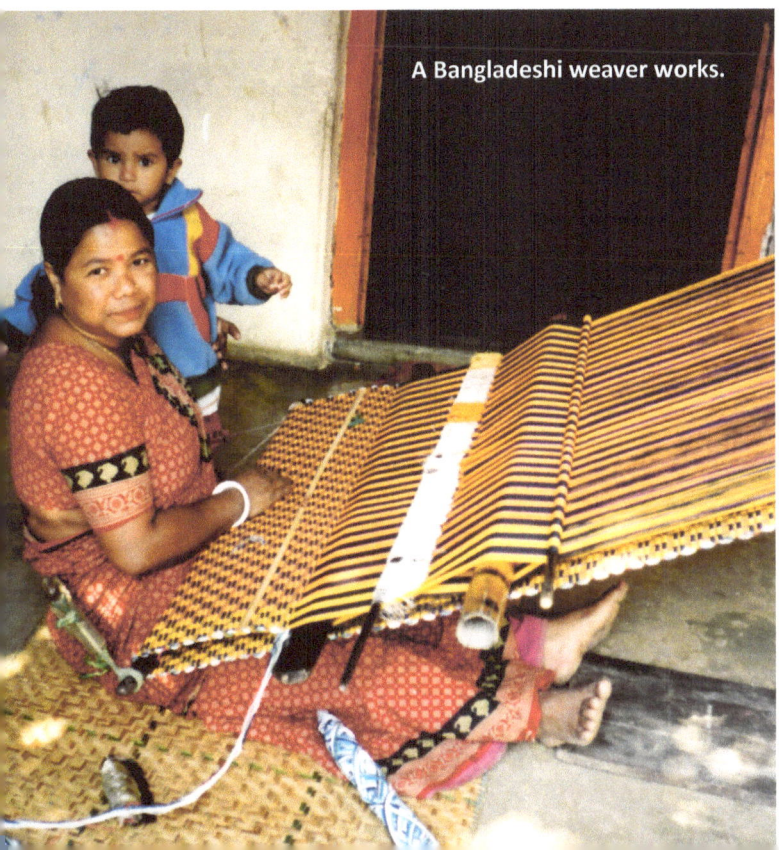

A Bangladeshi weaver works.

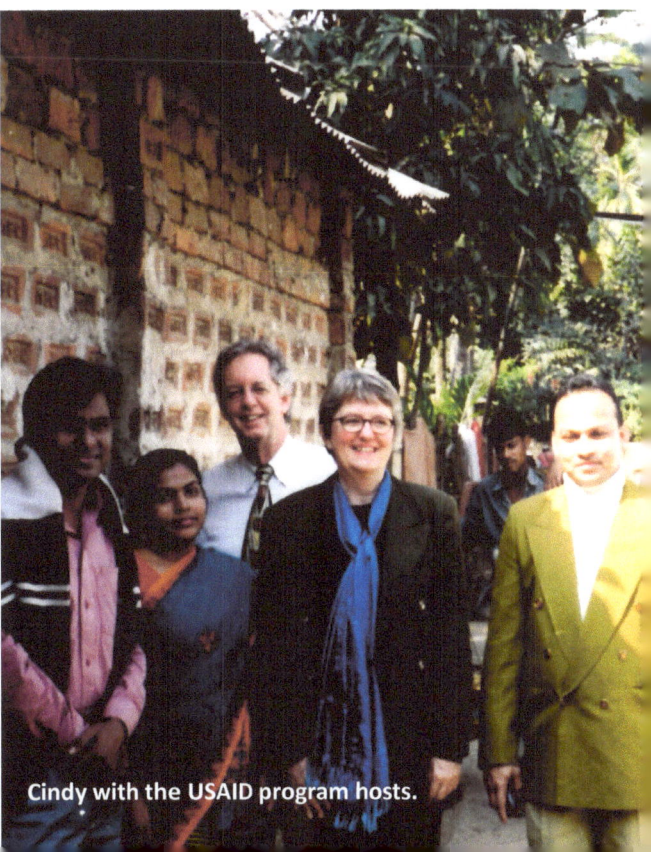

Cindy with the USAID program hosts.

The Adivasi mats did appear at the New York show. ABC Carpet and Linen, a large home interior store on 9th Avenue, ordered an entire shipping container of mats. But we had to turn down the order. There was no way the Bangladeshi village women could fill such an order with the three handlooms they used. Smaller orders, yes, but gigantic orders, no way. I would be heartbroken for the plight of the weavers, who are up against a scale of capitalistic consumption unknown to them. How would they survive without sales? Nevertheless, I would be forced to let go of this project because the funding had dried up.

For CHF International, an economic development agency in Washington, D.C., now called Global Communities, I traveled to the Republic of Georgia to conduct a survey of crafts across the country. The purpose was to determine if the craft sector could be a viable source of economic development. With a group of talented, knowledgeable Georgian textile artists, I traveled for three weeks from one end of the country to the other. We visited nuns who embroidered religious scenes with fine gold thread. Another textile artist created clothing with fine felted wool. In the mountainous Tusheti region, I saw women knitting multicolored slippers as they herded their sheep.

From remote village terrace banisters hung bright, patterned, hand- woven rugs. Georgia, with its own language, culture, architecture, diverse people, and Christian religion, was located on Marco Polo's northern route to Europe. Before Russia took over Georgia and wiped out much of its culture, Georgia was the origin of the word *wine* and, in fact, grows much of Eastern Europe's wine supply. On the spot and off the cuff, I created workshops as we traveled because the women I met along the way, from monastic nuns to institutional workers to remote mountain village people, were all hungry for outside stimulation and connection. Georgia is filled with exquisite detailed textile work handed down through generations of skilled women.

Near the end of my presentation, women quietly scurried around to hold hands in a circle. Chechen women who had traveled from their village six hours away treated me, their guest, to Caucasus folk songs and traditional dances. Lively strains of accordion music played by a mustached woman wearing a long dress, repaired many times over, accompanied songs known by all. I clapped my hands to the musical strains, twirled, and laughed. My heart overflowed with emotion as tears ran down my cheeks.

The magic of a coat is a gift of discovery. I thought I had much to offer others and I did, but what came back to me was so much greater. My discovery throughout my international work was a humbling reality check. No matter how little we Americans have, we have so much more than most of the rest of the world. I knew, at this part of COD's life, I at least had a coat to throw over my back. I had a roof over my head. Healthy food and clean water abounded. My family was safe.

The gift of discovery, however, doesn't stop with the life and plight of others. In the middle of Dhaka, Bangladesh, a city crushed with 15 million people, I strolled around a tiny lake near my hotel, where I watched women wash their naked children, scrub clothing with no soap, and fill aluminum pots with water to use for cooking. I witnessed throughout my five years of consulting work and travel how people survived on nothing, and I knew back home, COD and I would survive. I needed to recognize and honor this discovery. After all, COD had a dedicated staff, lots of fabric scrap from years of building coats, and electricity to run sewing machines. Back home at the Wallace Street factory, design and production was cranking up. I stayed home for a while to ride herd over another magical wave of change at COD.

I later made the decision to focus my work with indigenous cultures in a different direction. Instead of training them to produce thousands of products for large discount stores, catalogs, and retail chains, I wanted to help them expose their wonderful handmade products so that they would be appreciated by the outside world. When I was forced to drop my training in Pakistan and to leave the Adivasi weavers in northern Bangladesh in limbo at the New York show, I was as devastated as the artisans must have been. With so much hope riding on production training that could lead to viable income, a more stable life, and connection to the outside world, the outcomes had to be a tragic letdown.

In reflection, a wiser approach for the development agencies that hired me would be to help artisans find different markets for their goods. It would be a market that values the sustainability of existing skills and appreciates beautiful handmade native products. The Santa Fe, New Mexico, International Folk Art Market was organized to answer just such a need. The response both from international vendors as well as the crush of customers attending only reinforced my contention. I was able to introduce the Georgian textile artisans to this market, and they were successful for the three years they attended while their travel funds held out.

I was fortunate to ride a wave of funding that had been available for craft training within development projects. The funding that originally paid my way into the lives and traditional cultures of international artisans is limited today. I fear for the loss of international artisan skills as rural artisans seek livelihoods in urban settings. The population shift from rural to urban is the wave of the future in our own country as well as across the world. With this shift come new technologies that focus light years away from handmade. However, the number of festivals featuring handmade products organized worldwide, as well as the availability of online handmade training for anyone who has an Internet connection, is heartening.

CHAPTER 14

Oh, Precious Scrap

My home library of design books lay scattered around our house, each marked with a slew of sticky notes. For months now, I had mulled over ideas for sewing scrap pieces into new designs. Early one morning before anyone had shown up to work, I entered the Wallace Street factory. I turned on the lights and descended the stairs into the basement. I wore tattered overalls and a long-sleeved flannel shirt, outfitted for the task of crawling around among boxes of scrap. I needed to see and feel the scrap we had hoarded. I always loved being alone in the factory, with its old-building creaks and groans, fabric and people odors, silence, and the smell of possibility. I wasn't disappointed. Looming before me, stacks of scrap-filled boxes reached dangerous heights behind the swaying racks of coat patterns.

I pulled one box after another down and dumped the contents onto the long cutting table. I was convinced that before my eyes lay COD's emerging future. Mounds of handmade wool felt, heavy brushed wool, polar fleece, cotton velveteen, and wool melton called forth visions of small pieced products, likely decorative home accessories, such as pillows, blankets, holiday stockings, table runners, and Christmas tree skirts. I sat with the scraps for a while, a sort of dawn meditation.

Ideas flew around in my head. Silence can spawn flights of fancy. I raced upstairs to my office to grab a pen and pad of paper. Sitting on the high twirling chair pulled up to the cutting table, I sketched ideas for small pillows first. I looked over at the Omnistitch embellishment and blanket-stitch machines, two sewing workhorses, to gauge their input. The scrap collection had spoken to me. My excitement was palpable. I wanted to dance and sing on the production room sewing tables. Still alone in the wee hours of morning, I had finally landed on a way to use our 10-year collection of scrap. To celebrate the moment, I went into the break room and made a pot of strong coffee.

At this point, COD was about 17 years old. We had focused on making coats—that's what we were known for, and that was our business. For many years, we had often discussed what to do with this valuable mound saved from our past production. We didn't want to throw expensive fabric in the landfill. Remains of cut fabric yardage could be precious goods to a manufacturing business. After all, in one sense, scrap was free. We sold off some scrap at our annual coat sample sale. However, overflowing scrap grab bags couldn't reduce with any significance the boxed castle of scrap sequestered in the factory basement.

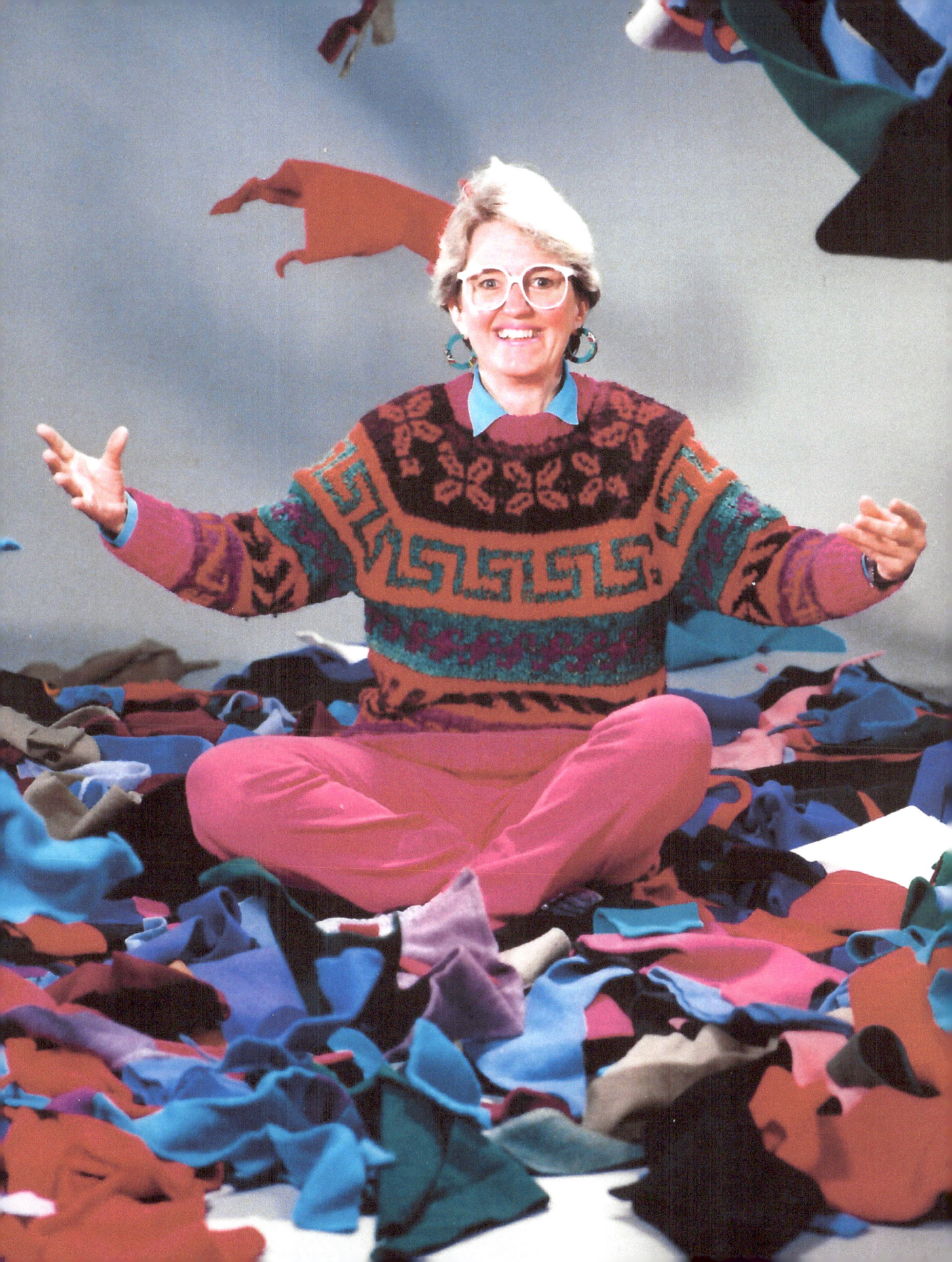

In the mid-1990s, a trend was "vintage rustic cabin" looks in home textiles, furniture, and house wares. I adored the "cabin" style with its cozy twig and log textures, bright-red and black color combinations, and vintage Hudson Bay blanket look. I would find writer Ralph Kylloe's 20-some books on "cabin everything" inspiring. Historically, Adirondack State Park in upstate New York is a hotbed of rustic styles with handmade birch bark furniture, lamps, and home accessories. Spending time where my husband's family camped in the Adirondacks exposed me to birch bark and tramp art from the Depression era. Also, "Montana log cabin" style had a strong influence on me. During frequent visits to the Angus cattle ranch of friends in Cinnabar Basin, 60 miles southeast of Bozeman, I stayed at their log ranch house. My memory of lying in bed below a giant log ceiling remains vivid. The smell of high mountain air and sitting around a fire telling stories solidified my love of Montana's rustic traditions.

COD's participation in the annual Cody, Wyoming, Western Design Conference Fashion Show would prove to be pivotal to my future designing. The show, in general, provided a venue for clothing and furniture designers from the West to show their work. We designed coats, jackets, and skirts, entire ensembles, with a western flair, just for this show. It was through this show that COD's famous blanket coat came to grace the interior pages of *Cowboys & Indians Magazine*. While I never saw COD's coats as "western" per se, our designs were "of the West," the surface stitching and expansive blocks of color being reminiscent of western landscapes.

At one of the early shows, I met my longtime mentor-from-afar, Ralph Kylloe. As keynote speaker, his passionate words opened my eyes to a world of rustic interior design, where the use of logs and other natural materials were what he considered "real stuff," and I agreed, "rustic" being the direction COD's new pillow collection would go in.

We piled the design studio tables with pillow tops, sewn concept samples. The Omnistitch embellishment machine figured strongly in surface design elements. This machine is a behemoth, a wild-animal industrial sewing machine. Think grizzly bear. Three strands, one of thread, one of yarn, and one of monofilament, must coordinate to make one stitch. As the machine clumps along, a raised pile is created on the surface of the fabric. Because there are no feed dogs to guide the fabric, the operator must guide the stitching by moving the fabric. With a pre-drawn guide, an operator could draw on fabric with this machine. The possibilities were endless.

The scrap stash contained sizeable scraps of black velveteen left over from the production of cuffs and collars on wool coats. Dreaming of all the "rustic cabin" imagery I had recently seen, I played with fabric chalk, drawing an array of forest-inspired designs. I drew pinecones, cabins, and pine tree sprigs. When I combined these images with words, eventually I landed on "Welcome to the Cabin." I created two "Welcome..." pillow possibilities. Both had the same words, but the center image on one was a red heart with a wooden button laid on top of pine sprigs. The second design was pinecone sprigs with a wooden button. With the pile stitching and the forest green with bright-red colors on a black

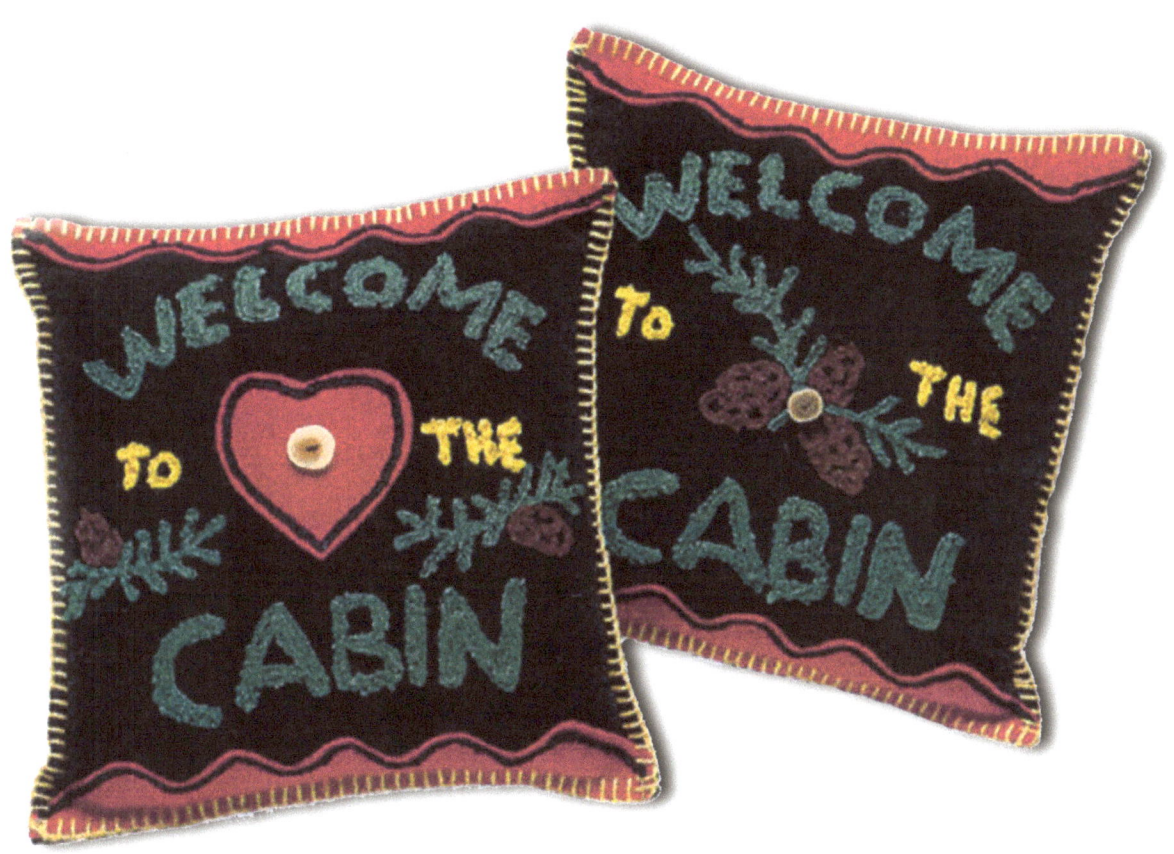

background, the pillow tops had a "vintage cabin" feel. We blanket-stitched in bright-yellow the backs to the fronts.

The two samples visually said "rustic cabin." I immediately called Deborah Cook in Minneapolis to get her read on this new product. I held my excitement in, but my heart fluttered. She asked to see samples as usual, so I sent the samples off. Deborah loved the pillows and suggested sending them on to a company and catalog called *Whispering Pines.* She then called Mickey Murray, the owner, along with her sister. Mickey said they weren't really looking for new products at that point, but she would still take a look. No guarantees (the usual retail buyer response to such questions). Deborah sent the pillows anyway.

I had been a catalog-aholic for many years. Catalogs provide a window into current trends. My collection of *Whispering Pines Catalogs* was a one-foot stack next to *Sundance Catalogs* and *Smith & Hawkens,* all dating back years. All three of these catalogs supported handmade artisan work.

When the phone rang, it was Deborah. She always spoke in one-liners. I thought for sure the news would be rejection. But when Deborah said you're in, I screamed, "Yes," as loud as I could. She nearly dropped the phone as she laughed and explained that Mickey and her staff loved the pillows. They not only wanted one—they wanted *both* pillows.

Unbeknownst to me, they would feature the two pillows on the cover of their fall catalog. They promptly placed orders for 150 pillows in each style.

I had been inspired by *Whispering Pines'* rustic theme and their whimsical approach to "cabin" and "vacation home" decor. I was over the moon with joy to think COD pillows would be front and center. I leafed through my collection of *Whispering Pines Catalog*s, my hands shaking and sweaty. The reality of our situation pulled me down to earth. I sat with a clunk at my kitchen table for lunch. I blathered to the salt and pepper shakers as I tried to eat a grilled cheese sandwich. Here is where we stand, I explained into the silence. Although I was delighted, making 300 pillows would be daunting. At this point, I had downsized my factory in all ways. I employed a handful of sewers and had a limited number of sewing machines.

Later, back at work, when I laid out our situation, those of us present put our heads together and decided to try to meet the deadline with the present staff and present machinery. This decision carried with it a certain amount of risk. On the other hand, we had not expected such a positive reception to "Welcome to the Cabin."

When the fall catalog came out in September, *Whispering Pines* could not fulfill all the customer orders. They had underestimated the response and hadn't ordered enough stock. They quickly doubled their next order, and before the end of December, five members of COD's production staff would make 2,500 to 3,000 pillows in the two styles.

The workroom was a frenzy of activity. Everyone had dark circles under their eyes. The radio blared rock songs over and over to feed our energy. The cutting/sewing production line had never worked so smoothly and with amazing hast. I wondered how we could possibly keep up the pace, but we did. We were each in our own daze. We would work long hours, long days, and frequent weekends to hold up our end of the obligation. We were all exhausted, but the popularity of "Welcome to the Cabin" fueled our excitement, giving us the energy we needed to work and make our deadline.

Scraps quickly turned into the necessity to order fabrics. Steel template dies had to be ordered to die-cut hundreds of hearts, waves, and pillow tops. Here we go again, I said to myself. A desperate sort of panic swept over me. My skin prickled with nerves. I paced sleepless nights again. How would we fund this latest upsurge in business?

I dipped into my personal savings. We scrambled to try to automate the sewing process, but still each pillow top had to be sewn by an operator. *Whispering Pines* staff conjured additional pillow ideas. We made "My Heart Is in..." (you fill in the blank). Hundreds of place names, like Aspen, Chicago, White Bear Lake, and of all places, Suck Lick Run, were individually written on each pillow. Bright-red velveteen pillows by the hundreds shipped, each to individual customers.

The business we did with *Whispering Pines* launched the concluding years of my pillow business. My "rustic cabin" designs also brought me contract design work with big companies like Big Sky Carvers, Michaelian Home, and Land of Nod. One "Bronco" pillow I designed would be offered in the *Land of Nod Catalog* for three years running. Our "Gone Fishin'" pillow graced many a kid's single bed.

I designed a line of what I called "souvenir pillows." These tiny pillows incorporated early photos of Yellowstone Park, plus other early camping images all from postcards I had gathered over the years. One group of pillows used images heat-transferred from my own paint-by-number painting collection. A couple of the paint-by-number "Horse" and "Cowboy" pillows were featured in *Country Living Magazine*. "Welcome to the Ranch" pillows graced the pages of *Crow's Nest Catalog*.

When I decided to display COD's pillow collection at one of the largest wholesale gift shows, The Atlanta Gift Show, I designed a birch forest backdrop. The backdrop was an actual photo of a floor-to-ceiling birch forest provided by a Bozeman sign company. The pillow samples hung in the trees camouflaged. As buyers stepped into the booth, they entered the forest. They looked around and surprise came over their faces. As I greeted people, I welcomed them to my secret woodland. The white birch environment was my favorite booth design. I always tried to "color outside of the lines" visually and creatively in order to connect urbanites with rural wild places like Montana. At the very least, the birch tree forest offered me a quiet place to hang out for 10-hour days during the five-day show.

The pillow business was fun. It never seemed quite as serious as making coats had become. Pillows were small, playful, relatively inexpensive to make, and popular with customers. When I chose to leave the fashion scene, the decision pulled at my heartstrings. People often asked why I had made this decision, and I would answer with this story:

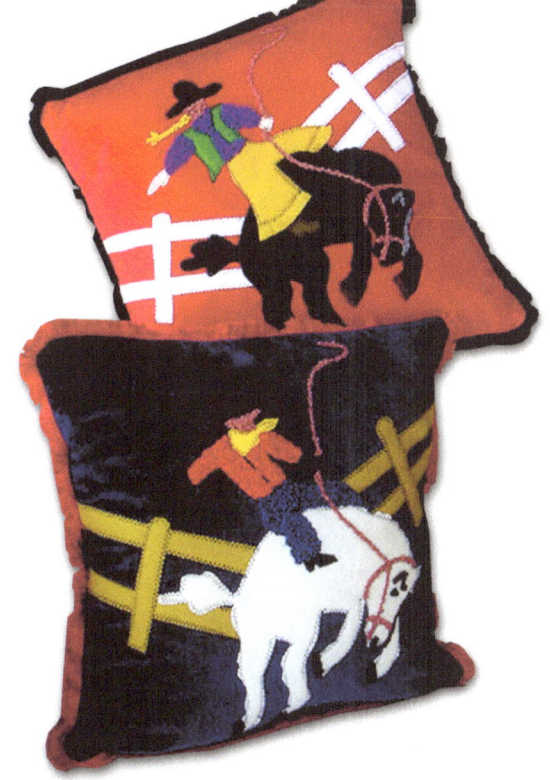

"I paddled a canoe in Minnesota's Boundary Waters many years ago. The weeklong trip required our group to portage from lake to lake. At the outset, such a hike, carrying a pack and a canoe, seemed impossible to me. My backpack was so heavy that when I bent over, I flipped forward from the weight, was thrown off-balance, and landed right in a wild rose bush. Others had to right me up, pack and all. I cherished the Woolrich red-and-black-checked lumberjack wool shirt I wore throughout the trip, my North Country talisman. The smell of our campfires buried deep in my clothing was rustic perfume to me. During a final lake crossing, our canoe nearly flipped over in a windstorm. My partner and I paddled like crazy. The crossing was terrifying as the wind blew

The Bronco Pillows Series.

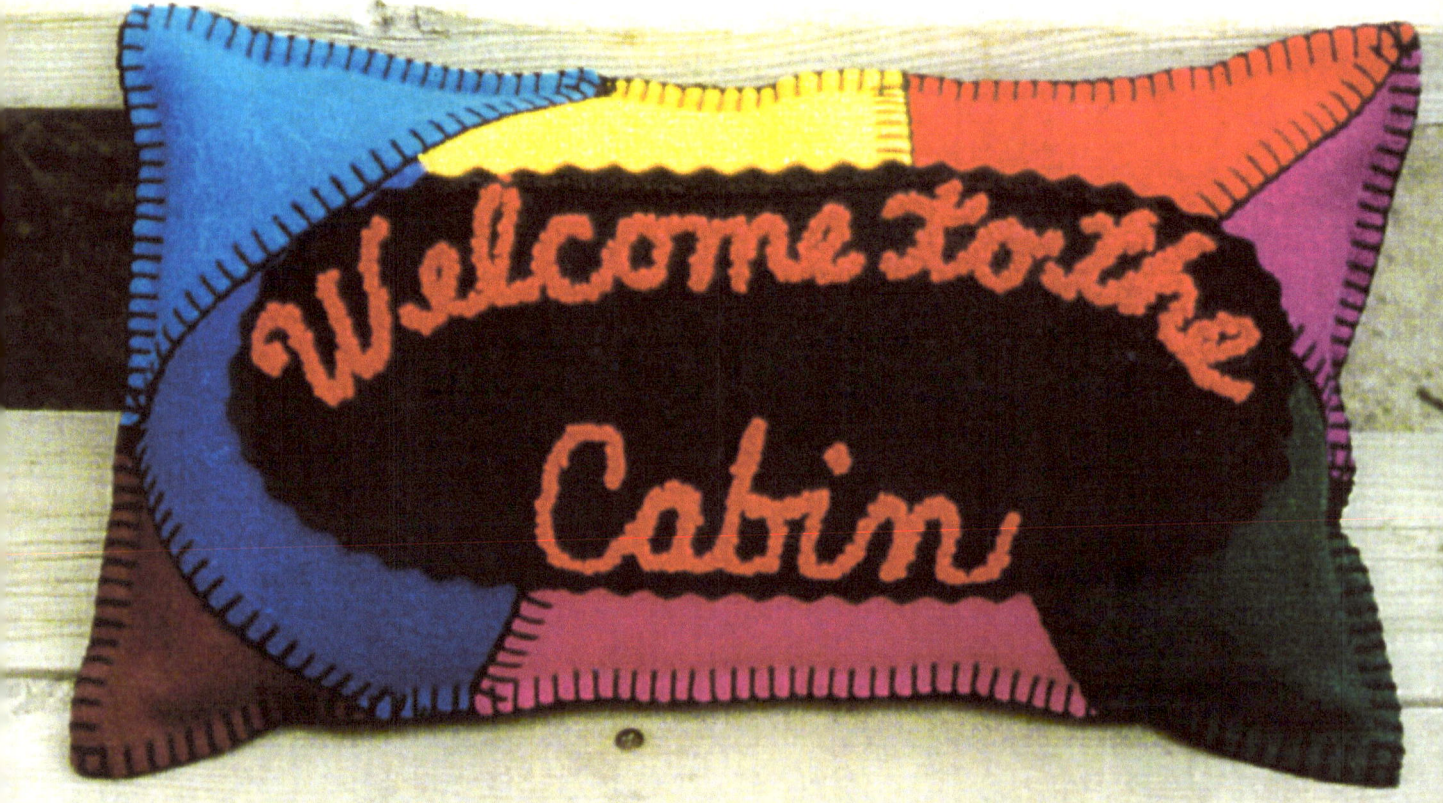

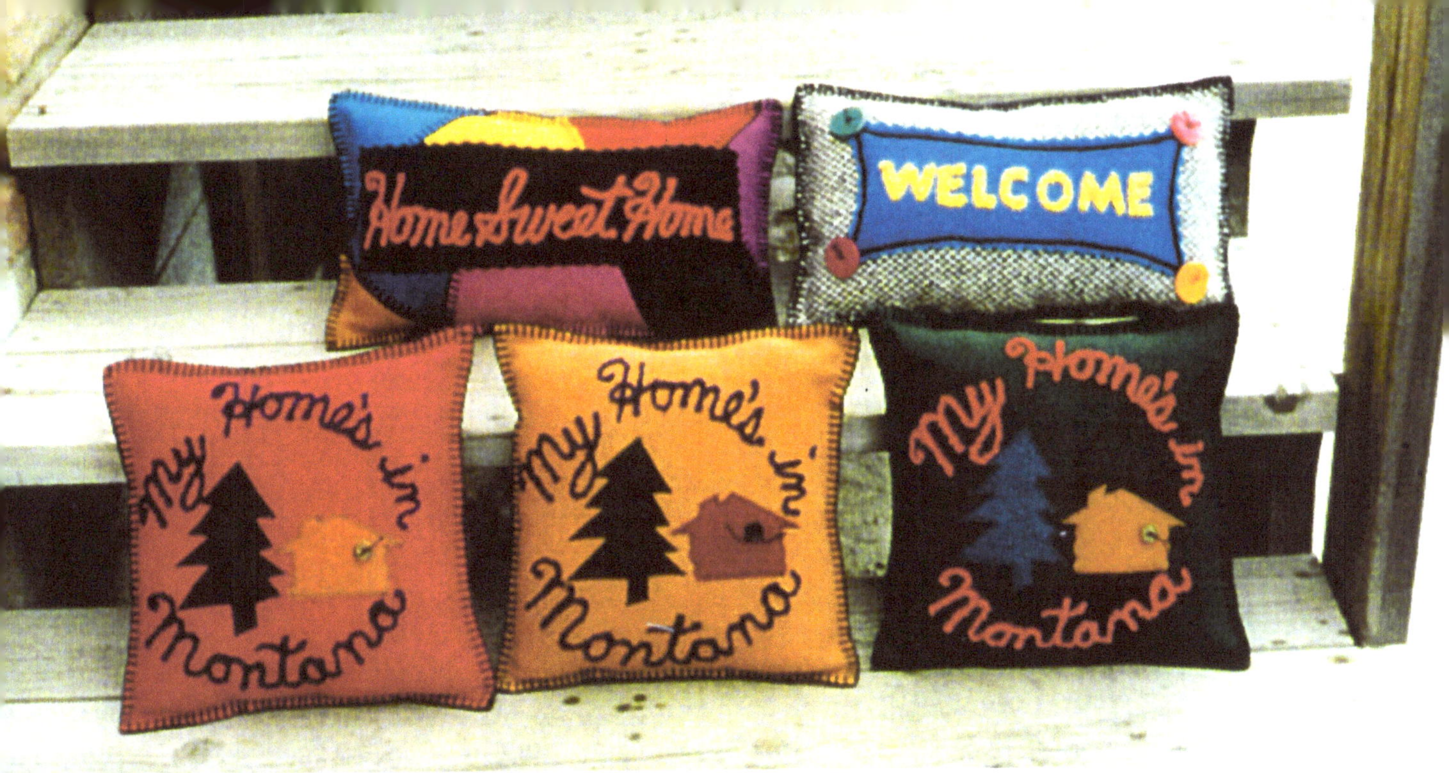

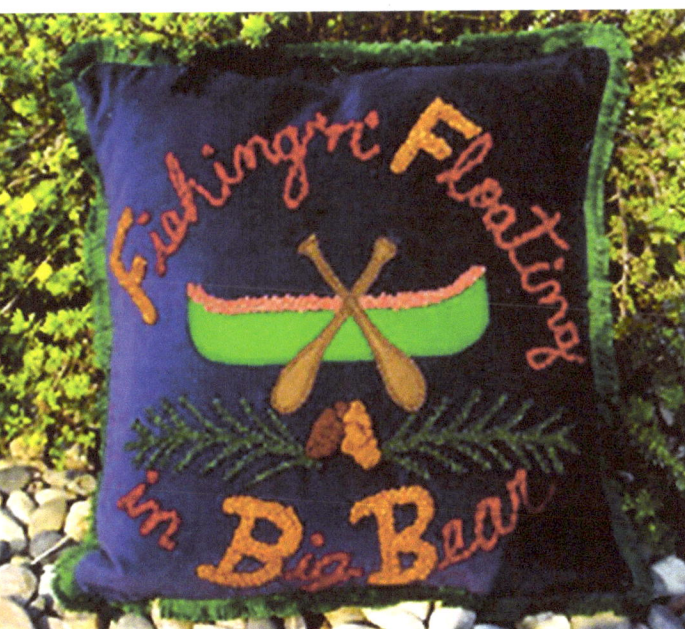
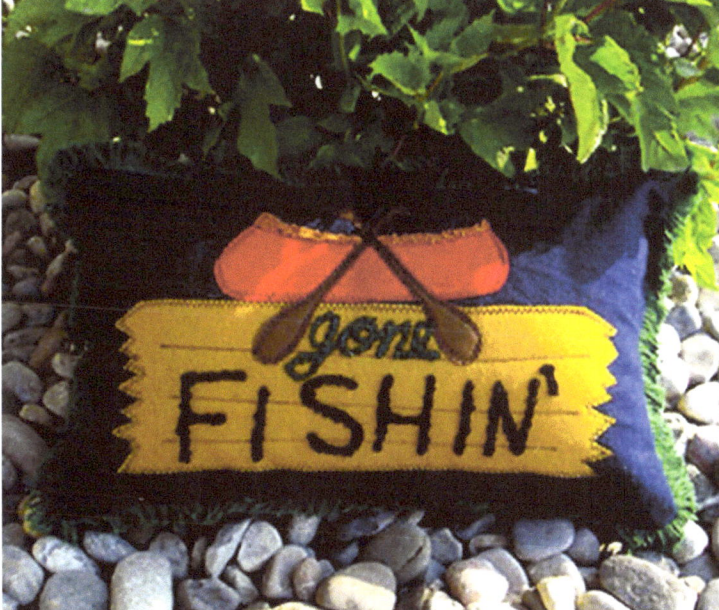
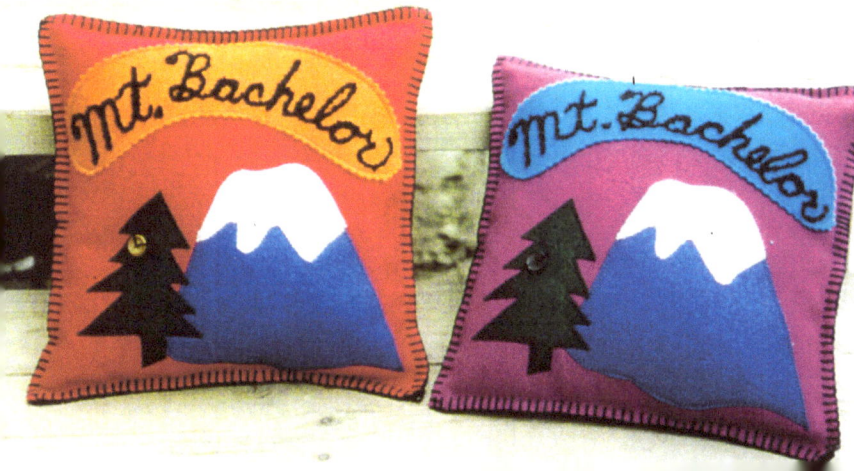
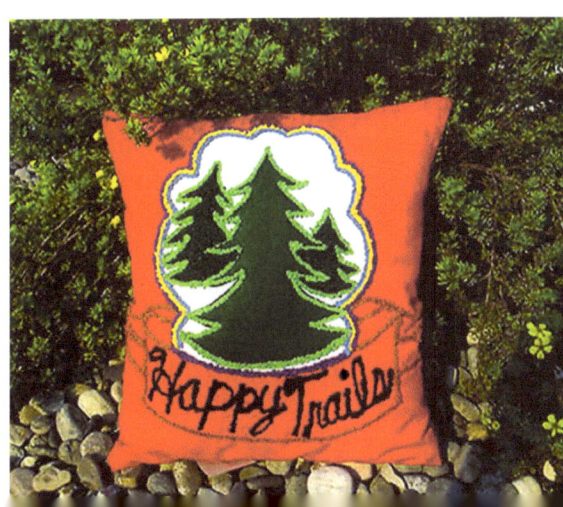

our canoe off-course. Exhausted, wet, shivering, and scared, we finally reached shore. We fell to the ground to kiss the forest soil. We were alive. I wept in relief. Likewise, ending the fashion part of my business was a welcome relief."

One day in the late 1990s while staying with friends in Ennis, Montana, I walked into their guest cabin carrying my suitcase. There on the bed lay two tiny 12-inch-square pillows with black velveteen backgrounds, evergreen sprigs in the centers, and red waves on the tops and bottoms. Each said, "Welcome to the Cabin." My friend told me her sister-in-law had given her the pillows for Christmas. I could barely believe my eyes. My friend was shocked when she turned each pillow over to see my name.

Another time, I opened Ralph Kylloe's book, *Rustic Traditions,* to see the same "Welcome to the Cabin" pillows gracing a large log bed in a snazzy Adirondack cabin. The "Welcome..." pillows were my designs, spread far and near through *Whispering Pines Catalog* sales. The creation story of the "Welcome..." pillow and its entry into the marketplace would once again be another COD connection through serendipity and magic.

"Wonders of the West" pillows, including "Welcome to...," "My Heart Is in...," "Gone Fishin'," "Happy Trails," and "Howdy," were some of COD's final pillow creations. Not only were the people who sewed my designs wonders of skill, craftsmanship, and tenacity, but also the products they made were unforgettable. When I opened *O, The Oprah Magazine* to see a "Welcome to the Cabin" pillow featured on the "Love That!" page, I knew that I, as a self-taught textile designer, had reached a pinnacle beyond my wildest dreams. My designs had a broad reach to masses of people beyond my Montana home. The products COD made would be timeless.

And, yes, we eliminated about one-half of the mountain of scrap in the factory. Scrap became COD's magic pot of gold. It provided hope and paved a path leading out of hard times. On the back of thousands of pillows, plus international consulting, I was also able to pay off the debt I owed, though it took seven years.

I wondered often how debt made or broke my business. Without capital, a business cannot survive. I was not wealthy. I turned to a local bank, the SBA (the federally funded Small Business Association), and friends and family, who became my angels, to help provide funds to pay workers, market my products, and grow my business. But what would I give up if I paid back my debt? First, I would give up many sleepless nights worrying about paying back the debt that hovered over me. Secondly, as a business goes deeper and deeper into debt, its activities become limited by interest payments and the need for more and more funding. Debt is a thankless circle.

In 2003, after shutting down my business, I started to pay the final debt of $40,000 owed an angel. It took until 2007 to pay it all off. He wrote me a note saying that of all the many businesses he had ever loaned money to, I was the only one to pay him back. Regardless, I was finally free.

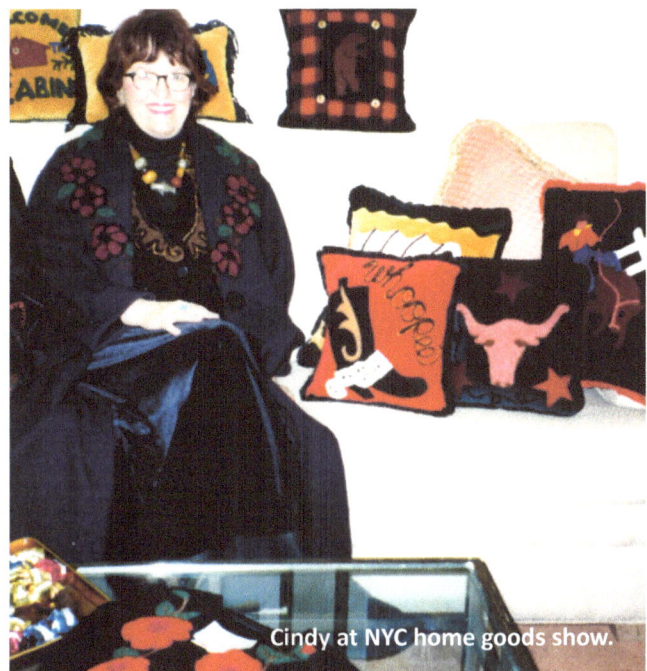
Cindy at NYC home goods show.

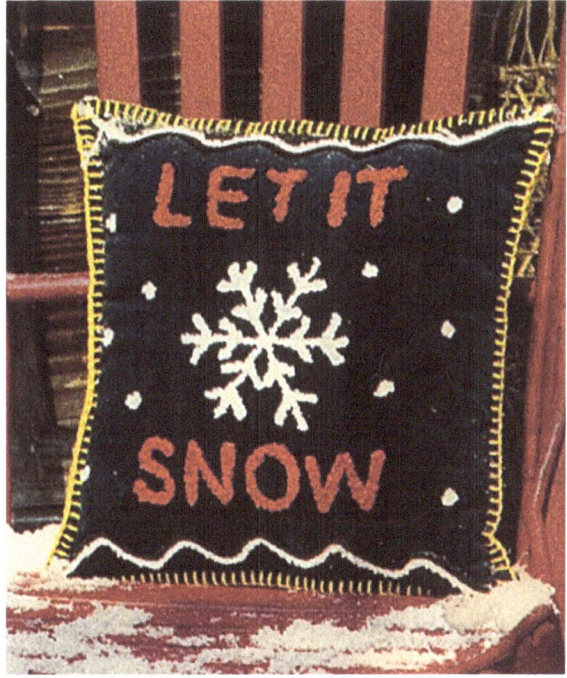

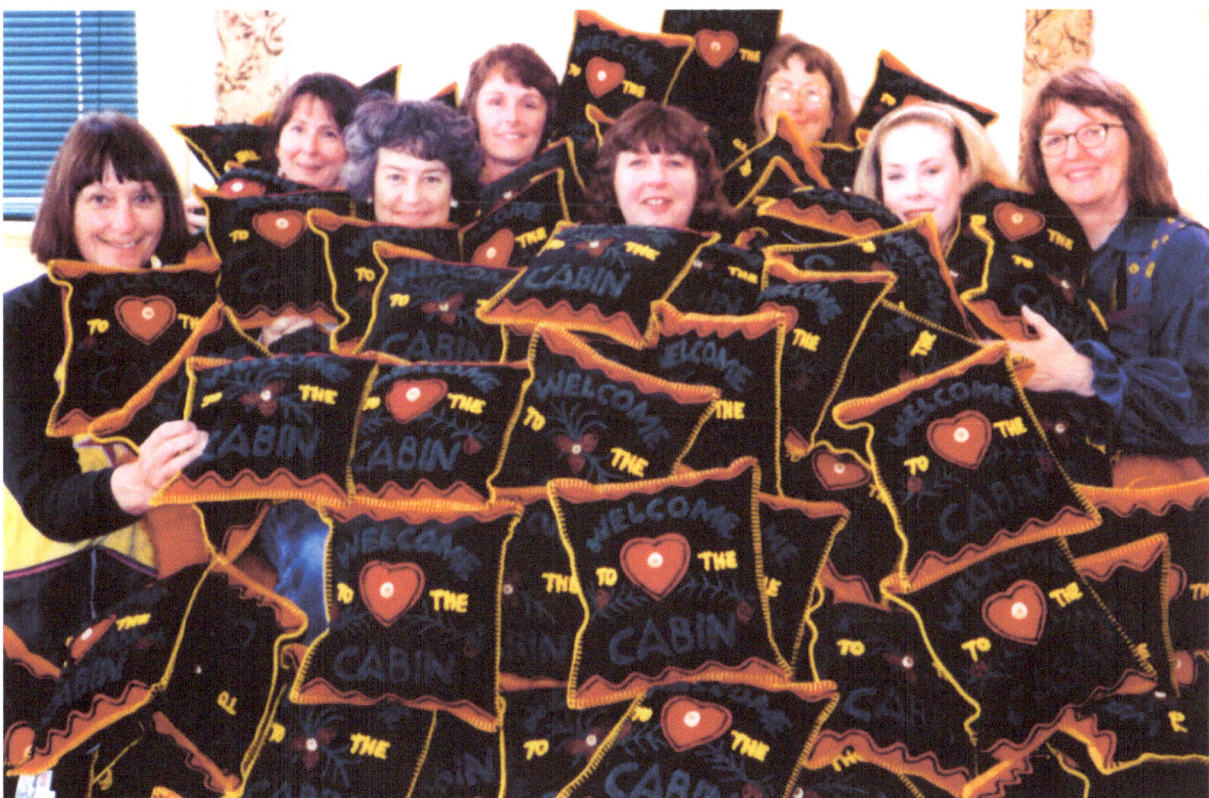
Cindy (right) and staff with mountain of completed Welcome To The Cabin pillows.

CHAPTER 15

Petunias Grow Forever, Almost

Every box that left COD's factory carried a sense of handmade celebration. The pride for our work was ancestral, buried deep in the by-hand traditions of our community. How could I hail other artisans dedicated to doing quality handwork and trying to make a living at the same time? I felt that a place needed to be carved out within my business to sing the praises of handmade. Petunias in the Factory, our tiny retail shop, was born.

Share the fun, so to speak. Concrete garden figures from Bridger, Montana, were assembled, up-cycled wooden icons appeared from Alabama, life-sized papier-mâché kitties skipped in the door, and huge blown-glass globes sparkled with light, all mixed in with COD coats. Handmade, colorful, whimsical treasures from all over crept into our midst. An onsite shop would also allow direct retail sales of coats. Since I was always working at the factory, I decided to open the shop in the factory. Red bricks on the face of the building still display a faded sign. I loved the idea that our factory continued an industrial manufacturing tradition in a town that used to be known for its sweet pea processing.

Most folks think of Petunia as a pig. In fact, a friend said to me in astonishment, "How could you name your store after a pig?" But I wanted to name my store after my favorite flower. Petunias are the only dependable Northern Rocky Mountain flower that blooms through freezing temperatures well into fall. The name Petunia, in a Native American language, means "she knows." But I only cared that the name Petunias would be recognizable and unforgettable. And so it was.

The front space where the shop would be located needed extensive remodeling. My future husband, Graham, took on the job to strip and refinish the pine floors, rip out the ugly drop ceiling, paint, and restore the entryway. I hired a friend to paint (reverse glass) a whimsical bird and floral design on the front two windows. Between the windows another friend painted a large rococo *trompe L'oeil* gold leaf frame. I found a tiny romantic couch that I upholstered in bright-red mohair fabric from our stash of scrap. Freestanding display shelves and cupboards came

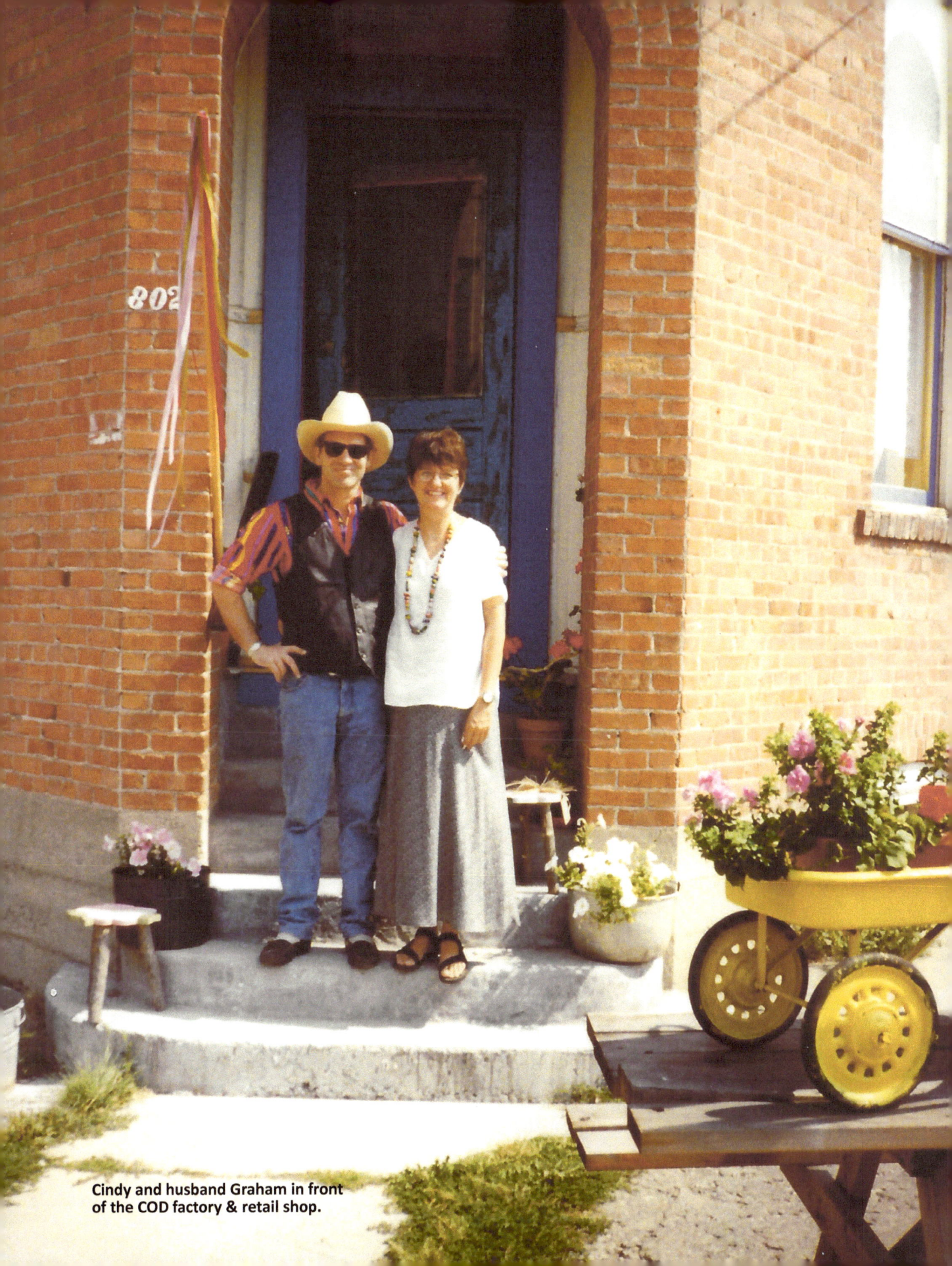

Cindy and husband Graham in front of the COD factory & retail shop.

through Ralph McHenry, who sold furniture in Bozeman. He brought in lively antique Mexican pieces that had been made and painted bright colors by Mennonites living in Mexico. My favorite Mennonite piece was a bookshelf fashioned of old fruit crates.

Petunias in the Factory, while remote and out of the way, attracted a strong following of intrepid shoppers. Maybe it would be the treasure hunt aspect that brought people eight blocks north of Main Street to shop. Regardless, Petunias became a destination spot to find colorful folk art, baskets from South Africa, tiny house boxes, beautiful coats, concrete garden art, bottle cap jewelry, and unusual textiles from around the world. As a quirky shopper myself, merchandising Petunias for me was great fun. June Safford, a well-known Bozeman artist, painted a piece showing Petunias in the factory and its sky blue entry as part of her running series of historic Bozeman.

Shoppers began to pour in like a river. A good thing would become a not so good thing, however, with the constant interruptions. Someone from COD's production or office staff had to be at the ready during open hours with the clang of the doorbell.

When Petunias was about a year old, we decided the shop needed to move. With great excitement, we found a space on the corner of Main and Willson in the corner of the Baxter Hotel. I vacuumed the carpet of the space and we moved Petunias to downtown Bozeman. What a great location with great exposure. But a whole new set of challenges faced COD's tiny shop. How would we stay on top of inventory and who would work in the shop?

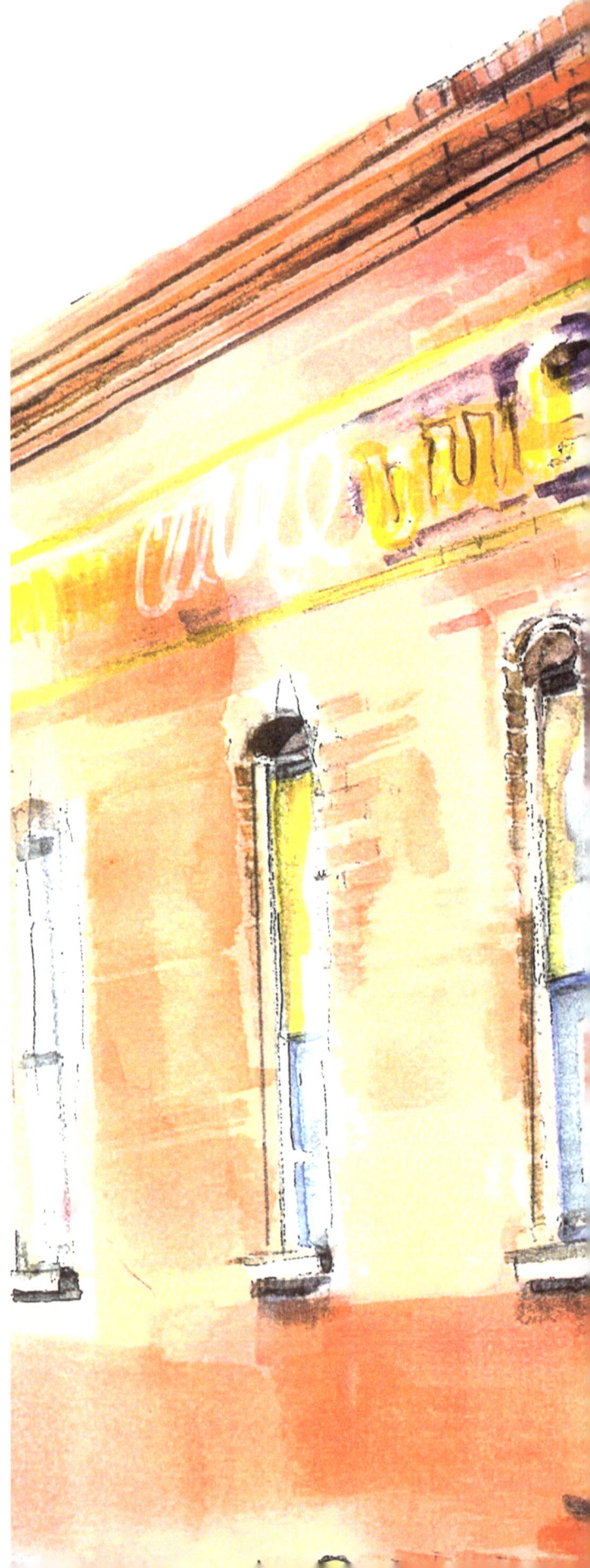

Petunia's retail store breathed new life into Bozeman's former Coco-Cola factory. Artist June Safford painted the watercolor of the facade.

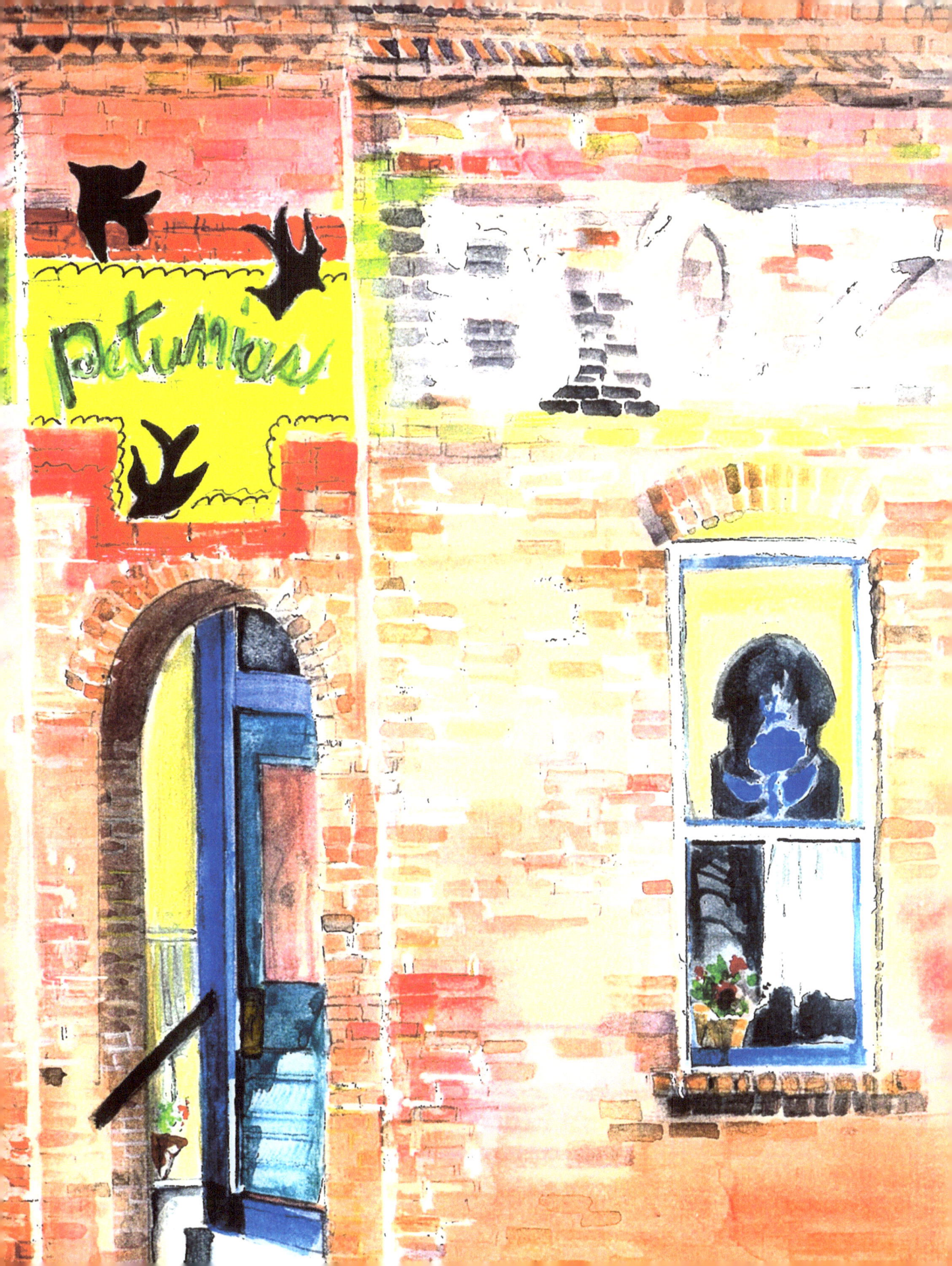

For the 30 years of my life in Bozeman, I observed the ebb and flow of downtown retail. Many of Petunias' display cases and tables came from the Chambers-Fisher Department Store when it closed. Across the street, Bungalow Drug closed its doors. Longtime men's and women's clothing shops folded. High-end art galleries would come and go like the change of seasons. Upscale, funky, and elegant haberdasheries, eateries, and coffee shops of all ilk slipped into high-rent spaces only to find out competition was stiff. When a longtime women's store kitty-corner from Petunias closed its doors, our sales dived. Downtown retail could be fickle and capricious.

One hot summer day, Petunias' heavy, swinging, glass front door shattered with a bang like a gunshot. Everyone in the store hit the floor in confusion. The solid glass door had broken because the glass was old, and I later found out could not be repaired. My heart sank. I knew the big bang was the death knell of retail for COD. When the Baxter Hotel landlord at the time refused to install a new door, Graham came to the rescue. My stalwart supporter installed a locking door. Petunias limped its way to the end of the year, and then closed its doors. National retailers and restaurateurs were entering the downtown scene willing to pay high rents. The interest in supporting local handmade retail grew and then wilted, leaving Petunias with a smaller piece of the downtown retail pie.

To this day, people tell me Petunias was their favorite store in Bozeman. On separate occasions at Petunias, two women brought family members near death in to see, touch, and connect with the joy of handmade. The experience would uplift saddened hearts by planting a seed of appreciation that could carry forward as a happy memory. I suspected Petunias struck a chord in the hearts of shoppers because we carried goods made by real hands, by real people. Why are people drawn to handmade? In a world overflowing with mass factory-made plastic goods, people yearn for the authenticity of a product made by a real person's hands from indigenous materials. It's about connection to our ancestral beginnings.

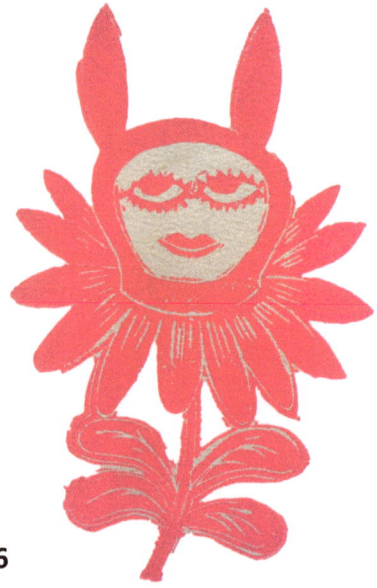

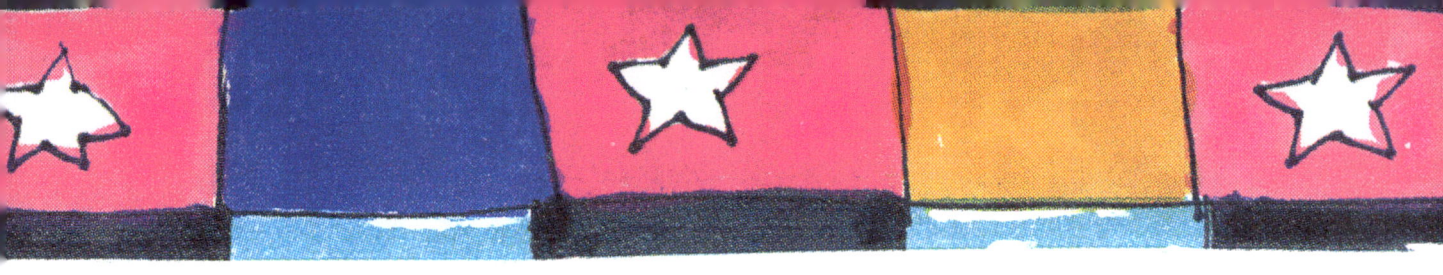

When you are in Bozeman visit our tiny shop - filled to the brim with whimsical folk art, hand painted furniture and the famous C.O.D. coats. Look for us in the Historical Brewery District.

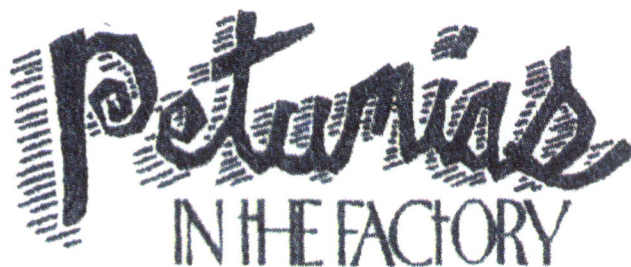

802 North Wallace
Bozeman, Montana
59715

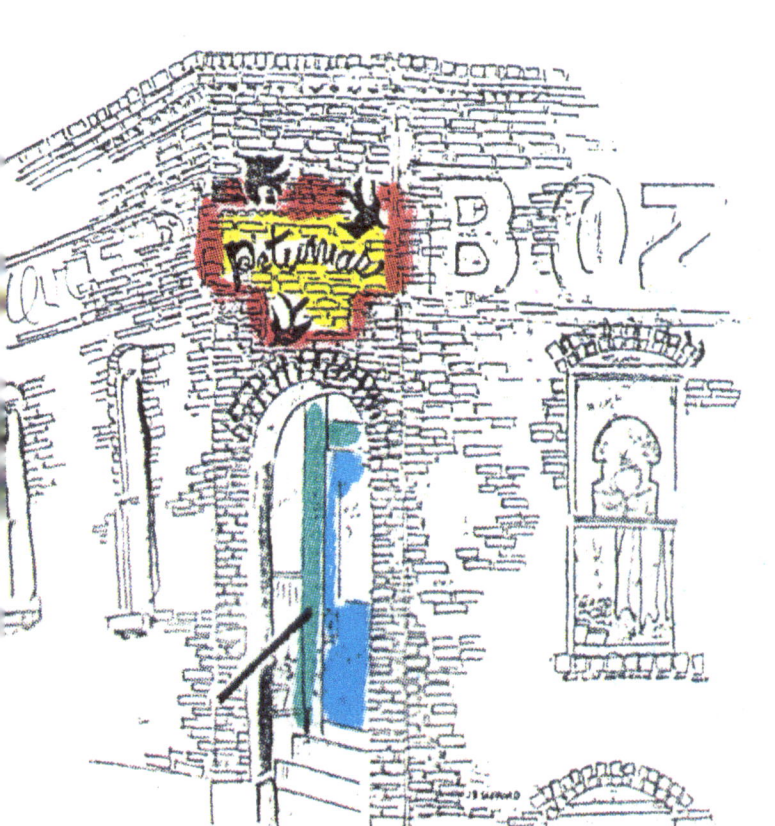

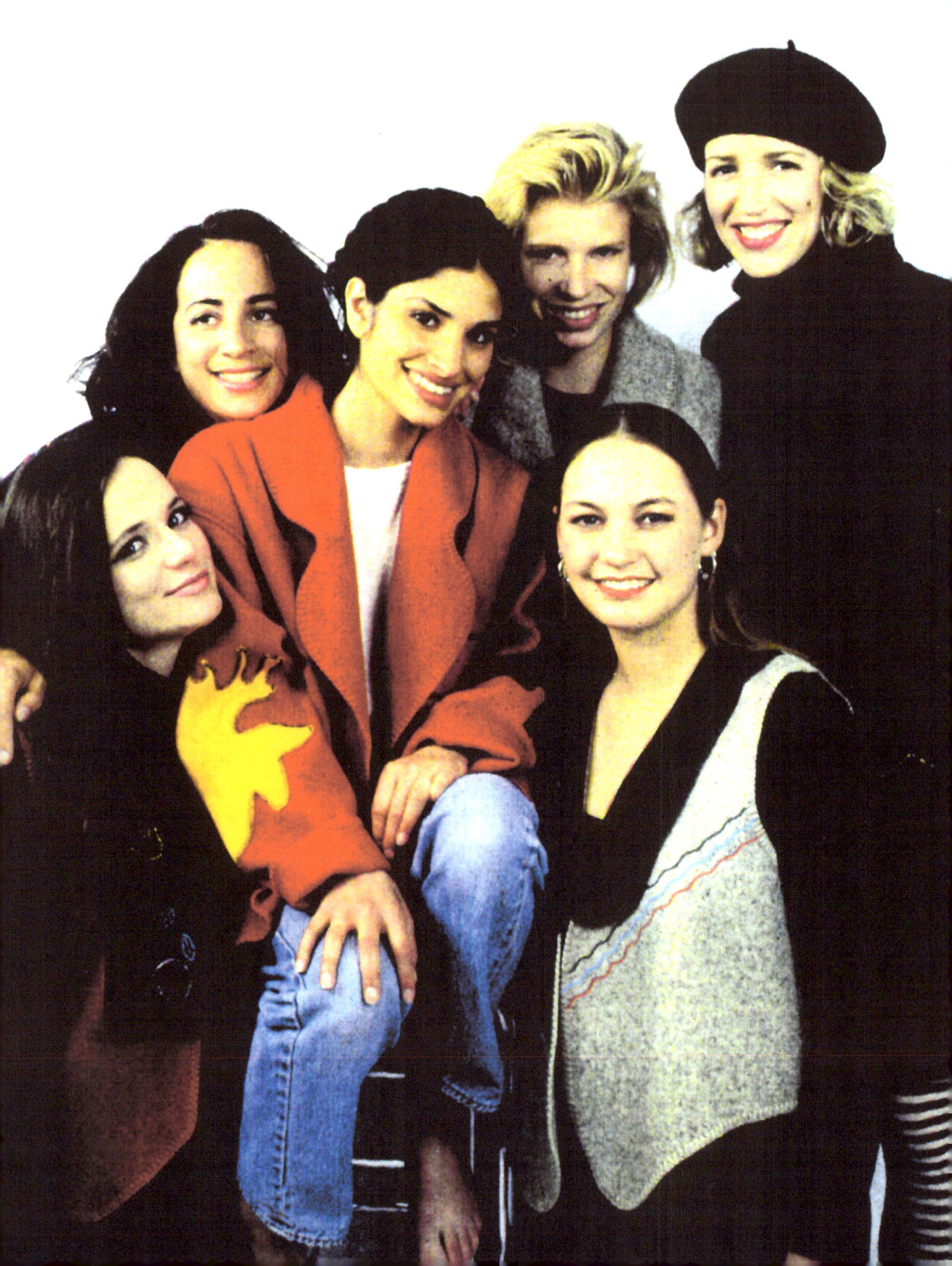

CHAPTER 16

Endings Circle Around to Beginnings

A coat is more than a coat. Even Virginia Woolf knew the true purpose of a coat.

Buried in the fabric of each COD coat would be the flowing of a river, the blowing of the wind, and the silence of falling snow. Wrapped in a wool coat, warm against winter cold, the wearer becomes the coat, with its inherent landscape. Secreted within this garment would be the possibility of relationship and connection with moose, bear, trout, and the vastness of the West. Kept safe and warm by this coat of many colors, the wearer would be free to waltz into a world at once unfamiliar filled with unknown but sought-after understandings.

Clothes opened my own world and changed it along the way. During stays with my grandparents as a teenager, I cared only about visits to fabric stores in Denver. I would open the door to Hancock Fabrics in Cherry Creek, hit with the musty smell of bolts of fabric. I stood stock-still as my eyes would skip around the store. What was new? Glittering taffetas and silk satins shimmered on upright rolls, while cotton dress yardage stood end to end on bolts filling table after table. A print caught my eye. I pulled the bolt out to unfold the fabric. Huge strawberries lined one side of the yardage. I would buy enough fabric to make a gathered-skirt dress to wear to the Monday-night canteen dance back home. Canteen would be my own private fantasy designer runway. I would create a new dress ensemble for each dance through the entire summer months during high school.

When my family sorted the final possessions of my parents, I was astounded to find a treasure trove of COD early coats. I had no idea they were here. I had grown up in a family that didn't care about and couldn't afford fashionable unique clothing. Living on the rivers of the West called for dressing practically, not fashionably. A couple of pairs of jeans, a few shirts, and a sturdy coat were the expected attire. I was an aberration. When I learned to sew in home economics classes at school, my mother helped me hone my skills at home. But when I started sewing expensive dresses, my mother objected. Our family lived from hand to mouth. I got a job at age 14 to help pay for my dressmaking. My mother had purchased the coats, but had never worn some of them, a quiet testament to her support of my business. In the final years of my mother's life, she wore only one coat, a COD fleece coat with a hand-woven Guatemalan fabric yoke. I wrapped her ashes in this coat at her burial.

Leaping ahead to Henri Bendel's in New York City. During one of my requisite visits to this outrageous store, featuring up-to-the-minute fashions, I would swish my hand along a rack of cotton velveteen evening jackets by the Italian clothing designer, Romeo Gigli. His voluminous silhouettes and elaborate draping swept me away. I knew I had to have a Romeo. I would try on a few of his signature pieces. A tulip-bottomed, black velveteen evening capelet with a puffed collar caught my fancy. I bought the evening wrap. I would be a fashion queen for each moment I wore the jacket. This fanciful piece of Italy would accompany me home to Montana. So unlike my own COD coat designs, my fashion flights of fantasy would be essential to the dreams I would transform into real coats.

COD, the business, shut down in 2003. Upon the heels of the end, I decided it was time to leave town, so I moved, lock, stock, and barrel, 45 miles southwest of Bozeman to the majestic Madison River Valley. I sold the Lindley Place house, and another tenant bought the building that housed the Wallace Street factory and remodeled it. COD's 23-year-old phone number was assigned to another party, who called me to say how tired he was of answering calls from people who wanted coats. With the gentrification of the Northeast side, structures from Bozeman's industrial history would be lost. Regardless, COD would be forever stitched into the fabric of that rich history.

Coats would not be far from my life, past, present, and future, however. Recently, I was sitting eating a chili-covered baked potato in Ennis High School's cafeteria when three women joined me at my table. We were volunteer judges for the statewide speech, debate, and drama finals. My judge packet lay beside my fork. The women glanced in my direction, their eyes falling to my name written large on the packet, and one woman asked me if I was a designer.

"Yes, I am a designer," I replied.

She then asked, "Are you *the* Cindy Owings who made all of those beautiful coats?"

"Yes, that was me," I said.

Then she went on to exclaim how famous I was and how unforgettable my coats are.

"Maybe once, but now I am anonymous," I replied.

When they asked how that felt, I answered, "It was a welcome relief, poignant, but now I can wear COD coats anonymously, knowing secretly who the designer is."

The conversation warmed my insides. I smiled and walked to my next judging session.

Once a woman from Ireland emailed me, saying she had spent Christmas in New Orleans and had bought one of my coats from a secondhand store there. She had tracked me down through Google. She went on to say how lovely her COD coat was, how she loved wearing it, and how she treasured it. For months, we maintained a lively correspondence.

On the other hand, I receive coats from friends and former customers who no longer want heavy wool coats taking up space in their closets. Heart-wrenching though it is to collect worn coats, I treasure the journey of these coats. I have saved these coats to be part of my coat archives. My home is filled with traded artwork that through the years came to me because of COD coats—a cast aluminum birdbath, paintings of Madison mountain sunrises, a three-part screen emulating the Yellowstone fires of 1988, a great bear painting by a Crow artist.

As I look back on the rainbow of coats I created, it amazes me that store buyers and customers alike placed confidence in COD's sense of design, whimsy, and color. To this day, I ask myself how COD could have convinced people to wear coats with kissing moose, bison, and trout. I ask myself, why were mainstream women interested in wearing my long, flowing, unlined, pieced-together "Zig Zag" blanket coats? I expected quirky people to wear my coats, but I was surprised by the response of mainstream customers. What would be behind their love of COD's multicolored trapeze and swing coats sometimes sporting hearts, kitties, or dogs? What could be the attraction to elegant long coats that had hidden, intricately stitched elk heads on the sailor collar, or, more outrageous, black motorcycles printed on white satin short jackets? I privately asked myself if I could get away with these flights of fantasy in my coat designs. But I was to discover that people wanted a connection to nature and to show who they are through the clothes they wore.

The flowing river of my story stands as a testament to how a passion can turn into something bigger than self. Along the way, precipitous falls and swirling eddies can add danger to the river's course. The vagaries of changing markets, limited funding, competition, and exhaustion take their toll.

One day halfway into my business, I walked into Maurice's Store in the Bozeman mall. There hanging on center racks were copies of COD coats fashioned in Asia of nylon and other cheap fabric. COD's signature black-and-white "snake" graced every jacket. I knew that the only way to stay ahead of the knock-off industry is to constantly design fresh products.

I am fortunate to have had COD in my life. The experience strengthened me, opened doors to unforeseen relationships, friendships, and events. I would not have paddled the same river had I chosen to remain designing and sewing in the Lindley Place living room.

What's in a coat? My answer lies in the knowledge that some women (and men) enjoy stepping out of themselves, to show their world an artsy person, a fun person, a discerning person, without fear of inherent attention through what they wear. A COD coat didn't just provide warmth—it also provided a new way for its wearer to be seen and

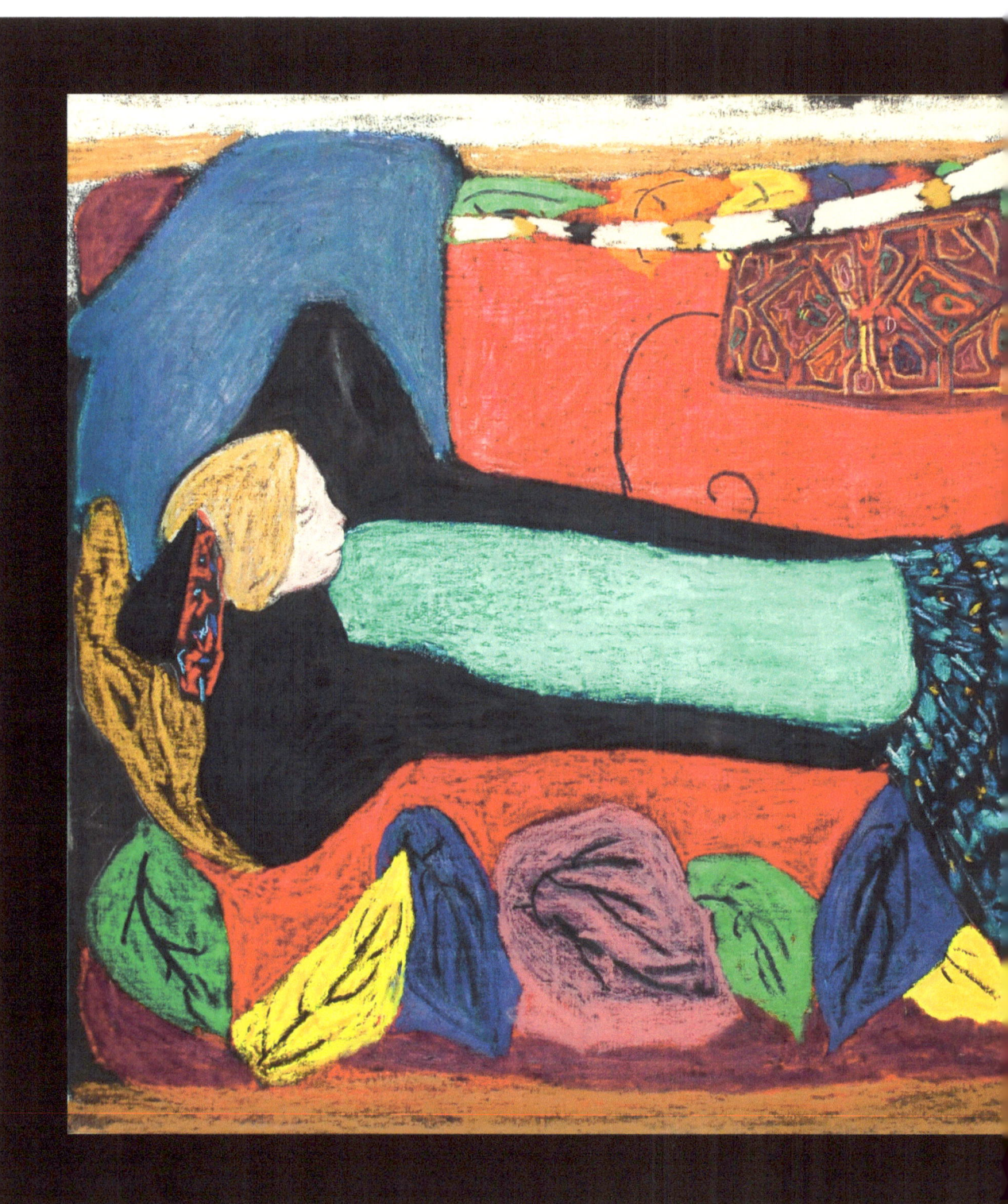

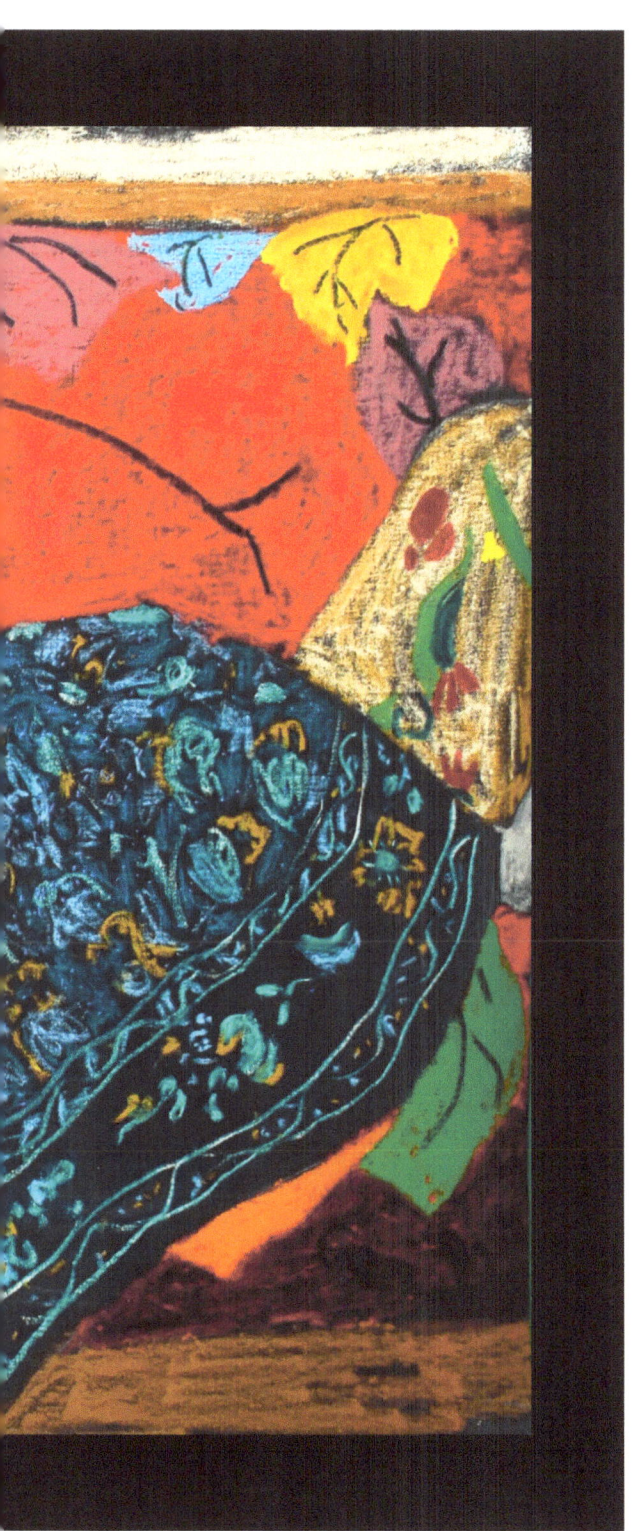

Left:
Cindy is honored that artist Gennie DeWeese featured a COD home goods blanket with a leaf design in her painting, shown here.

Below:
Gennie and her husband, Bob, were influential pioneers of the contemporary art scene in Montana. They supported Cindy when no one else did. In this image, Gennie is wearing a COD Arrow Jacket.

Images used with the permission of their daughter, Tina DeWeese.

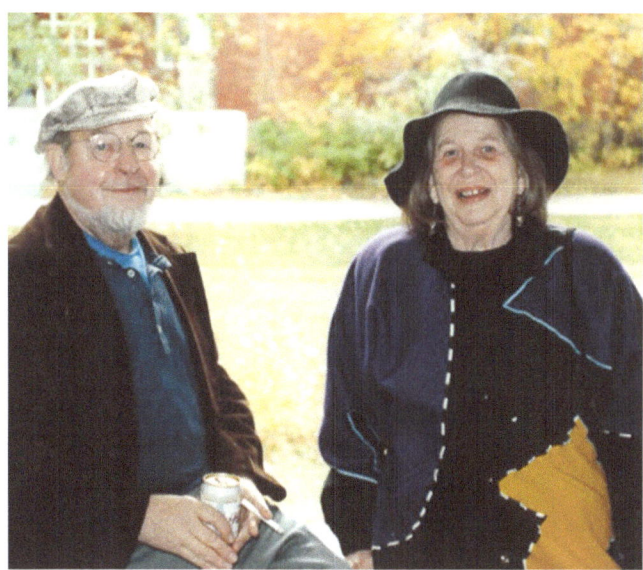

considered. Choosing to wear a coat with kissing moose heads required its wearer to step out of anonymity, to say, "Here I am!" What a person chooses to wear says a lot about the essence of a person, as well as one's understanding of colors, textures, and patterns.

My colorful coat enterprise would live on in a different way. Looking back is to look forward to collect my past to help mold my future. Now, late in my own life, two COD coats, a "Zig Zag" blanket coat and an "Arrow" coat, hang on the rack in my straw bale Bluebird Studio, a reminder of a rich and flamboyant era in my life gone by. Today, Bozeman women tell me they have as many as 10 COD coats in their storage closets. I know now that COD's legacy lives on when I see COD coats on eBay and in thrift stores across the country. One morning recently, I opened the *Bozeman Daily Chronicle* to see a photo of one of COD's short swing coats gracing a woman strolling down Main Street.

Fashion is self-decoration, self-definition. Maybe COD customers just loved wearing their inner selves outside—it was as simple as that. But it's still magic. And I'm happy to have taken part in that magic.

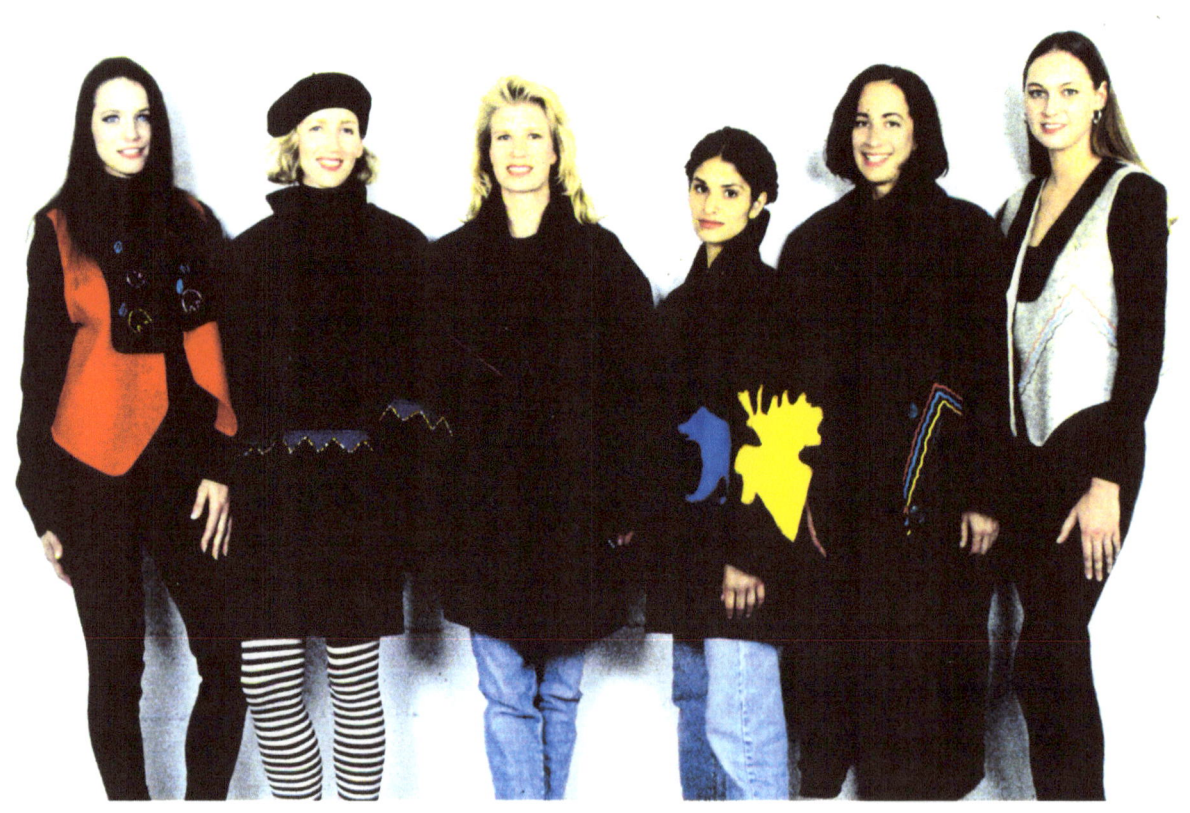

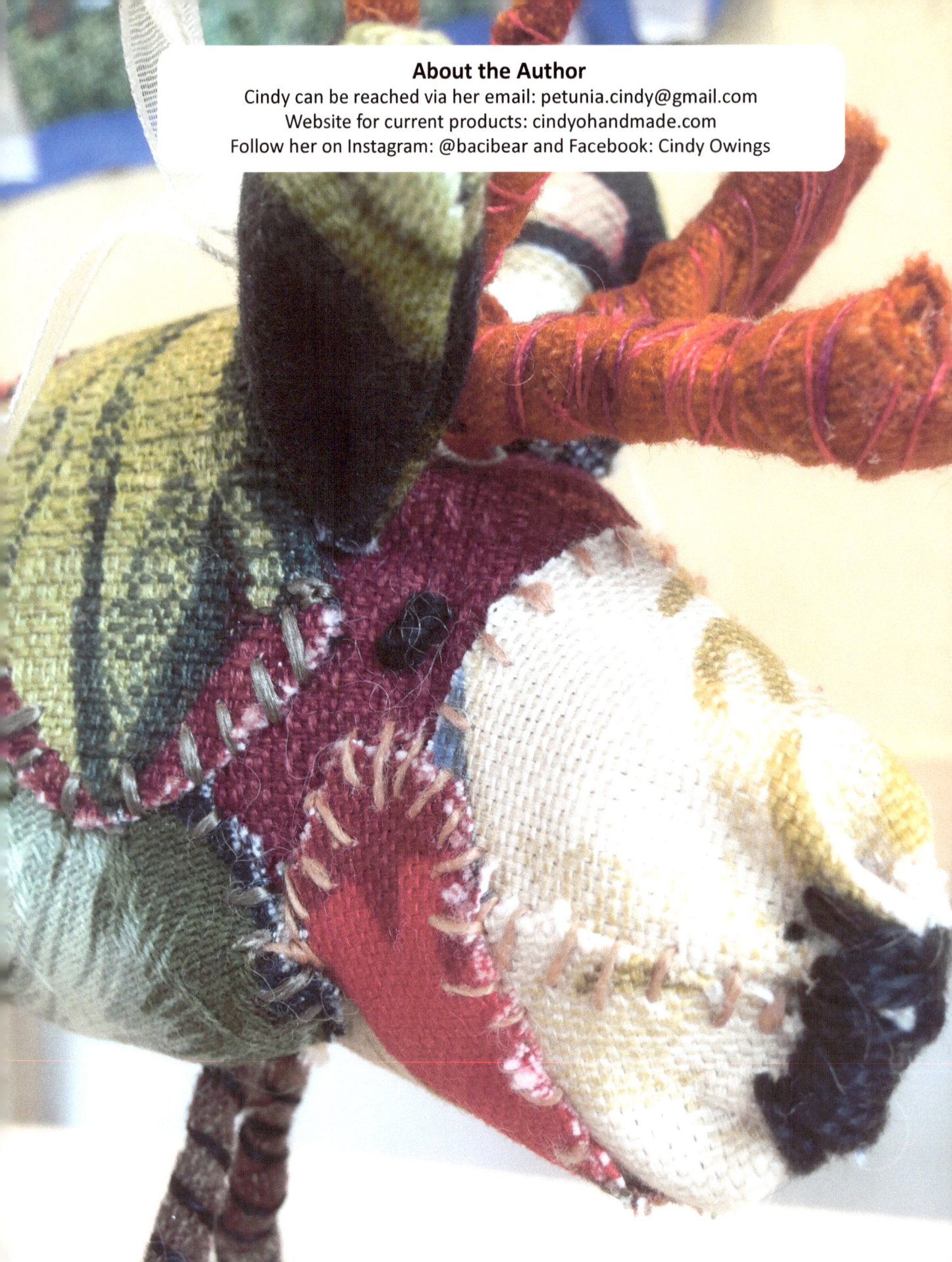

About the Author
Cindy can be reached via her email: petunia.cindy@gmail.com
Website for current products: cindyohandmade.com
Follow her on Instagram: @bacibear and Facebook: Cindy Owings

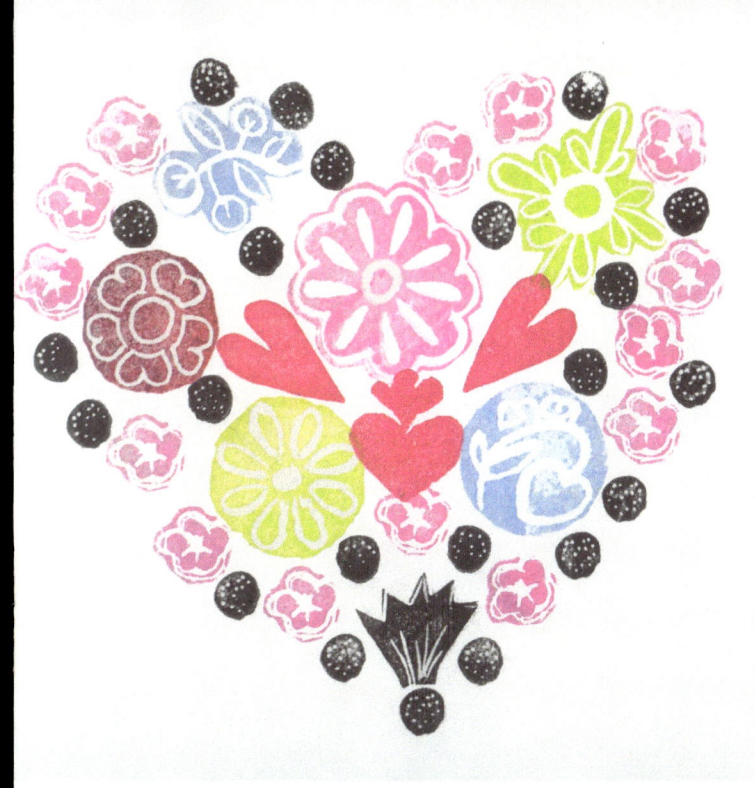
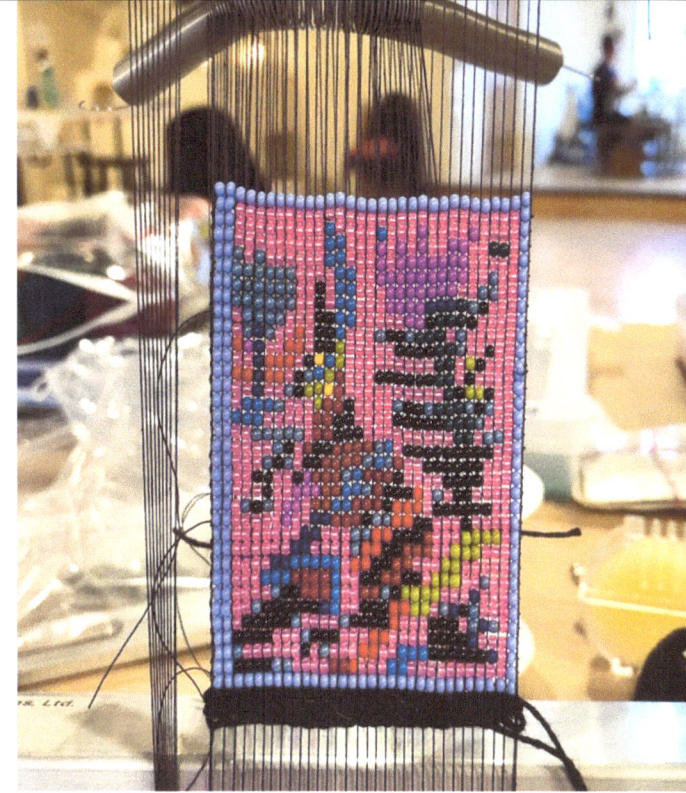
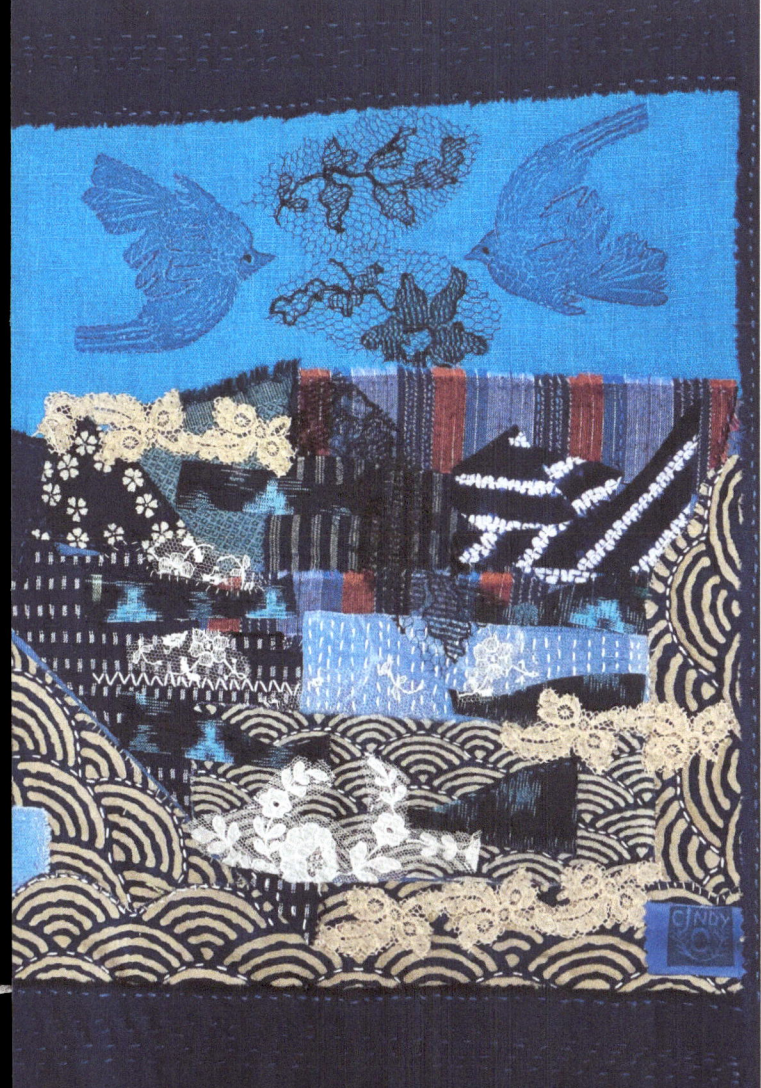
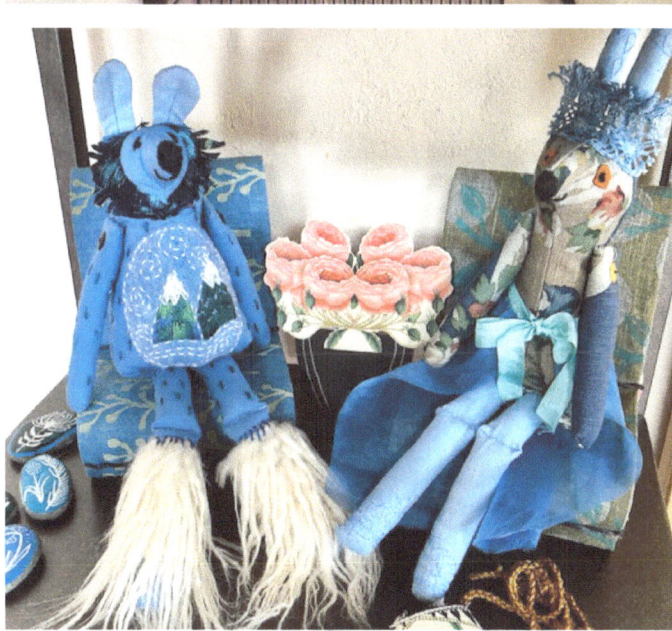
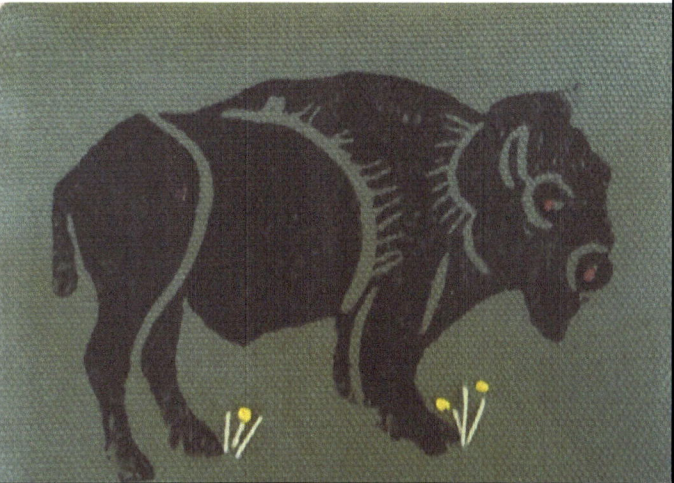

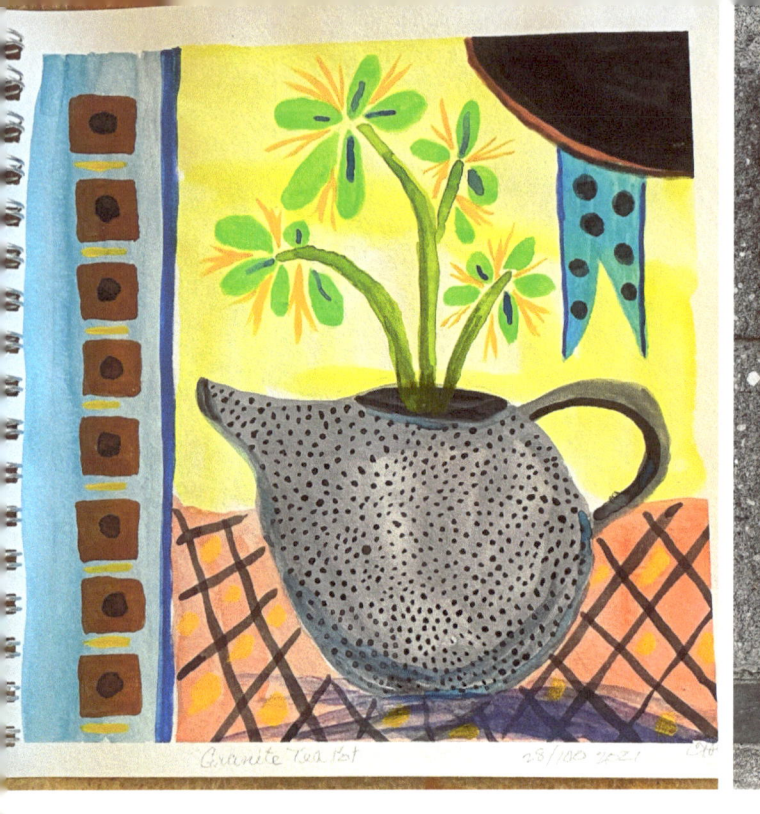
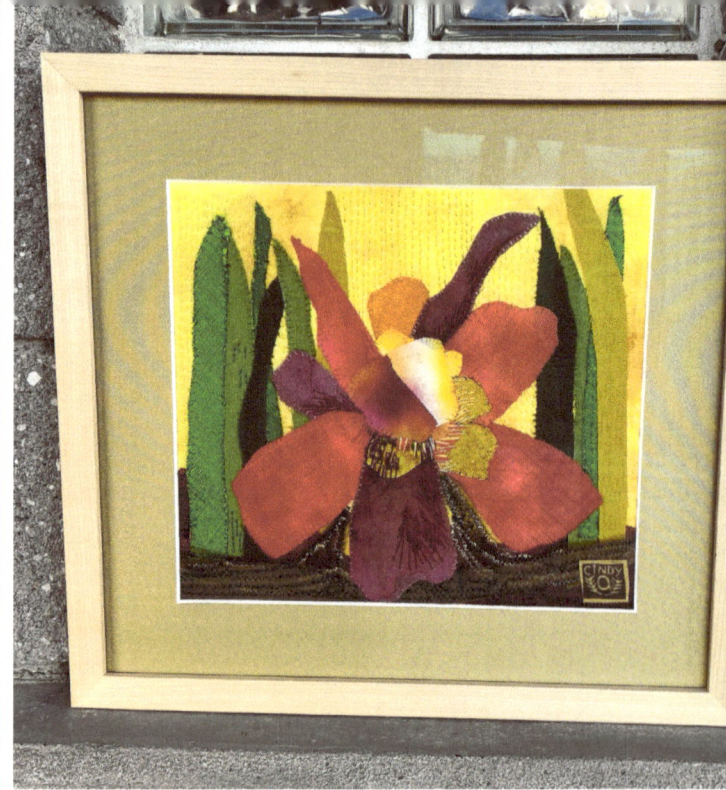

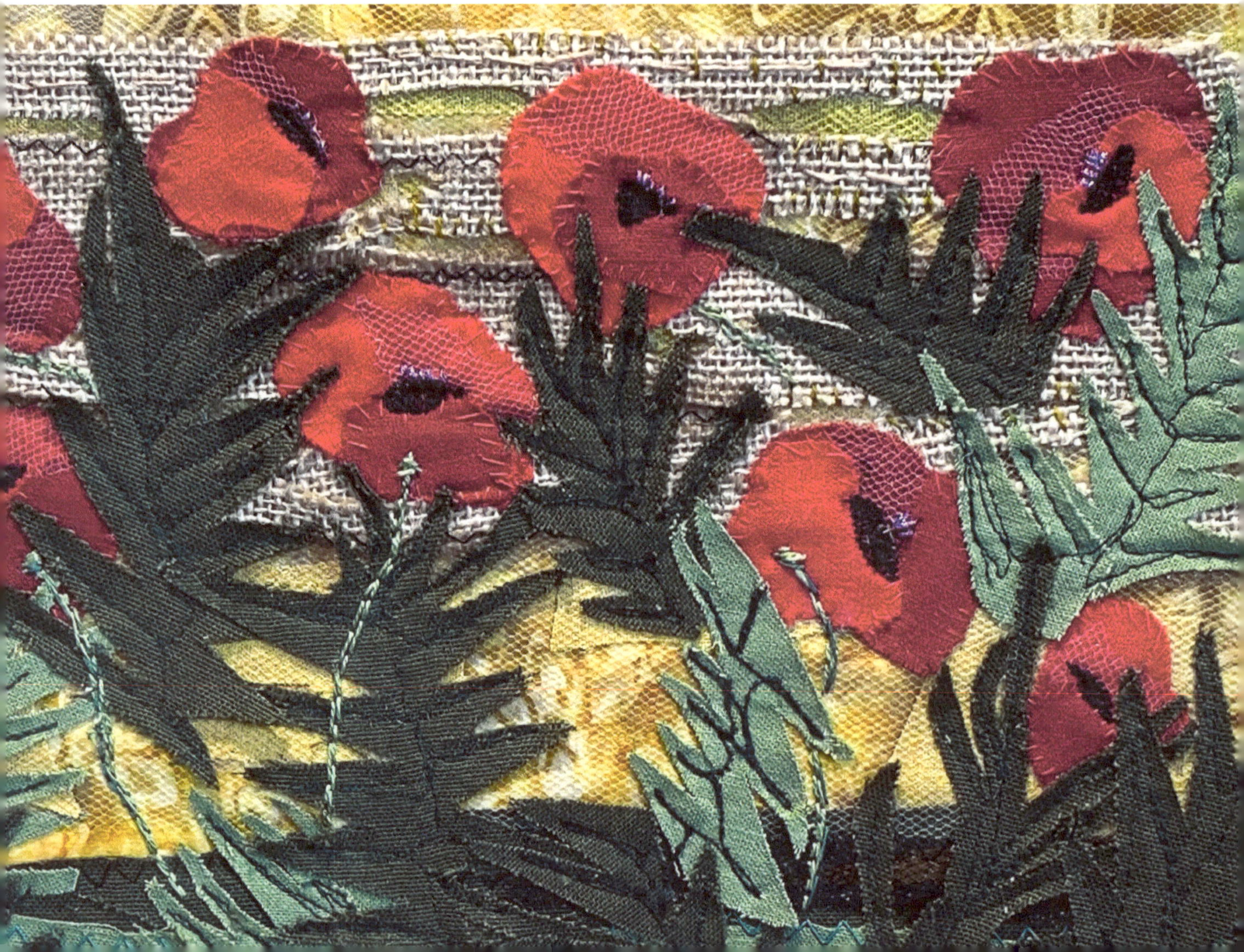

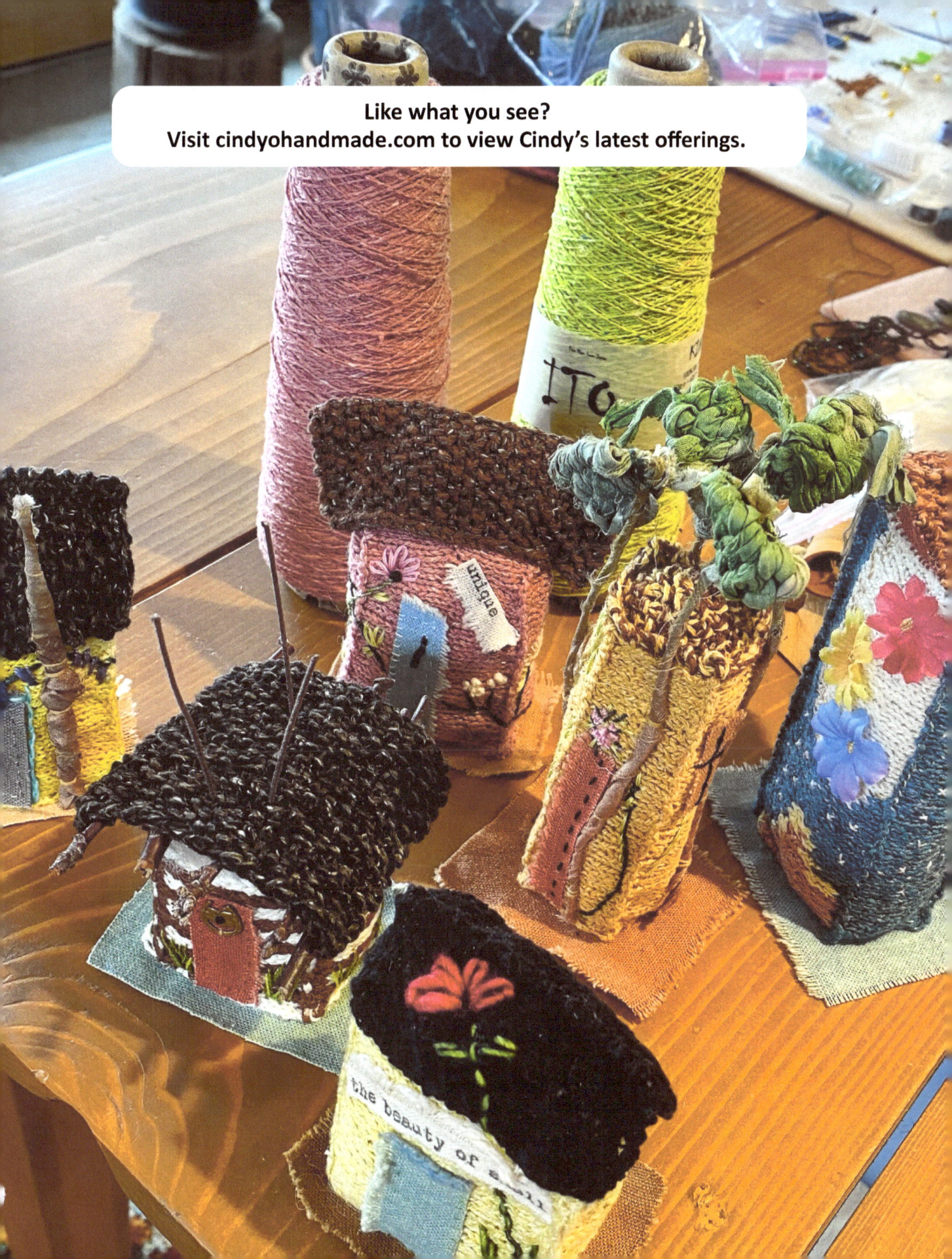

ACKNOWLEDGMENTS

"What is important about memory, I think, is not that it is always accurate (it isn't, of course), but that it is so powerful...the heart of history is the power of memory, the creation of tradition, the significance of place, the importance of stories, the richness of language, the meanings of silence, and the employment of imagination."
By Peter Iverson in his book, Dine: A History of the Navajo People

Thank you to my late parents Rich and Milly Hagan, who exposed my brother, Richard and me to the significance of place, the West, through their love of nature, wild animals, breathtaking campsites, and wandering road trips.

My two grandmothers, Hazel Hagan and Gladys Barnes, fed my imagination with their appreciation of vintage textiles in their homes surrounded by antique furniture, china, and paintings. While lacing up Gladys' corset she shared stories of her favorite dresses and which Denver department stores were her favorites. Hazel insisted I accompany her into the mountains of Colorado to hunt deer and catch fish. She taught me the value of silence.

I am grateful to friends and thoughtful first-round readers, Jim Madden and Linda Wallace who nudged me towards richer, more descriptive, and grammatically correct English language. Molly Caro May, author and writer guided and coached my writing to be the best it could be. Laurel Ornitz, literary editor, took a rough cut and fashioned a gem. The beauty and organization of The Purple Blanket are the creative endeavor and collaboration with graphic designer, Erica Evans Mita from Sparkle Bomb Studio, who worked on this book off and on for three years, as she held the power of memory and story. Thank you to Bitterroot Mountain Publishing House for inviting me to publish.

To all of those who became part of COD's colorful history over the 23 years of its existence (and you know who you are) I thank you for your devotion, creativity, technical knowledge, friendly demeanor, and team spirit. You helped to write COD's story. You created a Montana tradition through every stitch, every scissor cut, every phone answered, and every coat pattern drawn. You were the fabric of COD!

And, finally, thanks to all of COD's loyal customers. You chose to wear crazy colorful brightly patterned wool coats from that faraway place, Montana. Not only did you help write COD's story, you wore the story on your backs. You were the heart of COD!

PHOTOGRAPHY CREDITS

All photos are courtesy of Cindy Owings Design (COD), except those listed below.

Cindy Owings Design (COD) has made every effort to locate and credit the appropriate rights holders. We apologize in advance for any unintentional omissions. Please get in touch with the author to request changes. After consideration of the request, the author will coordinate any necessary corrections or revisions in future reprints.

Front Cover Rob Wilke (robwilke.com); **Page 17** Audrey Hall (audreyhall.com); **Page 20** Audrey Hall (audreyhall.com); **Page 22** Cowboys & Indians Magazine; **Page 24** (all) Cowboys & Indians Magazine; **Page 25** Cowboys & Indians; **Page 27** Magpie by Alena Kazlouskaya via Shutterstock; **Page 29** Bruce Selyem (grainelevatorphotos.com); **Page 33** (all) Bruce Selyem (grainelevatorphotos.com); **Page 36** Audrey Hall (audreyhall.com); **Page 44** Origami crane by Bennyartist via Shutterstock; **Page 39** Audrey Hall (audreyhall.com); **Page 47** Rob Wilke (robwilke.com); **Page 48** (all) Rob Wilke (robwilke.com); **Page 49** (all) Rob Wilke (robwilke.com); **Page 55** Bonwit Teller & Co. Ad; **Page 57** Jones & Co Ltd Ad; **Page 60** Rick Keating Photographer, RK Productions; **Page 63** (all) Rick Keating Photographer, RK Productions; **Page 71** Audrey Hall (audreyhall.com); **Page 78** (yellow coat) Rob Wilke (robwilke.com); **Page 82** Rob Wilke (robwilke.com); **Page 85** Rob Wilke (robwilke.com); **Page 105** Whispering Pines Catalog Ad; **Page 114 - 115** watercolor by artist June Safford; **Page 118** Audrey Hall (audreyhall.com); **Page 122 - 123** painting by artist Gennie DeWeese (courtesy of Tina DeWeese); **Page 123** (right) courtesy of Tina DeWeese; **Page 124** Audrey Hall (audreyhall.com); **Back Cover** (right side top and bottom) Rob Wilke (robwilke.com), (left side bottom) Audrey Hall (audreyhall.com).

www.ingramcontent.com/pod-product-compliance
Lightning Source LLC
Chambersburg PA
CBHW051911210526
45473CB00006B/1976